THE FRUGAL GOURMET COOKS ITALIAN

RECIPES FROM THE
NEW AND OLD WORLDS SIMPLIFIED
FOR THE AMERICAN KITCHEN

JEFF SMITH

Craig Wollam, Culinary Consultant

Chris Cart, Illustrator

Patty Smith & D.C. Smith, Research Assistants

AVON BOOKS NEW YORK

To Maria Guarnaschelli

Whose patient insights and Italian fervor
gave birth to this effort
and to many others

*La signora è più pregiata
di un ottimo vino Italiano!**

—J. S.
C. W.

*The lady is more precious than a fine Italian wine!

AVON BOOKS
A division of
The Hearst Corporation
1350 Avenue of the Americas
New York, New York 10019

Copyright © 1993 by The Frugal Gourmet, Inc.
Line illustrations copyright © 1993 by Chris Cart
Published by arrangement with William Morrow and Company, Inc.
Library of Congress Catalog Card Number: 98-8499
ISBN: 0-380-72391-3

First Avon Books Printing: July 1995

AVON TRADEMARK REG. U.S. PAT. OFF. AND IN OTHER COUNTRIES, MARCA REGISTRADA, HECHO EN U.S.A.

Printed in the U.S.A.

OPM 10 9 8 7 6 5 4 3 2 1

Acknowledgments

I suppose it is hard for anyone outside the television business to understand how many people are behind a show. It is the same with a cookbook. I need to thank so many wonderful folks on this American continent and Italy. Many thanks!

When I prepared the list of persons behind this book I realized that I should probably publish a second volume just to include the well-deserved thanks.

This book is dedicated to Maria Guarnaschelli, our editor. This is the ninth book that we have worked on together, the first one coming about in 1984. Both Craig and I have learned so much from this wonderful and brilliant woman.

Bill Adler, our book agent, is always behind us . . . no, usually ahead of us, as is the head of William Morrow, another fine Italian, Al Marchioni. No, Bill Adler is not Italian!

Very special thanks must be given to Lynn Rossetto Kasper, author of *The Splendid Table* (see Bibliography). This woman seems to know everybody in all of Northern Italy, and she was a great help to us. She really should have her own television cooking show.

Fulvia Sasani, who teaches Venetian cooking in a Venetian palace, was so very kind to us . . . and she did a show with us as well. Such an elegant lady!

Lidia Bastianich, of Felidia's Restaurant in New York, has taken us under her wing. Such a fine place to be.

Carlo Middione, a longtime friend and author of *The Food of Southern Italy* (see Bibliography), returned my every phone call within a moment. This man is so kind and so insightful.

Salah, from Salah al Lago in Seattle; Bobby Estanzo, from Prego's in San Francisco; and John Chikulas, chef at Scuzzi in Chicago, also contributed to our shows and to our fun. In addition, Carmine, from Carmine's Il Terrazzo in Seattle, and Sue Wilkins, owner and chef at Little City Antipasti Bar in San Francisco, added their talents to the book and to the show.

Two other persons turned out to be grand stars on the show. Kevin Clash, the genius behind the muppet "Elmo," got into it with Father Joseph Orsini, a Roman Catholic priest from New Jersey and author of *Father Orsini's Italian Kitchen*. The result of this unrehearsed conversation simply points to the brilliant wit that belongs to each of these fine men.

Now, to Italy.

During the time that we spent in Italy preparing for this book we were under the guidance and care of Dr. Micaela Bolzoni. She lives in Rome with her neat husband, Roberto, and the two of them seem to be able to set up anything that one might wish to experience in Italy. Such a pair! Our driver during this time, Giorgio Bellini, of Cary in Milan, became a dear and treasured friend. Lord, that man is funny!

Mille grazie to those who put up with us during our travels:

Mr. Nano Morandi of the Giuseppe Giusti Shop in Modena

The Staff at Leonida Restaurant in Bologna

Atti Pasta and Pastry in Bologna

Chef Ermina Marasi at Trattoria Vecchio Molinetto in Parma. One of the best meals we had in Italy.

Dr. Leo Bertozzi, of the Parmigiano-Reggiano Cheese Consortium

The Staff at La Prima Market in Milan

The Staff at Peck's in Milan

The Staff at Il Salamaio di Monte Napoleone in Milan

The Bessi family at Da Bruno Restaurant in Milan. Wonderful!

Carlo Freni at Fratelli Freni candy in Milan

The Blitz Bar for Sandwiches in Milan

The Samarani Bar Caffè for Sandwiches in Milan

Bagutta Restaurant in Milan. First Class!

Ms. Raffaella Bologna of Braida Di Giacomo winery in Asti. Wow!

Teresio Vaschetto, President of the Truffle Hunters of the Piedmont region

The Staff at Pasticcio De Filippis, Turin

Salumeria Garibaldi Delicatessen, Turin

Dr. Montuschi of the Parma Ham Consortium, Parma

The Umberto Iotti Family of the Spardarotta Cheese Factory in Reggio Emilia

Dr. Rino Alvisi of the Magnani Aging House for Parmesan

Dr. Orlandini, President of CIBUS in Parma

Count Paolo Giudotti Bentivoglio of the Consorzio Aceto Balsamico Tradizionale in Modena

Mr. Giovanni Tamburini and his fine food shop in Bologna. One of the greatest!

Buca dell' Orafo Restaurant in Florence

Alla Madonna Restaurant in Venice. Wonderful!

The Staff at Fattoria del Corno, Tuscany. Wonderful wine and olive oil.

Albergaccio Niccolò Machiavelli in the Tuscan Hills.

Such great food!

Perini Delicatessen, Florence

Chef Pasina, of Alla Pasina in Trevisio. Terrific!

In this country:

Peggy Green of Mutual Travel in Seattle can move mountains, elephants, television crews—anyone anywhere. She is the best and still she amazes us. Not one slip, not one, in all of our travels.

We must also thank:

The Di Palo Cheese Store in Little Italy, New York

The Italian Food Center, New York

The Fretta Sausage Company, New York

Joe Pace and Sons Italian Market, Boston

La Piccola Venezia Ristorante, Boston

Armando at Mottola Pastry, Boston

Esposito's Meats, Philadelphia

Di Bruno Cheese, Philadelphia

Caludio's Cheese and Olives, Philadelphia

Geno's Steak Sandwich, Philadelphia

The Giovannucci Family of Fante's, Philadelphia

Superior Ravioli of Philadelphia

Criniti's Pastry, Philadelphia

Criniti's Restaurant, Philadelphia

Lanci's Bakery, Philadelphia

Cilione's Cheese and Delicatessen, Philadelphia

Michael Anastio Produce, Inc., Philadelphia

Panelli Bros. Italian Delicatessen in San Francisco

The Florence Pasta Company, San Francisco

DeLaurenti Italian Market, Seattle

Rose and Walter at Ital Foods in San Francisco

Lorenzo and Bruno at The North Beach Restaurant in San Francisco

The Gang at Molinari's Italian Foods, San Francisco

Globe Ceramics attempted to teach us about the grand things coming from Sicily. Vitantonio brought wonderful pasta machines. What neat people.

If it were not for the In-Sink-Erator corporation, inventors of the sink waste disposal, we would probably not even be on the air. What a blessing it is to work with a company that is so responsible and so easy to work with.

Our television crews must be thanked as they tasted all of these dishes and wasted no time in making creative comments. Nat Katzman and Geoff Drummond, our executive producers, are brilliant. Lonnie Porro, our producer, can calm anyone down at any time. I know. So can Stephanie Worley, the assistant producer. John Anderson, our production assistant, remains a very quiet delight of a person. Chef Mark Hogan stood by our side, and Marion Schiewe, our set Mother, watched all of this come down . . . and she watched with a squinted and questioning eye. Janice Vaughns watched me like a hawk. She is great. Mike Riolo, an editing genius, also played time as our director. I like a director who loves to eat!

The studios at Pinnacle in Seattle were watched over by J.P. and Vance. I think they are still walking around in a daze since we left.

The television crew offered us by Northwest Mobile continues to be one of the best crews that we have ever worked with.

You would not believe the fun we had in Italy with our East Coast on-location crew. Penny Locke, our assistant road director, is still trying to figure out what went on. Geoff Drummond, our director in Italy, brought one of the best on-location cameramen we have ever worked with, Herb Forsberg. Our sound person, Rebecca Patsch, was equally skilled. Such comfortable working conditions.

I must thank my wife, Patty, who read and corrected my Italian history and who wrote the great article on Italian wine. D. C. Smith, our regular research assistant, offered some weird insights into that land called Italy, but then his insights are always weird. David Camp, who runs our office, along with Dawn Sparks, must be congratulated for not screaming at me once during this whole process. This is probably due to the fact that I could not hear them above my own screaming.

Jason Lynch and Angelo Ortego tasted and tested and cleaned up the mess, over and over again. Good insight from these fellows.

Chris Cart deserves some kind of new award for the illustrations that he created for this new book. I am always amazed at the fact that he understands the nature of a project before I can even figure it out. Further, Steven Rothfeld created the most beautiful color photographs of our food that I could ever hope for.

National PBS also must be thanked . . . well, I guess that is actually you, our reader, for supporting our efforts for so long.

Finally, as always, I must thank Craig Wollam, our chef, sidekick, and culinary consultant. I say "as always" because this is the seventh cookbook that we have worked on together. The other day a reporter asked me this question: "What do you think other T.V. cooks should have in order to be as comfortable on television as you are?" I replied, "Craig Wollam, but you are not going to get him!"

Thanks to all, and the wonderful people of Italy.

Contents

Introduction

This is not a romantic cookbook. We are not trying to tell you about how a little lady in a rustic Italian village cooks a particular dish. The reason is simple. You do not have that kind of kitchen nor do you have the romantic three days to cook the food.

Rather, we want you to cook Italian style regularly, and that means that recipes need to be simplified for the American kitchen and table, but we don't believe that you have to give up a great deal in terms of taste.

So this is to be a practical rather than a romantic collection of recipes . . . from both the Old World and the New. They are usable on a regular or even a sometimes basis, but most of all, they are aimed at a generous celebration of one of the most creative cuisines in the Western world.

We are convinced that the true flavors in Italian cooking come from the peasant stock. I am not ashamed to say that nor are they ashamed to receive the compliment. It was the peasant cook who taught the aristocracy how to eat . . . and the aristocracy took this wonderful cuisine to the rest of Europe. Witness the influence that Catherine de Médicis (1519–1589) had on France when she moved to Paris to marry Henry II in 1533. She brought her chefs with her from Florence. Many chefs! She had heard that French cuisine was very different from her own culinary upbringing and thus the caravan of Florentine chefs.

All Italian chefs claim that their people taught the rest of Europe how to cook, including the French. That may be a bit much, though it is safe to say that the Italians have had more influence upon the cooking of Western Europe than any other people since the founding of Rome.

This is not to say that we are not going to gossip together about the romantic background of a particular dish. We are just saying that the romantic background is not the point. The translation of such a dish to your American kitchen is the point!

We have attempted to construct regional recipes in such a way as to offer you some basic yet stupendous flavors without quite as much fuss and time as might be involved in the Old World method of preparation. Therefore, understand that these dishes are not necessarily for the purist but rather for the household cook who wishes to have the kitchen smell like Italy not just on special occasions but regularly, maybe constantly.

We have not included every region. That is impossible! Italy is a country of countries, and we cannot deal with all of them. If you lament the absence of Roman cooking, please understand that we did a previous cookbook titled *The Frugal Gourmet Cooks Three Ancient Cuisines— China, Greece and Rome.* In it we show how the land that we now call Italy influenced, indeed directed, the cooking of the whole of Western Europe.

Finally, this book is for fun in the kitchen. We don't want you to see Italian regional cooking as complex and painful since it need not be. And the stories that we want to tell you in this volume should help you see the element of fun in Italian cuisine.

So, to the kitchen without any pretense whatsoever. Just be sure to have plenty of good fresh garlic on hand, along with lots of good-quality olive oil, and we will be ready for feasting on the cuisine that remains among the finest in the world.

—Jeff Smith
Craig Wollam

ITALY

A Little History,
A Little Affection

It took me some time to understand this, but when we visited this wonderful country we did indeed find an "Italy," but we found very few people who called themselves "Italian." An Italy without Italians?

The reason for this strange circumstance goes back to times prior to written history. The great peninsula was then, and is now, inhabited by many different tribes speaking diverse languages. These tribes saw themselves as strictly autonomous, maintaining city-states. The keynote of the city-state was absolute independence, and this independence seems to have held to this day.

When Greece invaded what we now call Italy, it did so in the name of Greek city-states, such as Athens, Corinth, or Syracuse, rather than "Greece." Thus the Greek invaders furthered the Italian sense of village, city, and regional independence.

The Greek city-states founded colonies in Sicily and Southern Italy around 750 B.C. At about the same time the

Etruscan civilization was developing in the north-central area of the peninsula. The origin of the Etruscans is still debated today. Some, like Herodotus, believed that the Etruscans came from Asia Minor, while others agree with Dionysius of Halicarnassus who wrote, "The Etruscan nation emigrated from nowhere. It has always been there."

Whatever their origins, the result of that early division of the Italian peninsula between the Etruscans and the Greeks was a contrast that seems to have persisted to this day. Polenta in the North, seafood soup (brodetto) in the South. This gastronomic frontier divides the country in terms of most of the basics: butter and flat noodles in the North and olive oil and tubular pasta in the South. One division, the veal line, which cuts across Italy just south of Florence, is geographic, not cultural. This is the line that separates the lush pasturage of the North from the poor grazing of the South. In the North animals are raised for milk; in the South they are generally used as draft animals. For this same reason the poverty line divides the prosperous North from the poorer South.

Many attempts have been made to unite the country into one nation. Napoleon tried, King Victor Emmanuel II tried, and Mazzini, Cavour, and Garibaldi fought long and hard to create a nation. I don't think it has ever come about.

Even the language of contemporary Italy is a foreign tongue to a majority of its citizens. After all, it is often language that is used to define nationality. English people speak English, French people speak French, German people speak German. Language even defines extraterritorial nationalities as Arabs speak Arabic from Morocco to Oman. But not the Italians. "Standard Italian" is based on Tuscan, the mother tongue of Leonardo, Michelangelo, and the brave Dante, who first composed literature in that vernacular. But in our time a Milanese speaks Lombard, a Genoan speaks Ligurian, and on and on . . . Piedmontese, Emilian, Neapolitan, Calabrian. In 1875, the five hundredth anniversary of Boccaccio's death was celebrated by the publication of one of his stories in all the extant Italian dialects. When finished, they had printed approximately seven hundred different versions. You still meet people in Italy who are primarily committed to their regional language, not to the national tongue.

This fierce regional pride results in the belief that the local cuisine is the best, of course. The production of prized food items is carefully controlled by consortiums. Balsamic vinegar, Parmigiano-Reggiano cheese, Parma hams and the like are all so skillfully watched over and so legally defined that one is amazed at the concerned organization. Yet these are the same people who cannot get a phone call from Rome to Naples! Why? Because these wonderful Italian individualists care about food, and wine, and music, and art, and religion, and family, and the good life. To Hell with the government! At the time of the writing of this article the Italian government was in the midst of another turmoil, scandal, whatever. So what! Dinner will be served promptly at 1:30 P.M. and Grandma Petosa is bringing her special dish of cauliflower and peppers. The wine is coming via Uncle Orsini. Now sit down and relax. Everything will be just fine.

A Little Affection

When you travel in Italy, please think regionally. The food and wine vary from region to region and the specialties are often very exciting.

Please forgive us if we have not paid special attention to your favorite region or city. The following notes pertain to our several visits and to our own particular affections.

PIEDMONT

Such rich soil and food you have never seen! Long considered one of the great food regions of Italy, Piedmont is a must in terms of a culinary visit. Craig noticed that since the region borders France, there is a special attention to good food. . . . "No," he said, "it is closer to French confidence, almost arrogance." It seems to be a wonderful blending of two fine food traditions.

Alba

This city is the center of the great white truffle. The markets are often underground as the great truffle is taxed heavily and thus the black market in this treasure of the fungi world. The restaurants will serve you well during the white truffle season, which occurs during October and November. The white truffle is so significant that there are even parades and festivals during the season.

Asti

One of the great wine-producing areas of Northern Italy, Asti can boast some of the best food that we found on our journeys. Asti Spumante wine, vermouth, and terrific Barbera are common in the city, if you can use the word *common* about such treasures.

The Ristorante Gener Neuv serves particularly fine food and we urge you go. Ristorante Guido also offers a lovely dining room and fine food, really fine.

This is also the region of Bagna Cauda, so be prepared for fine dishes.

Turin

This lovely city has one of the finest outdoor city markets we found in all of Italy. Further, the indoor market, fully covered and clean as can be, was an even greater delight. We nibbled from stall to stall, wineglasses in hand, and found only top-quality food of every description for sale. This market is a must when in Piedmont. Stop by the Baratti Bar for coffee and wonderful candies and pastries. The place has been there for generations and it is very "Torino."

LOMBARDY

This wonderful region boasts the least Italian city in all of the great peninsula. Milan is its own mother and father, and it draws in adopted trends from all of Western Europe. The region is rich with veal and seafood, also risotto, and surely the most beautiful women in Italy.

Milan

The fashion center for clothes and luxuries, Milan is not the normal tourist town. La Scala opera house and the great Cathedral, the Galleria, and more. The city has such class. Food is included in this city of luxuries. You must go see Peck's markets, and Salumeria di Montenapoleone will startle you with such gorgeous food. La Prima is a new fine-food market that will tickle you with its beauty. You can even have an espresso and brandy while you shop.

One of the most wonderful things that you will find in Milan is the sandwich bar. I know that this sounds odd to Americans but the Milanese are the sandwich masters. Try the Blitz Bar or the Samarini Bar Caffè.

For good restaurant food try the Bagutta or the Da Bruno. You will be treated with respect. Bice is very famous and very full of tourists, but on a good night you will do fine.

Be sure to visit the Fratelli Freni candy shop. They make Sicilian marzipan fruits and vegetables—even hot dogs and false teeth—that will delight you.

VENETO

The land of Romeo and Juliet, the land of romantic Venice, the land of the best seafood that you can find in Italy. Eel is so popular, as is polenta and salted fish.

Asiago

We traveled up into the hills to see the making of the famous Asiago cheese. The cheese maker uses equipment that is hundreds of years old, and the cheese is worth every minute of that history. The whole town lives and loves around this great cheese, and any meal there will offer you flavors of their cheese-filled history.

Treviso

Located very close to the water, and very close to Venice, Treveso boasts fine food traditions that have been influenced by many foreign powers and several invaders.

One restaurant that you must try is called Alla Pasina. The owner, Mr. Pasina, is very skilled and he is an absolute sweetheart on top of it. My only bad thought about this place is that we had time for only one meal. Bad planning!

Venice

I am always asked about my favorite eating city in Italy. It is a toss-up between Venice and Rome. Some days I do not even understand the toss!

Try the grilled eel at Alla Madonna. No, the American singer has nothing to do with this place. It has been very popular with real Venetians for generations. The cold crab will do you in.

The public market, just behind the Rialto Bridge, is a daily stop for most citizens of this city of islands. The fish market located there has just got to be one of the best things I have ever seen!

You will also have a delightful lunch at Harry's Dolce, located a bit down the main canal.

If you feel that your wealth has exceeded your ability to spend, hire a taxi (motorboat) and head for the island of

Torcello. The restaurant Cipriani will do you well. Just do not try to feed the sweet little wild kitty cats that will come to your table. They will tear your leg off!

Please also be comforted by the fact that you are in the midst of very civilized company. The Venetians introduced the use of the table fork and the napkin to the rest of Europe. You can't get more civilized than that!

EMILIA-ROMAGNA

While it is true that most regional Italian cooks claim that their region and local food are the best, I must side with the people of Emilia-Romagna. This is the home of the great Parma ham, the wonderful Parmigiano-Reggiano cheese, and of course, balsamic vinegar. If you were to produce only one of these food products you would qualify for international respect and attention . . . but this region produces all three.

Bologna

You will have a field day in Tamburini's fancy food shop located in the public market in Bologna. It is surely the most diverse and complete, the most lovely and creative, market that we found in all of Italy. Go!

Lunch or dinner at Leonida's will surprise you. Not expensive, not filled with tourists, and fine Bolognese cuisine. For a second hop you might try Diana, though the food will be a bit more inconsistent and the guy at the next table will introduce himself as a merchant from New Jersey.

Parma

In this little city the pigs that give us Parma ham eat the whey left over from the production of the most famous cheese in Italy, the Parmigiano-Reggiano. There is a pride here in frugality and simple cooking, and it is great.

One of the most well-known restaurants in the region is called Trattoria Vecchio Molinetto. The chef has been there for some forty years and she is a jewel. The food is simple and profound.

The food shops are just wonderful. See Salumeria Garibaldi.

Modena

The home of balsamic vinegar, one of the greatest medicines, condiments, perfumes, and elixirs ever to be produced for the joy of man-and womankind. Stop at Giuseppe Giusti and smell the flowers.

The cathedral and city square are wonderful and the whole of the community will make you feel most comfortable.

Reggio Emilia

Parma and Reggio Emilia battle all the time about who has the best food. Craig and I vote for Parma.

Incidentally, when eating in Italy, watch out for the old "I'll give you the tourist menu" trick. This happened to us only once in Italy; such a scam is against the law. However, at a place in Reggio Emilia, a joint called Scuda d'Italia,

Craig and I were given the English menu. Our best friend and guide, Micaela, from Rome, was also given an English menu. When she asked for an Italian menu (My Lord, is she Italian!), the manager responded. We then discovered that the prices for the tourist or English menu and the Italian menu were not even in the same camp. That is very naughty, naughty.

When I confronted the owner with the discrepancy he told me that the Italian menu was outdated. "How then," I asked, "could both menus have the same specials and the same date listed on the top?" Watch out for this sort of nonsense. I was later told that I should have called for the police as the Italian government is anxious to support the tourist trade. Craig responded, "We are to go out and call a policeman into the restaurant? He'll just think that we want to buy him dinner. No way!"

TUSCANY

This rich region of the best olive oil and some of the best wines in Italy is a must. Further, the affection for beans and innards is historical.

Tuscans are great red-meat eaters, more so than perhaps any other region in Italy. The steaks are wonderful, the Chianti wine superb, and the markets are filled with first-class food.

Florence

Near the Ponte Vecchio there is a downstairs joint called Buca dell'Orafo. Yes, you will find a lot of tourists about but the food is very good, not expensive, and the guys that run the place are a gas! Their Tripe Florentine is superb.

The White Boar is near the same bridge and the food is excellent.

In the same neighborhood you will find a place called Mamma Gina. Good food, fair prices, and lots of fun.

ABRUZZI

This region close to the sea seems to have the best of several worlds. The seafood is terrific, it is the center of the only saffron-growing region in Italy, and the home of Maccheroni all Chitarra.

L'Aquila

A wonderful little town set up in the mountains. Don't go unless you are willing to hike up and down small hills to get to the market, the square, the restaurants, the hotel, whatever. In any case it is worth it. The city market is a delight, held regularly in the city square. I promise you that you can buy any kind of foodstuff imaginable, including roasted pork and chicken, and a thousand other things. You can also buy things that you did not realize were for sale.

Stay away from the fancy tourist restaurants. Stick to the back-street restaurants or those on the smaller square. In any case, be prepared for a good time.

CAMPANIA

Invaded many times by Arabs, Greeks, Romans, and just about everyone else, this region is the home of great fruit and the famous fresh mozzarella cheese, made from the milk of the Asian water buffalo. The food is heavy with seafood and lots of tomato sauce. Most Americans think of "American Italian Restaurants" as being from this region, and indeed, until very recently they were. The heavy use of tomato is typical of the region, and when coupled with the fact that a majority of Italian immigrants to America came from the South—Naples and Sicily—one can understand our common image of Italian cooking. However, this image is changing very rapidly.

Naples

This is the crazy city. Absolutely crazy! Even the Neapolitans will tell you that. The traffic is bizarre, as if each cab driver is protected by some secret patron saint. I have never even heard of these saints! The rush to run over someone else is a matter of civic pride, and you really do lose the color in your knuckles when riding across town . . . if you make it.

When you tell someone in the North that you have just come back from Naples, they generally say, "I am sorry!" What they mean is that you have finally learned about the argument between the North and the South. They will never understand each other.

However, if you go out onto the top-floor deck of your hotel in Naples, and if you can ever get a cup of coffee out of the waiter, you will relax in one of the most beautiful places that I have ever seen. The harbor is filled with fishing boats (who is working at this time of the morning? It's only ten o'clock) and above this beauteous harbor is Mount Vesuvius. The Mountain holds court as you sip your coffee and brandy, and then HE (The Mountain) allows you to decide on the fine waterfront restaurant in which you will have a glorious and heavy lunch. The varieties of seafood celebrated in this community are carefully brought to the table with both freshness and pride.

Forget about the taxi driver!

The Public Market, the street market, goes on for blocks and blocks. Be prepared to spend a day walking this strange blend of Arabic street market and Italian grocery.

On Eating in Italy

I first traveled to Italy in 1960, a kid just barely twenty-one years old. My friend Jerry Yost and I saved up enough money during our college days to visit most of Western Europe during a six-month trip that changed my life.

I fell in love with Italy.

A few nights ago I read through my journal from that trip. I remembered buying our Austrian motorbikes—mopeds—and the daily travels all over Europe. I remember the fact that we lasted in Europe for six months with only $1,000 in each of our pockets. I remember meeting a Finn from Argentina and eating fresh bread and jam in the mountains of Norway. I remember Paris. But most of all, I remember Italy.

The people of Italy seem much different to me now over against my memories of thirty years ago. But then I must confess to a very limited budget that certainly did not allow us to eat in good restaurants or hang around with the well-educated crowd in Rome—or any other place for that matter. We ate in small and very inexpensive restaurants, and the only dish that I actually mentioned in my journal was

Trippa Florentina, tripe cooked in the manner of Florence. Since that first journey I have been back to Italy nearly a dozen times and now I know a very different crowd. Such charmers, these Italians. Tourism is even more important now than it was in 1960 and the Italian citizens recognize that fact without being arrogant or nasty about it. They are gracious and accommodating and for the most part very kind. I don't know if some of the other countries in Western Europe will ever catch onto this.

Italians are very anxious for you to enjoy their food. The pride in the food you see in the various regions is just beautiful, and this pride carries through to the variety of regional dishes. The food alone will help you remember that Italy is still made up of many different countries!

You can even get a good meal on the wonderful Italian railway when it is running. Strikes are rather common. Still, it is great fun to travel by rail and sip wine while you watch the beautiful countryside come to you and then pass by.

The open food markets that you will find in any major city will cause you to wonder whether we have given up too much for the sake of the ever-efficient American Supermarket. The fresh ingredients offered in the open stalls in Italy are much more seasonal than those in our markets, what with our storage and freezing methods, our hydroponic farms, and our great greenhouses. We seem to have lost a sense of the seasons.

Further, we seem to have lost our sense of history when it comes to food. A TV dinner has no memories, certainly not in terms of our past. In Italy recipes are offered that go back to the first century, and all kinds of restaurants call themselves Antica, ancient or old-style. The wines go back to before the Christian era. I found edible history everywhere. Sipping coffee and brandy on the roof of our hotel in Naples while watching the sun rise on Mount Vesuvius. Pouring olive oil on my bread in the very inn where Machiavelli wrote *The Prince*. Sitting in St. Mark's Square in Venice and eating a sandwich while thinking about the fact that the Islands of Venice have been populated since the Roman Empire by people wishing to escape everything from Attila the Hun during the fifth century to the great plague of 1348. What a place to have a cup of espresso! And the elegant coffee bars that have been in business for generations throughout Italy are enough in themselves to justify the whole manner of Italian eating and life-style.

The diet is quite different from our own and I believe it to be much healthier. More starch is eaten, and less animal fat. Olive oil, which is really quite good for you, is everywhere, as are pasta, rice, and polenta. And cold cooked vegetables with a simple oil and lemon dressing. We rarely serve this in our country and the combinations are really wonderful. You will have to read the chapter on innards in order to understand my affection for tripe and sweetbreads.

Craig, my chef, and I were amazed and amused by the fact that everyone in Italy has a recipe to share. "What are you doing here in Italy?" "Working on a cookbook," we reply. "Listen, have you ever tried cooking pasta with black Italian olives and red peppers flakes?" That one is from the bartender at our hotel in Milan.

I warn you that the cost of eating out in Italy is simply astronomical! But then, so is the cost of everyday food. The Italian is willing to spend a much greater percentage of his/her income on food than we do in America. The cost of Parmigiano-Reggiano cheese, Parma ham, balsamic vinegar, or mushrooms and truffles will put you into a coma. But then you can always have some beans, and nobody does a better job on beans than the cooks of Italy.

Why do the Italians spend so much on food? I think it has something to do with pride, a very important sense of pride. It has something to do with knowing that the whole of the Western world has come to appreciate regional Italian cuisine. We did a TV show in which there were five chefs and one cook on the set at the same time. All were skilled in regional Italian cooking. One chef was a Greek, the second Lebanese, the third from the Philippines, and the fourth from Mexico. I am Norwegian and Craig is German. How can you get more international than that?

Then again, the Italian sense of pride in food and history may be linked with the confidence that comes from knowing that the Renaissance was theirs, and that they were the ones who taught the French how to improve their cooking.

And remember, while many Italian dishes go back to very ancient times, the cuisines of Italy are still ever changing and growing. Stay away from the tourist traps and you will have a hard time finding a meal in Italy that is not superb.

Glossary

Basic Ingredients for the Italian Kitchen

INGREDIENTS, CONDIMENTS, AND FOOD DEFINITIONS

Anchovies
Buy flat anchovy fillets packed in olive oil. The Italian product is excellent, but you can also buy canned anchovies from other countries such as Spain, Portugal, or Morocco and you won't pay as much. A good brand is Roland and is readily available. Keep refrigerated.

Arborio Rice:
See page 237.

Baccalà or Dried Salt Cod
Codfish that has been cured with salt. Common in Mediterranean cooking. Must be soaked in water for at least eighteen hours, changing the water several times, before you cook it. Buy in Italian delicatessens or seafood shops.

Beef Stock:
See page 115.

Cannellini Beans
A slender medium-size white bean, also known as a white kidney bean. Find dried or canned in Italian markets, or substitute any white bean. Dried beans must be soaked for several hours before use.

Capers
Pickled buds used in salads and dressings. Found in any good supermarket.

Cheeses:
See page 465.

Chicken Stock:
See page 116.

Couscous
A fine semolina grain brought to Sicily by the Moroccans or Arabs. Buy the regular noninstant variety. Available in most supermarkets.

Dijon Mustard
A style of mustard from France. A good American brand is Grey Poupon.

Fresh Fennel
A vegetable with stalks and a white bulb. It has a mild licorice flavor and usually only the bulb part is used. After the bulb has been trimmed you can use the tops to flavor stocks or sauces.

Garbanzo Beans or Chick-peas
The Italian name is *ceci*. Purchase in Italian markets dried. They must be soaked in water several hours before use.

Grappa
A dry, usually colorless Italian brandy made from the distilled residue of the wine press.

Leeks
These look like very large green onions in the produce section. Wash carefully because they are usually full of mud.

Mortadella
Famous sausage made in Bologna. Domestic brands can be found in Italian markets and delicatessens. Delicious served as an appetizer, sliced paper thin or cubed.

Mushrooms, Dried:
See page 415.

Olives:
See page 485.

Pancetta
Italian-style bacon with a flavor all its own. Find in Italian markets and good delicatessens. Regular bacon can be substituted but it is not as good.

Pesto Sauce
A sauce of northern Italian origin, made from fresh basil, olive oil, garlic, cheese, and pine nuts. Great on pasta or in soups and on vegetable dishes. Best to make your own or purchase frozen in Italian markets.

Pine Nuts
Expensive little treasures that actually come from the large pine cone of Italy. Find in Italian markets or substitute slivered almonds.

Polenta
Coarse cornmeal used in Italy. Buy this in bulk in any Italian market.

Porcini:
See page 415.

Prosciutto di Parma:
See page 355.

Quick-Rising Yeast
There are a couple of brands on the market now that will cause the dough to rise in half the time. Both Red Star and Fleischmann's manufacture such a thing. You can find these in any supermarket.

Radicchio
Resembles our purple cabbage, but smaller in size and has a slightly bitter taste. Find in most supermarkets. Expensive.

Saffron
Real saffron is from Spain and is the dried stamens from the saffron crocus. It costs $2,000 a pound. Buy it by the pinch or use Mexican saffron, which includes the whole flower and is very cheap. This works well, but just remember to use much more. Available in threads or powdered.

Sausage Casings:
See page 350.

Semolina
A very coarse-ground flour made from hard durum wheat. Buy in an Italian grocery. Ideal for making fresh pasta, and the flavor is superior to farina, which may be used as a substitute.

HERBS AND SPICES

Buying, Storing, and Grinding Herbs and Spices
Herbs and spices are some of the most important ingredients in your kitchen. You want to keep them as fresh as

possible, so don't buy them in large amounts. Keep them in tightly sealed jars. Try to buy most herbs and spices whole or in whole-leaf form; they have much more flavor that way. Crush the leaves as you add them to the pot. Or use a mortar and pestle (page 47). For seeds that are hard to grind, I use a small German electric coffee grinder (page 33). I have one that I use just for spices; it works very well.

Try to buy in bulk the dried herbs and spices that you use most frequently, and then put them in your own spice bottles. The saving realized here is about 70 percent. Hard to believe, but it is true. Find a market that has big jars of spices and you will be amazed at the difference in flavor.

Most supermarkets now offer a good selection of fresh herbs. These little bunches or packages of herbs are convenient but expensive, so you might try growing some of your own. Fresh herbs will give a clean bright flavor to your cooking, and in many recipes only the fresh will do. In other dishes, dried herbs are preferred or will do just fine.

If you want to substitute a fresh herb for a dried herb in a recipe, remember to use twice the amount of fresh herb to dried as the dried is more concentrated in flavor.

Good regional Italian cooking does not require too many exotic ingredients. This is especially true with the use of herbs and spices, so you are probably familiar with the ones used in this book. The following is a list of the most common herbs and spices used in the Italian kitchen.

Basil (fresh and dried)

Bay leaves

Coriander seed (an ancient spice but not very common)

Dillweed

Fennel seed

Garlic (always use fresh)

Mint (fresh and dried)

Mustard, dry (Colman's is a good brand)

Oregano (fresh and dried)

Parsley (Always use fresh flat-leaf Italian parsley, not the curly type that has no flavor. Dried parsley is used in this book only for sausage recipes.)

Peppercorns, black (always freshly grind your own)

Red pepper flakes, hot

Rosemary (fresh and dried)

Sage (fresh and dried)

Thyme (fresh and dried)

White pepper, ground

Cooking Techniques and Terms

Al Dente

This is a wonderful Italian term that means to cook "to the teeth." It means nobody wants soggy pasta. Cook pasta to the teeth, or until it is barely tender, still a bit firm. It is much better that way ... and the way Italians intended it to be eaten.

Blanching

Plunging a food product into boiling water for a very few minutes. The food is then removed and generally placed in cold water to stop the cooking process. The purpose is to loosen the skin of the vegetable or fruit, to set the color of a vegetable, or to cook a food partially in preparation for later completion of the dish.

Dash

Generally means "to taste." Start with less than ¹⁄₁₆ teaspoon.

Deglazing a Pan

After meats or vegetables have been browned, wine or stock is added to the pan over high heat, and the rich coloring that remains in the pan is gently scraped with a wooden spoon and combined with the wine or stock.

Dice

This means to cut into small cubes; the size of a cube is generally stated in the recipe. For instance, a ¼-inch dice means a cube of that size. It is accomplished very quickly and easily with a good vegetable knife.

Dredging in Flour

Meats and fish, generally thinly sliced, are rolled about in flour in preparation for frying or sautéing. The flour is usually seasoned with salt and pepper.

Dusting with Flour

Dusting of meat or fish in flour and patting or shaking off all the excess flour. The idea is to have a very light coating on the food.

Grilling

An ancient method whereby the food is cooked on a rack, heavy grill, or skewer over hot coals or an open flame.

Julienne Cut

Cut vegetables into thin slices, stack the slices, and then cut the slices into thin sticks, like matchsticks. The width and length of the cut varies.

Marinating

Meats or vegetables are soaked for a time in flavoring liquid such as wine, oil, or vinegar. The time of the marinating varies with the recipe.

Mince

Vegetable or herb that is chopped very fine. This pertains especially to garlic, onion, and herbs. The process is done by hand with a knife or a food processor.

Pinch of Herbs or Spices

Usually means "to taste." Start with less than 1/16 teaspoon, and then increase if you wish.

Poaching

Gently cooking fish, meat, or eggs in stock or water at just below a simmer. The liquid should just barely move during the poaching process.

Puree

When you wish to make a sauce or soup that is free of all lumps of any sort, puree the stock. This means that you put it in a food processor and mill it until it is free of all lumps, or run it through a strainer or sieve.

Reconstituting

A procedure used for preparing dried foods whereby the product is soaked in fresh water for a time. The food absorbs the water, so that its "life" is restored and it can be used properly in a given recipe.

Reducing

Boiling a sauce or liquid over high heat until it is reduced in volume, generally by half. The result is a very rich concentration of flavors.

Roux

A mixture of oil or butter and flour cooked together. This forms a pasty substance used to thicken sauces and gravies. If a white or "blond" roux is desired, the mixture is cooked a short time over low heat. If a brown roux is desired, the mixture is cooked longer to achieve a slightly brown color.

Rubbed

When whole-leaf herbs, such as sage or bay leaves, are crushed in the hands so that their oils are released, the herbs are then referred to as having been rubbed.

Sauté

This term comes from a French word that means "to jump." In cooking, sauté means to place food in a very hot pan with a bit of butter or oil and to shake the pan during the cooking process so that the food jumps about. Thus one can cook very quickly over high heat without burning the food.

Scalded

Generally this term applies to milk in recipes and it simply means to heat the milk to just under simmering. The milk is scalded when it becomes very hot. It is not a boil at all.

Shot

A liquid measurement that amounts to very little or to taste. A shot of wine is about an ounce, but a shot of Tabasco is less than $\frac{1}{16}$ teaspoon.

Sweat

To sauté over low heat with a lid on. This method causes steam and expedites the cooking time.

Kitchen Equipment

KNIVES

Knives are the most important pieces of equipment in your kitchen. When purchasing knives you should be mindful of the following points:

1. Please do not buy knives that are cheaply made and designed to go in the dishwasher. (No good knife should ever be put into the dishwasher. Low-quality knives may be made of stainless steel so that they are hard enough to take the dishwasher, but they cannot be sharpened.)

2. I prefer the standard old French chef's knife, not a designer gadget. The old model is hard to improve upon, and I have seen no improvement in function with the new "modern"-looking knives. Form follows function. A knife is for cutting. Buy one that does just that. Sabatier makes fine knives.

3. Buy good-quality knives of high carbon steel. They are now made to be nonstaining but are not stainless steel. Use a sharpening steel on them often to keep a good edge. Please do not consider buying an electric knife sharpener . . . no matter who tells you to do so. I find that people who use such devices simply sharpen their knives to death. There is no point in doing such a thing.

4. Good knives need sharpening and care, so never just throw them in a drawer. Keep them in a rack, and in good repair. A dull knife is very dangerous since you have to work harder and thus are more apt to let the knife slip and cut yourself.

5. I use the following knives constantly, but you may wish some other sizes. (I have about fifty knives. You don't need that many. Neither do I but I love good knives!)

> 10-inch-blade chef's knife
> 8-inch-blade chef's knife
> Boning knife
> Paring knife
> Long slicing knife (thin)
> Sharpening steel

Chinese cleaver:
There are several thicknesses available. A thin one is used for slicing and chopping vegetables and a thicker one for cutting meat and hacking poultry. Do not bother buying a stainless-steel cleaver. You cannot sharpen it.

POTS AND PANS

Good pots and pans make good cooking easy. Pans that are thin and flimsy can offer only burning, sticking, and lumps. Buy good equipment that is heavy. You will not be sorry.

Tips for Buying Good Equipment

1. Don't buy pots and pans with wooden or plastic handles. You can't put them in the oven or under a broiler.

2. Buy pans that fit your life-style, that are appropriate for the way you cook. They should be able to perform a variety of purposes in the kitchen. Avoid pans that can be used for only one dish or a particular style of cooking, such as upside-down crepe pans.

3. I do not buy sets of pans but rather a selection of several different materials that work in different ways. Most of my frying pans are heavy stainless steel or aluminum with SilverStone nonstick linings. I have aluminum stockpots and saucepans. No, I do not worry about cooking in aluminum since I never cook acids such as eggs or tomatoes or lemon juice in that metal . . . and I always keep aluminum well cleaned, remembering never to store anything in aluminum pots or pans. I have copper saucepans for special sauces and some stainless-steel saucepans as well. These are heavy stainless with plain metal handles, with an aluminum core sandwiched into the bottom. I also have a selection of porcelain-enameled cast-iron pans, Le Creuset being my favorite brand for that type of thing.

4. The pots and pans I use the most:

> 20-quart aluminum stockpot with lid
> 12-quart aluminum stockpot with lid
> 12-quart stainless-steel heavy stockpot with lid
> 4-quart aluminum sauteuse with lid
> 10-inch aluminum frying pan, lined with Silver-Stone, with lid
> Several cast-iron porcelain-coated casseroles, with lids
> Copper saucepans in varying sizes, with lids
> Chinese wok—I own six of them.

MACHINES AND APPLIANCES

Please do not fill your kitchen with appliances that you will rarely use. I do not own an electric deep-fryer or an electric slow-cooking ceramic pot or an electric egg cooker or . . . you know what I am saying. Other pieces of equipment will work for these jobs, and have other functions as well. But I do use an electric frying pan often because I can control the surface cooking temperature easily, and it's a versatile appliance.

I also have:

Food mixer

Choose a heavy machine, one that will sit in one spot and, using the different attachments available, make bread dough, grind meat, and make cake batters. I prefer the KitchenAid and have the large model with the five-quart bowl. For bread making, you'll need both the paddle-blade and dough-hook attachments. The meat grinder and sausage attachments make for easy and fun sausage making.

Food processor

While I use this machine less than my mixer, it is helpful.

Food blender

I have a heavy-duty model that will take a beating. Don't skimp on this machine. It should be able to puree solids easily—not make just milk shakes.

Electric coffee grinder, small size

I use this for grinding herbs and spices, not for coffee. It is from Germany.

SPECIAL EQUIPMENT

Pick and choose among these. Most of them are amazingly helpful:

Garlic press

I cannot abide garlic in any form except fresh. Buy a good garlic press. Be careful in purchasing as there are now many cheap ones on the market and they just do not work. I use a Susi made by Zyliss.

Lemon reamer, wooden

This is a good device, but many companies have recently been producing copies that are just not the right size and shape for proper use. Buy a good one, even if you have seen a cheaper model.

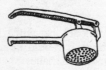

Potato ricer/spaetzle press

Buy one that comes with two removable plates. The plate with the small holes will rice potatoes to make Potato Gnocchi (page 212). The plate with the larger holes is necessary for making Passatelli (page 132).

Gnocchi strainer

An old utensil used to remove Potato Gnocchi (page 212) from boiling water. New designs of this ancient strainer are handy for removing any type of dumpling and most pastas from the kettle.

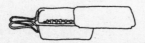

Stove-top smoker

This is a wonderful device put out by Cameron and it is made entirely of stainless steel. The idea is to place it on top of your stove with a bit of alder or hickory sawdust in the bottom and you can smoke things in just a moment in your kitchen. These are an investment, but you will find yourself smoking all kinds of things. Other sawdusts come with the device and can also be purchased in additional quantities. I remain partial to alder and hickory. IMPORTANT: You must have a strong out-of-the-house-exhaust fan to use this, or use it outside directly on the barbecue.

Stove-top grill
This is great for grilling peppers, bread, and other things right on top of the burner. It is called an asador, and it works very well.

Le Creuset stove-top grill
This device is a rectangular piece of cast iron with ridges on the surface. It fits directly on the stove top across two burners. Great for grilling indoors if you have an exhaust fan that draws smoke out of the house.

Grill racks
Choose one or two sizes of these racks for grilling on top of a griddle or on the barbecue. They are especially helpful in holding a fish together while you grill it.

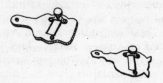

Truffle cutters

A very fancy gadget specifically designed for slicing truffles (page 423). It does a great job on slicing thin bits of hard cheeses. I also use mine for shaving chocolate. There are both wooden and metal versions. Find in gourmet cookware shops.

Chopper/noodle cutter/breadstick maker

An Italian cutting device that I find just great for making noodles and breadsticks. It also works well for cutting fresh herbs such as basil, parsley, et cetera.

Cheese graters

The hand-held stainless-steel graters are wonderful for grating hard cheeses on top of pasta and salads. Use in the kitchen or right at the table. You may also find other fancy graters like the box grater that catches the freshly grated cheese in a little drawer.

Meat pounder

This malletlike device will flatten out slices of meat so that they are very thin. Great for chicken, beef, and veal dishes.

Plastic sheeting
Sheeting is very helpful when you are pounding meat thin.
It is inexpensive and available in most lumberyards or hard-
ware stores. Ask for clear vinyl sheeting 8 millimeters
thick. *Do not store food in this sheeting.*

Fire extinguisher
A must for your kitchen. Buy one that will work on elec-
trical fires as well as stove fires. Talk to the salesperson.
You will sleep better at night.

Marble pastry board
These can be purchased in several sizes. Ideal for making
pastry, breads, or fresh pasta.

Stainless-steel steamer basket
This is a great help. I have two sizes, and they are adjust-
able for different pan sizes. Great for steaming vegetables
and not expensive.

Steamer stand
This aluminum stand sits in the bottom of your kettle. A
plate of food is placed on top and the pan becomes a
steamer. You can also use this rack as a double boiler.

Fine strainer for skimming oil
If you do get into deep-frying, this very thin mesh strainer
will help you keep the oil clean. From Japan.

Baking tiles
These will help you get a good crust on your bread.
Whether or not you use a pan, the tiles keep your oven
temperature even. Salday makes these.

Pasta rolling machine

This is the easiest way to make pasta. I prefer rolled pasta to extruded, and this machine can also be used for making other thin doughs. You can purchase many different cutting attachments.

Roasting racks, nonstick

At last, a roasting rack for a serious chicken lover. These work very well as the bird or roast does not stick to the rack.

Kitchen scale

Buy something that is fairly accurate. It will be helpful in baking perfect breads and in judging the sizes of roasts.

Plastic cheese baskets

Replicas of the old woven baskets used to form freshly made cheeses and drain them of excess liquid.

Large stainless-steel bowl

All-purpose mixing bowl 15 inches in diameter. Ideal for making bread dough and covering it while it rises.

Big wooden salad bowl

A good one will cost you some money, but if you like salad, you know that the greens will just not taste as good in metal or glass as they will in wood.

Copper polenta pot

A large heavy copper pot with a handle. Used in the old days for cooking polenta. You don't need one of these because they are expensive and polenta is easily cooked on the stove top in a good heavy conventional pot.

Baking sheets

I think the age of burned rolls and cookies is over, and it is about time. Buy insulated or air-cushioned baking sheets and pans. Wilton has a line called Even-Bake. I have tried them and they work! Bagels, rolls—breads of any kind—turn out much better than you could possibly expect. These are first class!

Insulated focaccia and cake pans

These pans have an air-cushion just like the baking sheets (above). These are also made by Wilton and they work great.

Perforated pizza pans

These aluminum pans work great because heat can pass through the little holes in the pan. This prevents the buildup of moisture underneath the dough and makes a crispy crust. Purchase a few 14-inch-diameter pans and you will have great success with the pizza recipes in this book. Made by Wilton.

Anchor Hocking freeze, heat, and serve dishes

So convenient for people cooking for one or two. Made of a special plastic that goes right from the freezer into the microwave, or even into a conventional oven up to 400°.

Glass baking dishes

Anchor Hocking offers several shapes and sizes. They are very inexpensive and durable. Find in good cookware shops and department stores. An absolute must for the kitchen.

Oil can

Decant your peanut oil or olive oil into this can and keep it by the stove for cooking. The oil is dispensed through a very small spout, which means you'll probably use less oil in your cooking. The can will also protect the oil from sunlight, which could spoil it. Find in good cookware shops.

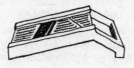

Mandoline

This is a wonderful device for cutting vegetables into thin slices or into julienne-style matchstick cuts. Be sure that you get a good one and be careful with it. You can cut yourself unless you use the guards properly.

Big dinner and serving plates

A dinner is much more exciting if served on large plates or platters. You can also find wonderful old serving platters in antique and junk shops.

Large skimmer/strainer

This has a long handle and an 8-inch-diameter head with holes. The handle allows you to reach into deep kettles, and the large holes in the head strain food very quickly. Very versatile and ideal for straining pasta without having to drain the kettle.

Parmesan-cheese knife

There are many different sizes of this special knife. The largest knife is rather heavy and may be 9 inches long with the handle. This knife is designed to split open whole wheels of Parmigiano-Reggiano cheese (page 465). The smaller knives, which look the same, are used for cutting smaller pieces of the cheese. They can also be used as a serving utensil on your buffet when you present a large piece of this great cheese to your guests. Simply let them cut off whatever amount they wish and serve themselves.

Mezzaluna

Chops vegetables and herbs using a rocking motion on a cutting board. It is also used to chop in a wooden or plastic bowl designed to accommodate its crescent shape. Available in a single- or double-blade version. Mezzaluna means "half-moon."

Soft-cheese knife

This unusual knife is serrated and has holes in the blade. Soft cheeses are easily cut because the slices won't stick to the blade of this knife. The forked tip allows you to use the knife for serving cheeses as well.

Wooden spoons and spatulas

I never put metal spoons or utensils in my frying pans or saucepans. Metal will scratch the surface, causing foods to stick. Buy wooden utensils and avoid the problem. I have grown very fond of tools made from olive wood as it is very hard and will last for years, even with regular use and washing. They cost more to start with but they will outlast the others by three times at least. I have also found some very durable plastic spoons, spatulas, and gadgets. These are made of an extremely high-heat-resistant plastic. They are the only plastic tools that I have ever found durable. Robinson makes them and they are called Ultratemp. Do not bother with buying cheap plastic.

Pasta wheel

The fluted wheel of this gadget makes a decorative edge when cutting fresh pasta or pastry doughs. It is commonly used for cutting out ravioli.

Assorted pasta cutters

These devices are simply rolled over sheets of fresh pasta to form a variety of shapes and sizes of noodles.

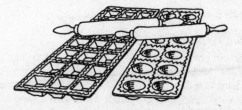

Ravioli presses

Makes a dozen or more ravioli at one time. A sheet of fresh pasta is fitted onto the form with plenty of overhanging dough. Filling is added to the cavities of the mold and another sheet of pasta covers the entire device. A rolling pin is run over the press firmly. The edges in the press will form and cut ravioli with a decorative edge.

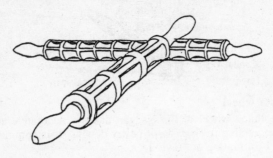

Ravioli pins

Forms ravioli by rolling the pin over large sheets of pasta with filling in between. The ravioli are then separated by cutting them with a pasta wheel (page 43). You will probably have better luck using a ravioli press (above).

Plastic pouring spouts

Use in wine bottles for oils, vinegars, et cetera. Buy in gourmet shops or restaurant-supply stores. I do not use metal pouring spouts as they corrode when used with soy sauce, wine, or vinegar.

Sausage funnel

Some electric mixers have sausage-making attachments, or you can use a sausage funnel to stuff casings by hand. Buy in gourmet shops.

Ravioli stamp
Used for cutting out individual square ravioli.

Heat diffuser or tamer
This is an inexpensive gadget that you place on your gas or electric burner to even out or reduce the heat. It will save you from a lot of burned sauces.

Tomato shark
This little gadget takes the stem out of the tomato in nothing flat. Be careful—there is a phony one on the market that doesn't work half as well.

Instant response thermometer
Calibrated from 0° to 220°. Use for making yogurt, bread yeast, and cheese, and for testing roasted meats for doneness. These are not designed to stay in the oven during cooking. Buy in gourmet shops and restaurant supply stores.

Pepper mill

The flavor of freshly ground black pepper is very different from that of the pre-ground. Find a good mill and grind your own. I have several mills, but my favorite is a Turkish coffee grinder. These are expensive, but if you are a pepper lover you will love this device. Be careful that the one you buy comes with a guarantee that it can be adjusted for pepper.

Poly cutting board

White plastic cutting board that is soft enough that it won't damage your good knives. Place this board in the dishwasher for easy cleaning (unlike a wooden cutting board).

Pizzelle iron

This hinged device is used directly over an open flame. A thin batter is poured onto the heated iron and then the iron is closed. This creates thin cookies with an attractive pattern. You can form the cookies into cone or tube shapes after you remove them from the iron and the cookie is still hot. You may prefer to try an electric pizzelle iron, which works very well.

Old-fashioned mortar and pestle

A replica of the antique ones made of heavy marble. Used with a wooden instrument, the pestle, for smashing foods and crushing herbs and spices. You might be lucky and find an old set in an antique shop or buy the new version from the address below. They are expensive but you will use it often in your kitchen.

Biordi Art Import
412 Columbus Avenue
San Francisco, California 94133

Porcelain mortar with wooden pestle

A less expensive option to the mortar and pestle above. Purchase a porcelain mortar and pestle set with a bowl that is about 3 inches tall by 6 inches in diameter. Replace the porcelain pestle with a wooden one. You might find individual wooden pestles for sale in antique shops or have someone who is good at wood working make one for you.

Television Shows and Recipes

Note: Dishes marked with an * were simply displayed and described. A recipe or demonstration was not given for those dishes. However, you will find a full recipe for the dish on the designated page.

901 SAUCES

Fresh Tomato Sauce Sicilian (page 139)

Ragù (page 144)

Bolognese Sauce (page 142)

Tomato with Lemon Olive Oil Quickie Sauce (page 140)

Brown Butter with Sage and Parmesan Cheese Sauce (page 150)

Sweet and Sour Sauce with Fruit (Agrodolce) (page 148)

902 PARMA HAM

Prosciutto with Cantaloupe (page 92)

Tortellini with Prosciutto and Peas (page 162)

Tortellini and Panna, with Prosciutto, Peas, and Mushrooms (page 160)

Italian Chicken Rolls (page 303)

903 HEARTY SOUPS

Bread Soup (page 119)

Bean Soup with Fried Escarole over Bruschetta (page 409)

Basic Stocks

*Chicken (page 116)

*Beef (page 115)

*Fish (page 117)

*Mock Veal (page 116)

Fennel Soup with Fish Broth (page 118)

904 BOLOGNESE FOODS

Tortellini in Brodo con Pesto (page 164)

Mortadella (page 23)

Ragù (page 144)

Passatelli (page 132)

Sweet Tagliarini Tart from Guest Chef Lynne Rosetto Kaspar (page 509)

905 OLIVES AND OLIVE OIL

Lemon Olive Oil (page 489)

Bread and Tomato Soup with Olive Oil (page 122)

Bruschetta with Oil and Garlic Machiavelli (page 261)

Pinzimonio (page 147)

Black Olive Paste (page 490)

*with Polenta (page 232)

*with Pasta (page 491)

*with Roast Pork (page 345)
*with Roast Lamb (page 346)
Steak Grilled with Olive Oil (page 490)

906 RISOTTO

Basic Risotto (page 239)
Risotto with Fennel (page 241)
Risi e Bisi (page 249)
Risotto with Gorgonzola (page 246)
Rice and Tomato Timbale with Bolognese Sauce (page 247)

907 FRESH PASTA

Spaghetti Vodka (page 158)
Pasta with Eggplant Sicilian (page 173)
Maccheroni alla Chitarra (page 180)
Maccheroni alla Chitarra Ragù (page 179)
Pasta Carbonara with Saffron (page 182)
Fresh Pasta Dough (page 178)

908 ANTIPASTO BUFFET

Bagna Cauda (page 78)
Bagna Cauda Butter (page 79)
Fried Radicchio Filled with Cheese (page 73)
Caponata (page 64)
Shrimp Caponata (page 66)
Artichokes and Caponata (page 65)
Salami in Oil (page 91)
Cold Frittata with Onions and Herbs (page 462)
Mussels in Parsley Vinaigrette (page 83) from Chef Lidia

909 PARMESAN CHEESE

Parmigiano-Reggiano (page 465)
Cheese Custard Plain (page 471)

Cheese Custard in Phyllo Dough (page 472)

Carpaccio with Shaved Parmigiano-Reggiano Cheese and Arugula (page 90)

Celery and Parmigiano-Reggiano Cheese Salad (page 110)

910 BALSAMIC VINEGAR

Parmigiano-Reggiano Cheese with a Drop of Good Balsamico (page 473)

Onion Omelet with Balsamic Vinegar (page 461)

Chicken with Balsamic Vinegar (page 301)

Strawberries and Balsamic Vinegar (page 517)

Lemon Olive Oil and Balsamic Vinegar Dressing (page 498)

Beef with Balsamic Vinegar Sauce (page 342)

911 SAUSAGES

Italian Dried Sausage (page 351)

Italian Sausage with Lemon (page 352)

Italian Sausage with Cheese and Wine (page 354)

Sausage Cacciatore over Polenta (page 355)

Sausage and Spinach Polenta (page 234)

Italian Sausage, Sicilian Style (page 352)

912 MORE PASTA

Spaghettini Tonnato (page 155)

Spaghettini Caponata (page 155)

Pasta Made with Fresh Herbs (page 169)

Penne Fonduta (page 179)

Pasta al Pesto with Cream, Green Beans, and Potatoes (page 193)

Pasta e Ceci (page 197)

Macaroni with Arugula and Fresh Tomatoes from Guest Chef Carlo Middione (page 159)

913 TRUFFLES

The Truffle Hunt (page 423)
Mushroom Soup (page 421)
Tagliolini with Butter and White Truffles (page 425)
Spaghettini with Black Truffle Paste (page 198)
Risotto with White Truffles (page 425)
Truffle Oil over Pasta (page 170)
Fried Cheese Polenta with Truffle Oil (page 228)

914 SANDWICHES

Milano Toasted Sandwiches (page 282)
*Pullman with Mozzarella and Cotto Ham (page 282)
*Mushrooms and Mozzarella Toast (page 282)
*Parma Ham and Fontina, Grilled (page 282)
Mortadella, Provolone, Mayonnaise, Lettuce, and Tomato (page 283)
Prosciutto, Grilled Eggplant, and Cheese (page 283)
Fried Pancetta, Tomato, Mortadella, and Fresh Mozzarella (page 283)
Salami, Provolone, and Roasted Peppers on a Roll (page 283)
Frittata Sandwich with Lettuce and Mayonnaise (page 283)

915 DESSERTS

Cornetti (page 513)
Torroncino (page 506)
Tiramisù (page 503)
Macedonia (page 514)

916 VENETIAN FOODS

Zuppe di Pesce Venetian (page 446)
Crab, Venetian Style (page 445)
Tiny Clams in Tomato Sauce and Wine (page 442)

Grilled Fish with Lemon Olive Oil (page 434)
Salmon in Foil from Guest Chef Fulvia Sesani (page 450)

917 MUSHROOMS

Fresh Mushrooms
Frozen Porcini
Dried Porcini for Sauces (page 415)
Cold Mushrooms Creamed (page 420)
Potato and Mushroom Timbale (page 416)
Crepes with Porcini and Mushrooms (page 418)

918 BREADS

Bread Soup (page 119)
Italian Peasant Bread (page 254)
Bread for New York Sandwiches (page 262)
Dried Olive, Black Pepper, and Sage Bread (page 258)

919 BEANS

Beans in a Flask (page 405)
White Beans and Tuna (page 407)
Pasta e Fagioli (page 403)
Pasta e Fagioli Fried (page 404)
Cannellini Bean Salad (page 98)
Tripe with Cranberry Beans (page 363)
Pisarei (page 410)

920 ITALIAN WINES

List of Favorite Wines (page 521)
Wine Gelatin with Fresh Fruit (page 515)
Braised Rabbit in Wine Sauce (page 305)
Italian Sausage with Cheese and Wine (page 354)
Mushrooms and Marsala (page 422)

A Lesson on Italian Wines with Patty Smith (Jeff's wife) (page 521)

1001 PASTA
(STUFFED PASTAS)

Basic Cannelloni Crepes (page 207)

Cannelloni Stuffed with Ragù (page 189)

Ravioli with Cheese, Potato, and Spinach Filling (page 183)

Green Ravioli with Fonduta (page 196)

Tortellini and Gorgonzola Sauce (page 163)

Fantasia di Farfalle (page 205)

1002 RED MEATS I

Meatballs, Criniti Style (page 330)

Farsumagru (page 331)

Veal and Parma Ham Rolls (page 337)

Beef in Rosemary Butter (page 338)

Pork Roast Stuffed with Mortadella (page 344)

1003 POLENTA

Three-Cheese Soft Polenta (page 224)

Hard Polenta (page 225)

Fried Cheese Polenta with Lemon Olive Oil (page 229)

Polenta Lasagna (page 232)

Sausage Polenta with Sage Butter (page 230)

Poached Polenta Cubes (page 233)

1004 FISH I

Cioppino (page 430)

Cioppino over Bruschetta (page 432)

Creamed Baccalà over Polenta Crostini (page 432)

Shrimp and Ragù over Pasta (page 446)

1005 CHEESE II

Fonduta (page 80)
Fonduta Mayonnaise Vegetable Dip (page 82)
Broiled Scamorza (page 479)
Dried Ricotta Cheese on Bruschetta (page 470)
Baked Ricotta (page 480)

1006 RICE II

Seafood Risotto (page 242)
Fried Risotto Milano (page 244)
Risotto with Saffron (page 240)
Meatball and Cabbage Couscous (page 340)

1007 SALADS

Seafood and Saffron Rice Salad (page 442)
Osso Bucco Salad (page 97)
Fancy Greens with Warm Pancetta Dressing (page 96)
Bread Salad (page 100)
Bagna Cauda Potato Salad (page 104)
Russian Salad (page 107)

1008 DESSERTS II

Bellini Cocktail (page 502)
Lemon Sherbet with Vodka (page 507)
Frutta for Dessert (page 508)
Cherries in Brandy or Grappa (page 505)
Cheese with Grand Nuts and Honey

1009 GNOCCHI

Potato Gnocchi (page 212)
Potato Gnocchi with Garlic Butter and Dried Ricotta
  Cheese (page 214)
Potato Gnocchi with Gorgonzola Sauce (page 215)
Potato Gnocchi with Truffle Oil (page 215)

1014   POULTRY AND GAME

Quail Grilled with Rosemary (page 296)

Game Hens Stuffed with Sausage, Fennel, and Mushrooms (page 297)

Chicken Breasts with Lemon Sage Butter (page 299)

Chicken Salad Venetian (page 315)

Chicken Twice Cooked (page 308)

Chicken, Farmer Style (page 313)

1015   COLD VEGETABLE BUFFET

Asparagus and Mushroom Salad with Egg (page 102)

Artichokes and Fried Radicchio (page 396)

Warm Spinach Salad with Bagna Cauda (page 105)

Bitter Greens (page 390)

Artichokes in Oil (page 388)

Sweet and Sour Cipolline (page 386)

1016   RED MEATS II

Porchetta (page 334)

Little Tied Porchetta Roasts (page 335)

Short Ribs with Wine and Porcini Sauce (page 324)

Beef in Rosemary Butter (page 338)

Deep-Fried Veal Meatballs (page 336)

Braciole (page 329)

1017   FISH II

Linguine with Zucchini, Tomato, and Grilled Shrimp (page 194)

Scapece (page 435)

Baccalà in Tomato Sauce over Poached Polenta Cubes (page 438)

Baccalà Salad (page 437)

1018 SANDWICHES II

Shrimp Salad on White (page 283)
Artichoke Salad on White (page 283)
Spinach Focaccia Sandwich (page 284)
Boiled Beef Sandwich Florentina (page 291)
Roast Pork Sandwich, Philly Style (page 286)
Veal Sandwich, Philly Style (page 286)

1019 FLORENCE (INNARDS)

Ignudi al Ragù (page 474)
Tripe Florentine (page 365)
Veal Kidneys with Gorgonzola Sauce (page 362)
Tripe with Cranberry Beans (page 363)
Risotto with Sweetbreads and Mushrooms (page 364)
Tripe and Polenta (page 362)

1020 THE ITALIAN-AMERICAN COMMUNITY

Covered Filled Focaccia (page 274)
Italian Potato Salad with Green Beans and Red Onion
  (page 106)
New York Special Sandwich (page 285)
Escarole Soup with Tiny Meatballs (page 129)
Grilled Chicken and Pancetta Spiedini with Three Sauces
  (page 316)

ANTIPASTI

Most Americans confuse antipasti with hors d'oeuvres. Hors d'oeuvres refers to fancy little edible works of art that are to be consumed with a drink in your hand, and they are generally served while the guests stand and talk. Not so with antipasti.

Antipasti is the first course. The name means "before the meal," that is, before the main courses. This first course is no light little bit of nibbly but rather a serious display of fine food items that help you prepare for the rest of the meal. Antipasti are always eaten while seated, though you may choose from a buffet of several items. I have seen antipasti tables in Italy that have as many as thirty items for the opening offering.

Such an antipasti display could make a meal for most of us, but the Italians are only getting started. The meal has a purpose of its own, and that purpose is not simply to feed the body. It is an event that invites communication, affection, gossip, discussion, and, of course, good food and wine. We Americans tend to plan meals that are efficient in terms of our use of time, but the Italians plan a meal that will take hours to consume, and one is expected to be content in many ways before the meal is finished.

I would like to think that we are doing a better job in this country in terms of feeding all of the human hungers, and not just the tummy. The antipasti course can be a great beginning for a wonderful and fulfilling event. Choose any of the following recipes and spread them out for your guests. They will realize that you really do value their company. Further, I hope your family grows to expect "the plate before the meal."

In addition to the recipes in this chapter you may also

wish to see the recipe for Cold Frittata with Onions and Herbs (page 462). This works well as an antipasto.

CAPONATA

MAKES 1½ QUARTS

This wonderful relish takes a few minutes to prepare but it will prove to be one of the things you fall back upon when you need to add life to a dish. The sweet and sour flavor is a favorite in Italy and points to the fact that this is a very old dish.

2 pounds eggplant
1 tablespoon salt
4 tablespoons olive oil, more as needed
2 cups celery, sliced ¼ inch thick
1 medium yellow onion, chopped
⅓ cup white wine vinegar
1 tablespoon sugar
3 cups canned plum tomatoes, crushed
2 tablespoons tomato paste
2 tablespoons pickled capers, drained

6 large pitted green olives, drained and sliced
4 or 5 anchovy fillets in oil, cut in half
¼ cup golden raisins
½ cup toasted pine nuts (Simply pan-fry over medium heat with a tablespoon of olive oil.)
Salt and pepper to taste

Trim the tops off the eggplant and dice into 1-inch pieces. Place the cubed eggplant in a large bowl and sprinkle with the salt. Toss together thoroughly and remove to a large colander. Place the bowl underneath the colander and allow to drain 30 to 40 minutes.

Heat a large frying pan and add 2 tablespoons of the olive oil, the celery, and the onion. Sauté about 15 minutes or until tender. Remove to a 4- to 6-quart pot.

After the diced eggplant has drained, rinse it well in cold water. Drain well and pat dry with a cloth towel. Return the frying pan to the burner and add some of the remaining olive oil. Add the eggplant and sauté about 10 minutes. Do this in 3 small batches, using some of the oil each time. Add to the pot of sautéed celery and onion. Stir in the remaining ingredients except the raisins, pine nuts, and salt and pepper. Bring to a boil, cover, and simmer 15 to 20 minutes, or until tender. Stir in the raisins, pine nuts, and salt and pepper. Allow to cool. Serve at room temperature or cold.

This recipe makes a very versatile condiment for the kitchen. It keeps for two weeks sealed in the refrigerator. We use it as an antipasto spread for crackers. It also works great in a salad dressing, as a cold seafood relish, and as a sandwich topping.

ARTICHOKES AND CAPONATA

SERVES 6

We had a dish similar to this one night while guests in the home of Chef Carlo and Lisa Middione. Carlo is the author of The Food of Southern Italy *(see Bibliography) and has become a dear friend. The two of them run an outstanding Italian restaurant in San Francisco, and Craig and I make it our first stop whenever we are in Baghdad by the Bay. Our recipe is only a tiny bit different from his and you will find many other such recipes from the South of Italy in his wonderful book.*

6 large artichokes	3 cups Caponata (page
1 lemon, cut in half	64)
Olive oil for	
brushing	

Cut the stems off the artichokes so that they will sit upright. Break off the row of tough leaves around the base of one of the artichokes. Rub the base with a lemon half to prevent discoloring. Cut the top third of the artichoke off and dig out the fuzzy center. (A grapefruit spoon works well for this.) Rub the inside with lemon. Using a pair of scissors, trim off the top third of each leaf, which contains a sharp spine. Rub the artichoke all over with lemon. Repeat with the remaining artichokes, making sure to rub with lemon as you work.

Brush the artichokes with some olive oil and place them upright in a large stainless-steel or enameled pot (not aluminum). Add enough water to the pot so that it is ½ inch deep. Bring the pot to a boil, cover, and simmer 35 to 40 minutes or until the centers of the artichokes feel tender when a knife is inserted. Add water to the pot as necessary to prevent it from drying out and burning.

Remove the artichokes and allow them to cool completely. Brush the artichokes with additional olive oil to give them a nice shine. Fill the center of each artichoke with the Caponata. To eat, pull off a leaf and dip it into the Caponata. Pull the bottom of the leaf through your teeth to remove its meat. Don't forget to eat the delicious artichoke bottom once the leaves are gone!

SHRIMP CAPONATA

SERVES 4–6

If you have made some Caponata ahead of time, this dish is a snap. It is amazing how well the flavor of the shrimp and the eggplant relish go together. This one you have to try.

1 tablespoon olive oil
1 clove garlic, crushed
½ pound medium
   shrimp, peeled
¼ cup dry white wine
Pinch of salt to taste
   (easy on the salt)

2 cups Caponata
   (page 64), at
   room temperature

Bruschetta (page
   261) or good toast

Heat a large frying pan and add the oil, garlic, and shrimp. Sauté over high heat 1 to 2 minutes until just barely firm. Don't burn the garlic! Add the wine and toss together for 10 seconds or so, until the wine evaporates. Salt to taste, remove from the pan, and allow to cool. The shrimp should not be overcooked. Fold the cooled shrimp together with the Caponata. Serve as an antipasto with Bruschetta or toast.

MARINATED ROAST PORK SLICES

SERVES 6–8

This sounds rather heavy for a first course but the meat is to be sliced thin and served with this very tasty dressing. The antipasti plate will feature other lighter items, of course.

This is a good way to use up leftover pork roast. Cold meats with dressings are very popular in both Tuscany and Lombardy.

1½ **pounds boneless pork loin roast**
1 **tablespoon olive oil**
2 **cloves garlic, crushed**
1 **tablespoon Dijon mustard**
Salt and pepper to taste
2 **teaspoons fresh rosemary**

THE DRESSING
¼ **cup Dijon mustard**
3 **tablespoons water**
1 **tablespoon lemon juice**
3 **tablespoons olive oil**
1 **tablespoon capers, drained**

Rub the pork with oil, garlic, Dijon mustard, salt, pepper, and rosemary. Roast in a 350° oven until a meat thermometer inserted in the center registers 150°, about 1½ hours. Don't overcook! (Roasting times will depend on the thickness of the pork. For best results have the butcher tie together 2 small pieces of boneless pork loin.)

Allow to cool completely. Whisk together the ingredients for the dressing thoroughly and set aside. Slice the pork thinly across the grain and toss the slices with the dressing. Allow to marinate for at least 1 hour.

Arrange the slices neatly on a platter and brush with any remaining dressing. Serve on a buffet or use the pork slices as a part of individual antipasto plates.

STUFFED CLAMS ANTIPASTI

SERVES 4–6 AS AN APPETIZER OR MORE AS PART OF AN ANTIPASTI PLATE

Steamed clams in vermouth! What a marriage. This dish will be popular on the antipasti table and as a main course on a warm summer evening.

2 tablespoons olive oil

2 cloves garlic, finely chopped

3 pounds large steamer clams (at least 2 dozen), rinsed, scrubbed, and drained

½ cup dry vermouth

1½ tablespoons butter

½ cup minced yellow onion

1 tablespoon chopped parsley

2 tablespoons all-purpose flour

3 tablespoons heavy cream

2 teaspoons lemon juice

Freshly ground black pepper to taste

THE TOPPING

3 tablespoons butter, melted

½ cup fine bread crumbs

2 teaspoons finely chopped parsley

Pinch of salt

Heat a 6-quart kettle and add the oil and garlic. Sauté for 1 minute and add the drained clams and the vermouth. Bring to a boil, cover, and reduce the heat to a simmer. Steam the clams open, stirring once, about 7 minutes. Strain, reserving nectar, and allow to cool. Remove the clam meat, reserving the shells. Chop the clam meat coarsely and set aside, covered. Strain the nectar through a fine sieve to remove any sand and set aside.

Heat a medium-size frying pan and add the butter, onion, and parsley. Sauté until the onion is clear; do not brown. Stir in the flour and cook together to form a roux, about 2 minutes. Stir in ½ cup of the reserved nectar and simmer gently until a smooth sauce is formed (save the remaining nectar for another use). Add the cream, lemon juice, and pepper to taste. Combine the sauce with the chopped clams.

Break the reserved shells into half shells. Fill the half shells with the clam mixture (you should have at least 24 half shells filled). Combine the ingredients for the topping and sprinkle over the stuffed shells. Place on a cookie sheet and bake at 375° for 15 to 20 minutes until hot and lightly browned.

GRILLED EGGPLANT
WITH FONTINA CHEESE
AND LEMON OLIVE OIL

SERVES 4–6

Eggplant is so very rich that it works well as a cold anti-pasto. Be sure to use imported Italian Fontina since the Danish and domestic versions do not even come close to the original.

1 1-pound eggplant (buy a nice fat one!)

2 tablespoons salt

½ cup olive oil for grilling

¾ cup finely diced ripe tomato

1 tablespoon chopped parsley

1 tablespoon grated Parmesan cheese

2 tablespoons Lemon Olive Oil (page 489)

Freshly ground black pepper to taste (not too much)

¼ pound imported Italian Fontina cheese

GARNISH
Additional Lemon Olive Oil

Cut the eggplant crosswise at a 45° angle into ¼-inch-thick pieces. This should yield about 8 nice slices (use the ends for another dish). Sprinkle both sides of the slices with the 2 tablespoons salt. Place in a large colander inside a bowl and allow to drain for 40 minutes. Rinse, drain well, and pat the eggplant slices dry with paper towels.

Heat a stove-top grill (Le Creuset—see illustration, page 35) to medium-high. Brush one side of the eggplant slices with some of the olive oil and place the oiled side down on the hot grill. Grill until a deep golden brown and tender, about 5 minutes. Brush the uncooked side of the eggplant slices with more oil and turn over. Grill until brown on that side. Remove to a sheet pan to cool.

Combine the tomato, parsley, Parmesan cheese, Lemon Olive Oil, and black pepper to taste. Cut the Fontina into thin strips and place it evenly on one half of each cooled eggplant slice. Top the Fontina with the tomato mixture. Fold each eggplant slice over the cheese and tomato mixture to form a half moon.

Place on a serving platter and drizzle with additional Lemon Olive Oil. Allow to marinate for 1 hour at room temperature before serving.

STUFFED OLIVES WITH MEATBALL FILLING

MAKES 3 DOZEN

Do not let the instructions for this dish deter you from trying it. Really, it is easier than it looks, and a lot of older Italian men will tell you that their mothers made a similar dish in the old country. These are delicious!

The soaking and the blanching of the olives will help get rid of the excess brine.

36 pitted green olives (Colossal size)

THE FILLING
1 tablespoon olive oil
½ cup finely chopped yellow onion
½ pound mild Italian sausage (squeeze the sausage out of the casings if necessary)
½ pound fresh spinach, washed and finely chopped
¼ cup fine bread crumbs
¼ cup milk
1 egg, beaten

2 tablespoons finely grated Parmesan cheese
Salt and pepper to taste (easy on the salt)

THE BREADING
1½ cups flour
3 eggs, beaten
3 cups bread crumbs

6 cups olive oil for frying (use inexpensive olive oil and save it in the refrigerator for more frying at another time)

Place the olives in a colander and rinse with cold water. Remove the olives to a large bowl and add plenty of water to cover. Allow the olives to soak overnight. Rinse and drain the olives. Bring 4 quarts of water to a boil and blanch the olives for 1 minute. Drain and allow to cool. Pat dry on paper towels.

Heat a medium-size frying pan and add the oil, onion, and sausage. Sauté until the onion is clear and the sausage is crumbly. Add the spinach and sauté 2 minutes more, cooking off any excess liquid. Remove to a bowl to cool completely.

Combine the bread crumbs and milk together in a small bowl. Stir together until the bread crumbs absorb the milk. Add to the bowl containing the sausage mixture along with the remaining ingredients for the filling and mix together well using your hands.

Place some of the filling in a pastry bag with a small tip. (You will probably have to open the end of the tip slightly.)

Stuff the dried-off olives, leaving a little excess filling packed on the end of each olive.

Place the flour, eggs, and bread crumbs in three separate bowls. Heat the oil to 375° in an electric frying pan. Lightly coat the olives with flour, then beaten egg, then bread crumbs. Deep-fry in small batches for 3 minutes and remove to paper towels to drain. (The breading on the fried olives may crack or crumble a little but don't worry about it.) Serve hot or at room temperature.

Note: Use any leftover filling for ravioli, or sauté and stir into pasta sauce.

FRIED RADICCHIO FILLED WITH CHEESE

SERVES 4 AS AN APPETIZER

This dish is so rich that one leaf is enough for each guest. We first tasted something close to this at Carmine's Il Terrazo Restaurant, in Seattle. Carmine is a first-class Italian restaurateur.

1 large head of
  radicchio (must
  have 4 nice large
  outer leaves that
  are whole and in
  good shape)
2 tablespoons pine nuts
4 ounces chèvre (goat
  cheese)
4 ounces ricotta cheese
  Salt and pepper to
  taste
4 thin slices of lean
  pancetta (have an
  Italian deli do this
  for you)

1 tablespoon olive oil

GARNISHES
Finely julienned red
  bell pepper,
  sautéed
Julienned fresh basil
Drizzle of olive oil
Lemon wedge

Core the base of the radicchio using a paring knife. Carefully remove 4 nice outer leaves that are fully intact and set aside. If a leaf breaks, line it with part of another leaf. Use the remaining radicchio for a salad or another recipe.

Lightly toast the pine nuts in a frying pan over medium heat for about 2 minutes. Allow to cool and chop coarsely. Mix together the pine nuts, cheeses, and salt and pepper in a small bowl. Place ¼ cup of the cheese filling in the center of each radicchio leaf. Form a bundle by rolling and tucking the leaf around the cheese filling. (Be careful not to tear the radicchio.) Wrap the bundle with a slice of pancetta (uncoil the pancetta and wind around the bundle) and secure with a toothpick.

Heat a large nonstick frying pan and add the oil. Place the filled bundles seam side down in the frying pan and lightly fry over medium-low heat, covered, until the pancetta browns, about 2 minutes. Carefully turn the bundles once and brown the other side, covered. The bundles will collapse down a bit as the radicchio becomes tender and may leak a little cheese, but that's all right!

Remove to individual plates or a serving platter. Garnish with lightly sautéed julienned red bell pepper, a sprinkle of basil, and a drizzle of good olive oil. Serve with lemon wedges.

RED BELL PEPPERS

SERVES 4–6

The utter simplicity of this dish is one of the most wonderful things about it. You will see these on antipasti tables all over Italy . . . and we can be proud of the fact that the sweet bell pepper originally came from the New World.

2 medium red sweet
    bell peppers,
    cored and seeded
3 tablespoons olive oil
2 cloves garlic,
    chopped
½ medium yellow
    onion, thinly
    sliced

2 teaspoons tomato
    paste
¼ cup dry white wine
⅛ teaspoon red pepper
    flakes
Salt to taste

Cut the peppers into 1½-inch-wide strips lengthwise. Heat a large frying pan and add the oil, garlic, onion, and pepper strips. Sauté over medium heat, covered, until just tender, about 15 minutes. Stir in the remaining ingredients and cook covered over low heat for 5 minutes more. Allow to cool to room temperature.

BRUSSELS SPROUTS

SERVES 8-10

If you do not overcook these brussels sprouts, you will even have the kids eating them! Cold vegetables in dressing are common on antipasto tables all over Italy, and this simple dish is a gem.

⅓ cup finely chopped
    pancetta (page 23)
1 tablespoon olive oil
2 cloves garlic,
    crushed
¾ cup thinly sliced
    yellow onion
2 pints brussels
    sprouts, trimmed
    and cut in half
    lengthwise

THE DRESSING
½ cup olive oil
2 tablespoons white
    wine vinegar
Salt and pepper to
    taste

Heat a large frying pan and add the pancetta. Sauté until the fat is transparent and drain off the excess fat. Add the 1 tablespoon olive oil along with the garlic, onion, and cut brussels sprouts. Cook, covered, over low heat until the sprouts are just tender, about 10 minutes. Remove to a bowl to cool. Combine the ingredients for the dressing and toss with the brussels sprouts. Allow to marinate for 1 hour at room temperature, tossing a couple of times.

MARINATED MUSHROOMS

SERVES 6–8

This addition to the antipasti table sounds almost corny . . . but this version really is delicious when the vinegar and mushroom flavors blend on the plate with the rest of the opening tidbits.

1 pound fresh large button mushrooms	2 tablespoons chopped parsley
½ cup olive oil	1 teaspoon dried oregano, whole
2 tablespoons lemon juice	Salt and freshly ground black pepper to taste
2 tablespoons white wine vinegar	
3 cloves garlic, peeled and crushed	

Trim the stems off the mushrooms and save for another use. Bring a large pot of water to a boil and blanch the mushrooms for 2 minutes. Remove and drain very well.

Mix the remaining ingredients together in a medium-size bowl and add the drained mushrooms while they are still hot. Toss together, cover, and allow to marinate in the refrigerator for 4 hours. Toss the mushrooms a couple of times while marinating.

GRILLED EGGPLANT WITH FRESH MOZZARELLA

SERVES 6–8

I hope we are talking the American public into eating more eggplant. It is easy to prepare and most flavorful. Just remember that you must always salt it first and let it drain well. This removes the bitterness that seems to bother some children.

Prepare Grilled Eggplant (page 373). After the slices of eggplant have been cooked and cooled to room temperature, shingle the slices alternately with ⅛-inch-thick slices of fresh mozzarella (page 469) on a serving platter. Pour the dressing from the eggplant recipe over all and garnish with chopped parsley.

ASPARAGUS TONNATO

SERVES 4 AS A VEGETABLE OR MORE AS PART OF AN ANTIPASTO PLATE

Asparagus with tuna sauce will probably surprise some people but the flavors really do belong together. I could make a whole lunch from this dish!

1 pound medium asparagus	1 tablespoon olive oil
Pinch of salt	½ recipe Tonnato Sauce (page 143)

Break off the tough woody ends of the asparagus and discard. Bring a large enough pot of water to a boil and add the salt and oil. Blanch the asparagus a few minutes and drain. Rinse with cold water to stop the cooking. Drain well. Chill and serve with Tonnato Sauce. You will not need the whole batch of Tonnato.

BAGNA CAUDA

SERVES 4–6 AS AN APPETIZER

It sounds all too simple, but it really is this easy and the results are fantastic. This "hot bath," or hot dip, is just great for endive, celery sticks, green onions, fresh fennel sticks, and so forth. In the hills of the Piedmont region they also use sticks of cooked red beet. This makes a wonderful first course but I can see you eating this as a whole meal on a cool summer evening.

¼ ounce dried porcini
    (page 415)
6 large canned flat
    anchovy fillets
¾ cup olive oil
½ cup butter

6 cloves garlic,
    crushed
2 tablespoons brandy
Freshly ground
    black pepper to
    taste

Place the porcini in a water glass and add ¾ cup hot tap water. Allow to stand 45 minutes, then drain and chop coarsely. Set aside. Place the anchovies in a very small saucepan and mash the fillets with a wooden spoon. Add the oil, butter, and garlic. Bring the mixture to a gentle simmer. Add the reserved porcini, brandy, and black pepper to taste. Gently cook and stir for 2 minutes. Serve with an assortment of fresh vegetables and Italian bread for dipping.

BAGNA CAUDA BUTTER

Refrigerate leftover Bagna Cauda (page 78) until firm. This creates a versatile flavored spread with endless possibilities. Spread on good bread that has been toasted and then broil for great garlic bread!

BAGNA CAUDA PEASANT STYLE

SERVES 4–6 AS AN APPETIZER

This is a bit thicker than the classic version you will find on page 78. We have found that the addition of the sardines adds a certain richness without quite as much salt. Of course, if you are a purist, then you want only anchovies in your Bagna Cauda. But for a change, this is very good, and it is a little less costly than the original dish from Piedmont. Even in Piedmont you have trouble finding Bagna Cauda since the price of anchovies has risen so.

6 large canned flat anchovy fillets, packed in oil	**Assorted Raw Vegetables for Dipping**
½ cup virgin olive oil	**Red bell pepper strips**
¼ cup butter	**Cabbage leaves**
6 cloves garlic, crushed	**Fresh fennel bulb pieces**
2 tablespoons brandy	**Endive**
Freshly ground black pepper to taste	**Celery sticks**
	Green onions
1 ¾-ounce can sardines (boneless, skinless fillets packed in oil)	**Radishes**
	Good Italian bread for dipping

Place the anchovies in a very small saucepan and mash the fillets with a wooden spoon. Add the oil, butter, and garlic and simmer gently for 5 minutes. Add the brandy, black pepper, and sardines with their oil. Gently cook and stir the mixture 5 minutes more to break up the sardines. Serve with assorted vegetables and bread for dipping.

FONDUTA

MAKES ABOUT 4 CUPS

One of the truly fine cheeses to come to the New World from Italy is Fontina. Do not confuse this very rich semisoft cheese with the product from Denmark bearing the same name.

This recipe is common in the Northern regions of Italy, and it certainly points to the influence of Switzerland and its fondue.

4 tablespoons butter	4 egg yolks, at room
4 tablespoons flour	temperature
2 cups milk	Tiny pinch of
¾ pound Fontina	ground white
cheese (imported	pepper
Italian Fontina)	

Melt the butter in a small frying pan and stir in the flour. Cook together over low heat for 1 minute to form a roux (do not brown!). Heat the milk in a double boiler. Whisk the roux into the hot milk. Continue to cook the milk and roux together, whisking constantly until smooth and slightly thickened, about 4 minutes.

Cut the cheese into small chunks. Add to the thickened milk and whisk until melted and smooth. Whisk in the egg yolks a little at a time and continue cooking the sauce, gently stirring all the time.

Cook the Fonduta 5 minutes more or until nicely thickened, smooth, and hot throughout (do not boil!). Add the white pepper to taste.

Use as a cheese topping, or with pasta or toasted bread.

VARIATION: Try adding a bit of sautéed garlic and dried porcini mushrooms to Fonduta. Soak about ½ ounce of dried porcini in ½ cup of water for a half hour. Then drain, rinse, and chop. Sauté in a tiny bit of olive oil with a touch of garlic. Stir into the finished Fonduta. Garnish with grated Parmesan cheese and freshly ground black pepper to taste.

FONDUTA MAYONNAISE
VEGETABLE DIP

MAKES 3½ CUPS

We had this in a very formal Italian restaurant one night, somewhere in the North where such a thing might be expected.

This great dip can be used with any kind of raw vegetable. I am afraid that your guests might just want to spend the entire evening eating this dish.

2½ cups Fonduta **(page 80)**	**1 cup mayonnaise** **(use good** **quality!)**

Prepare the Fonduta and remove it to a medium-size bowl. Cover and allow to cool to room temperature. Whisk in the mayonnaise until smooth. Use as a raw vegetable dip.

CROSTINI WITH BAGNA CAUDA BUTTER AND
FONTINA

Toast was actually a Greek invention, not Italian at all. However, when the Greeks taught the Romans how to make toast, the Romans immediately began dousing the crunchy bread with garlic and olive oil. This recipe is a combination of several flavors that will make you a fan of "toast."

Toast thick slices of good Italian bread and spread the toast with Bagna Cauda Butter (page 79). Broil the buttered side for 1 minute, then top with a slice of imported Italian Fontina cheese. Broil again until bubbly.

LIDIA'S MUSSELS IN PARSLEY VINAIGRETTE

SERVES 6

I have eaten many times at Felidia's Italian restaurant in New York City, and each time I swear it is better than the time before.
   Lidia Bastianich is the chef and co-owner, along with her husband, Felice. She is known throughout this country and in Italy as a person of great charm and tremendous skill. She gave us this recipe while appearing on our Italian cooking series. More can be found in her excellent cookbook, La Cucina di Lidia *(see Bibliography).*

3 pounds medium-large mussels (see Note)	**3 tablespoons minced Italian parsley**
4 bay leaves	**3 tablespoons virgin olive oil**
6 tablespoons minced Bermuda onion	**3 tablespoons red wine vinegar**
6 tablespoons minced roasted pepper	**Salt and freshly ground pepper**
3 tablespoons minced seeded peperoncini (see Note)	**Lemon wedges and parsley sprigs**

In a nonreactive pot large enough to accommodate the mussels with room to spare, bring 2 cups of water to a boil, add the mussels, and cook, covered, about 5 minutes, shaking the pot occasionally, until all the mussels have opened. Drain the mussels in a colander, discarding any that have remained closed, and, if desired, reserve the liquor for another use. Remove and discard the upper shells of the mussels, leaving the meats attached to the lower shells. On a serving tray, arrange the mussels in a concentric, radiating pattern, like flower petals, and allow them to cool in the refrigerator.

In a bowl, blend all other ingredients except the lemon wedges and parsley sprigs. When the mussels have cooled sufficiently (they should not be overchilled), spoon about 1 teaspoon sauce over each and decorate with lemon wedges and parsley sprigs.

Note: Mussels may be scrubbed and rinsed in advance of use, but should not be debearded until just before they are cooked. Peperoncini, hot pickled green peppers, can be found in Italian groceries and most supermarkets.

BACCALÀ SALAD ON CROSTINI

Dried salt cod may not be your thing. If you were raised in an Italian household you probably ate a great deal of this stuff when you were a child. In small batches I enjoy it very much. This recipe is perfect for the antipasti table.

Prepare a batch of Baccalà Salad (page 437) and some good
Italian bread slices toasted with garlic and olive oil. Place
a bit of the Baccalà Salad on the garlic toast and garnish
with grated hard-boiled egg. The number of people this will
serve will depend on the size of the pieces of garlic toast.

MARINATED
MOZZARELLA CUBES
SERVES 6–8

*Cheese with good olive oil is almost enough for a meal.
On the antipasti plate it becomes one of those refreshing
bits in between bites.*

¾ pound mozzarella
cheese, fresh or
aged
¼ teaspoon red pepper
flakes
1 tablespoon chopped
parsley

2 tablespoons chopped
fresh basil
½ cup extra virgin
olive oil
2 teaspoons lemon
juice

Cut the mozzarella into ¾-inch cubes and place in a bowl
along with the red pepper flakes, parsley, and basil. Mix
the oil and lemon juice together in a small bowl and toss
with the cheese and herbs. Allow to marinate for at least 2
hours at room temperature.

EGGPLANT, FENNEL,
AND ONION ANTIPASTO

SERVES 10 AS PART OF AN ANTIPASTI PLATE

*This is a very light and lovely cold relish that is perfect for
the antipasti plate. The flavors of eggplant and fennel certainly let you know that this is Italian.*

1½ 1½-pound eggplant
1½ tablespoons salt
1 1-pound fresh
   fennel bulb
4 tablespoons olive
   oil
2 cloves garlic, sliced
1 medium yellow
   onion, peeled
   and sliced ½
   inch thick
½ cup dry white wine

THE DRESSING
½ cup olive oil
Juice of 1 lemon
2 tablespoons
   chopped parsley
Salt and pepper to
   taste

Cut off the top of the eggplant and quarter it lengthwise.
Cut the quarters crosswise into 1-inch pieces. Place the eggplant in a bowl and add 1 tablespoon of the salt. Toss to-

gether and remove to a colander and allow to drain 45 minutes. Rinse and drain the eggplant well; set aside.

Cut off the top of the fresh fennel and discard. Cut the fennel bulb in half lengthwise and cut out the core. Slice the fennel into 1-inch-wide by 3-inch-long strips.

Heat a large frying pan and add 3 tablespoons of the oil. Add the eggplant and sauté about 5 minutes until nice and tender. Remove to a sheet pan to cool.

Return the frying pan to the burner and add the remaining 1 tablespoon of oil. Add the fennel, garlic, and onion. Sauté over high heat for 1 minute. Add the wine, cover, and reduce the heat to low. Cook covered until the fennel is tender, about 7 to 10 minutes. Remove to a sheet pan to cool.

Mix together the ingredients for the dressing thoroughly. Combine the cooked vegetables in a bowl with the dressing and toss together. Place the mixture on a serving platter.

CRUDITÉS WITH GERMAN MUSTARD

MAKES ENOUGH DIP FOR 2–4

I had some trouble trying to figure this one out. It was served us in a very fine restaurant in Treviso, in the Veneto region. The place is called Alla Pasina and we had one of our best meals in Italy in this place. I was confused by the flavor of the German mustard, but after the kind chef told me what he had done, I then realized that such a dish should be quite common in the region. After all, it is very close to Austria.

2 tablespoons
   German-style
   brown mustard
2 teaspoons hot water
⅓ cup extra virgin
   olive oil

⅛ teaspoon white wine
   vinegar
Salt and pepper to
   taste

Dilute the mustard with the hot water in a small bowl. Add the remaining ingredients and whisk together. Serve with an assortment of raw vegetables for dipping. This dip will not mix together smoothly and is supposed to be slightly separated.

ROLLED CARPACCIO

SERVES 4–6 AS PART OF AN ANTIPASTI PLATE

This variation on the classic dish has real class. The dish is a bit easier to eat than the original, and it is very attractive.

Follow the instructions for preparing the sliced raw meat in the recipe Carpaccio with Shaved Parmigiano-Reggiano Cheese and Arugula (page 90). Use "beef eye of round" and omit the garnishes in that recipe. Lay each paper-thin slice of meat on a sheet pan and add a little salt and pepper to taste. Top with a thin slice of mozzarella cheese, and a few whole fresh basil leaves. Roll the meat up into a cigar shape and cut the roll in half crosswise. Arrange the cut rolls on a serving platter and drizzle with extra virgin olive oil.

CARPACCIO DI VITELLO
(BROILED)

SERVES 4

This is one of the most unusual dishes we found in Italy. The veal is served raw, just as in any carpaccio, but it is placed under the broiler for just a moment so that all warms and brightens. This is worth your trying, I promise.

½ pound boneless veal
    shoulder or leg
    roast, sliced paper
    thin

Drizzle of extra
    virgin olive oil
Italian bread for
    serving

GARNISHES
¼ teaspoon dried
    marjoram
½ teaspoon fresh
    rosemary,
    chopped

Have your butcher slice the meat for you or follow the instructions for slicing the raw meat in the recipe for Carpaccio with Shaved Parmigiano-Reggiano Cheese and Arugula (page 90). Omit the garnishes in that dish and top the raw sliced veal that has been arranged on a serving platter with the garnishes.

Place the platter with the raw veal slices and the garnishes under a preheated broiler on high for about 30 seconds. Don't cook the veal, just give it enough time to warm up and to color the meat slightly. Serve with good Italian bread.

CARPACCIO WITH LEMON OLIVE OIL MUSTARD SAUCE

SERVES 4–6 AS PART OF AN ANTIPASTI COURSE

The story goes that this dish was invented in Venice, at Harry's Bar. Many variations have been developed since, and I think ours is a very good one.

This is especially beautiful if you can use a piping tube or a small-tipped plastic mustard dispenser to decorate the carpaccio with the dressing. I buy these gadgets from any restaurant supply house, and you will be amazed at the fun you can have with them.

Arrange the thinly sliced raw beef on a platter as in the recipe for Carpaccio with Shaved Parmigiano-Reggiano Cheese and Arugula (page 90). Omit the garnishes in that dish and top the raw meat with the dressing and garnishes below.

THE DRESSING	GARNISHES
5 tablespoons Lemon Olive Oil (page 489)	Freshly ground black pepper to taste
3 tablespoons Dijon mustard	Sprinkle of chopped parsley
1 tablespoon mayonnaise	

In a small bowl, whisk the lemon olive oil into the mustard a little at a time. Whisk constantly to emulsify. Whisk in the mayonnaise until smooth. Place in a squirt bottle. Squirt a creative pattern of the dressing on the thinly sliced arranged meat. Garnish with black pepper and parsley.

CARPACCIO WITH SHAVED PARMIGIANO-REGGIANO CHEESE AND ARUGULA

SERVES 4–6 AS AN APPETIZER

Real Parmigiano-Reggiano cheese makes this dish. It cannot be any other way, I am convinced. Choose meat that is very lean since the olive oil will replace the fat in the meat.

½ pound beef eye of round or New York strip steak (The meat must be in a whole piece trimmed of all fat, bone, and gristle. If using New York strip, specify a piece of meat cut off the "small end," which should contain no gristle.)

GARNISHES

Shaved Parmigiano-Reggiano cheese (use a truffle slicer [page 36] or cheese plane [page 41])

Tender arugula leaves, washed

Drizzle of extra virgin olive oil

Freshly ground black pepper to taste (optional)

Place the completely trimmed piece of meat on a small sheet pan and place in the freezer. Freeze until very firm throughout but not rock hard. The amount of time in the freezer will depend on how cold your freezer is, so just keep checking on it. Slice the meat paper thin (you must have an electric meat slicer to do this) and shingle the slices on a large platter. Top with the garnishes and serve with good Italian bread.

SALAMI IN OIL

You see this simple dish all over Italy, and it is very good. Slice wine-cured Italian salami and place it on a serving plate. Drizzle with extra virgin olive oil and let it come to room temperature. Serve on an antipasti buffet. That's it. Simple and delicious.

PROSCIUTTO WITH CANTALOUPE

*Good prosciutto with fresh fruit offers a match made in
Italy, not Heaven. Heaven should be so good!*
*Remember that this wonderful Parma ham must be sliced
just before use. Even two hours will cause a loss of flavor,
though plastic wrap right at the deli counter will help a
bit.*

Thinly sliced prosciutto is often wrapped around a peeled
wedge of very ripe cantaloupe. The dish is served this way
all over the North of Italy. However, I like it even better
with fresh ripe figs. You are certainly welcome to think up
your own combination. Even apples are better with prosciutto. Pear wedges simply sing with prosciutto, as do
most melons.

SALADS

I love Italian salads, since the people, particularly in the North, take the creation of a salad as a very serious matter. Further, the salad is always seen as a separate course and rarely served on a side plate along with some other portion of the meal.

In recent times you can find very fancy salads that serve as a whole luncheon meal. While this was not the custom in the past, new eating habits and shorter lunchtimes seem to demand such creations in big business cities like Milan and Genoa.

Among the salad recipes we have tried to offer some things that are a bit unusual. Some of these salads are so heavy that they can be used as a main course in terms of an American meal—heavy salads such as the Osso Bucco Salad, which is great for entertaining. You make it a day ahead of time and relax! The Bread Salad is unusually good, as are the Chicken Salad Venetian and the Cold Pork Salad. For lighter fare please do not hesitate to try the Green Salad Bagna Cauda and the simple Salad with Lemon Olive Oil.

Please strive to serve the salad as a separate course, Italian style. And you can serve the salad at any time during the meal, even at the end. Dessert can wait!

In addition to the recipes in this chapter you may also wish to see:

Chicken Salad Venetian (page 315)
Cold Pork Salad (page 343)
Lemon Olive Oil and Balsamic Vinegar Dressing (page 498)

CAPONATA SALAD DRESSING

MAKES 1½ CUPS

I love caponata, that wonderfully tangy eggplant relish. In a fit of salad hunger one day I developed the following salad dressing recipe. I think it is just great!

¾ cup Caponata (page 64)

¾ cup extra virgin olive oil

1 tablespoon lemon juice

Salt and pepper to taste

Place all the ingredients in a blender and blend together until smooth and emulsified. Toss with your favorite greens.

FANCY GREENS WITH WARM PANCETTA DRESSING

SERVES 4

I have to hand it to Craig, my chef and assistant. He decided that pancetta, the bacon from Italy that is not smoked, would make a much better salad than our smoked pork product. This is what he came up with and if you try it you will not go back to smoked bacon again. Of course, the Gorgonzola cheese just does it!

¼ pound pancetta
(page 23), thinly
sliced and
chopped
⅓ cup olive oil
1 tablespoon white
wine vinegar
1 tablespoon lemon
juice
Pinch of sugar (not
too much)

Salt and pepper to
taste
2 tablespoons pine
nuts
¼ pound Gorgonzola
cheese, crumbled
1 pound assorted
fancy greens (use
a combination of
red leaf lettuce,
arugula,
radicchio, or
whatever you
like)

Sauté the pancetta until slightly crispy. Add the olive oil, vinegar, lemon juice, and sugar. Simmer for 1 minute. Add salt and pepper to taste.

Toast the pine nuts by heating them in a frying pan over medium heat until golden brown. Shake the pan while toasting the nuts to prevent burning.

Tear the greens up and place them in a large bowl. Toss the greens with the warm dressing, toasted pine nuts, and Gorgonzola. Serve immediately.

OSSO BUCCO SALAD WITH TUNA DRESSING

SERVES 6–8 AS SALAD OR MANY MORE AS A PART OF AN ANTIPASTI PLATE

I would like to see the family that has two pounds of cooked osso bucco just sitting in the refrigerator. I know this sounds extravagant, but this is one of the best cold-meat dishes that I have ever developed. I am sure you will appreciate it as well.

1 6- to 7-ounce can
  tuna
¾ cup olive oil
2½ tablespoons lemon
  juice
½ cup mayonnaise
  Salt and pepper to
  taste

About 2 pounds
  cooked and
  diced osso bucco
  meat (page 325)
  (no bones)
1½ cups thinly sliced
  white onion
⅓ cup chopped
  parsley
  Lettuce leaves for
  serving

Flake the tuna and place in an electric blender. Add the oil, lemon juice, and mayonnaise. Blend until smooth, scraping down the sides of the container as necessary. Stir in the salt and pepper to taste. Toss the dressing in a large bowl with the remaining ingredients except the lettuce leaves. Refrigerate for 2 hours, folding the salad a couple of times while chilling. Serve in lettuce leaves.

VARIATION: Add thinly sliced celery or julienned celery root to the salad.

CANNELLINI BEAN SALAD

SERVES 6 AS A SALAD

The Italian cannellini bean is very close to our northern white bean, but the texture and flavor are just different enough that I urge you to find the actual cannellini. They will not mush up as much as our normal white bean and for this reason they make a terrific salad. You will find this dish all over the Northern regions of Italy.

2½ cups dried
cannellini white
beans (Or use
northern white
beans. Note that
northern white
beans may take
a little less time
to cook.)
½ medium yellow
onion, sliced
4 green onions,
chopped
3 tablespoons
chopped parsley
2 tablespoons
chopped fresh
rosemary

⅔ cup olive oil
Juice of 1 lemon
Salt and pepper to
taste
2 cloves garlic,
crushed
2 tablespoons white
wine vinegar
½ cup prosciutto
(page 355),
thinly sliced and
chopped
(optional)

Place the beans in a bowl and add 6 cups fresh cold water. Allow to sit on the counter overnight. Drain and place in a 6- to 8-quart pot. Add 3 quarts of fresh cold water. Bring the beans to a boil, cover, and simmer 25 to 30 minutes until barely tender. Drain well and pour the beans out onto a large sheet pan. Allow to cool completely and remove to a large bowl.

Add all the remaining ingredients to the bowl. Toss and allow to marinate for at least 2 hours at room temperature before serving.

BREAD SALAD

SERVES 10–12

This dish is certainly the glory of peasant cooking. Nothing could be wasted in the days when bread was so expensive . . . and thus the saving of the old bread for soups and even salad.

I know that this may sound a bit strange to you if you have not already tried it, but if you have not tried it, you are in for a sensational salad. Who needs lettuce? We have old bread!

1 pound good heavy bread, cut into 1-inch cubes and dried overnight (use good Italian or French bread)

3 medium-size ripe tomatoes, cut in wedges

2 white onions, peeled and sliced

2 medium cucumbers, peeled, seeded, and sliced

¼ cup chopped parsley

3 tablespoons pickled capers, drained

½ cup coarsely chopped fresh basil leaves

THE DRESSING

¾ cup olive oil

2 tablespoons lemon juice

2 cloves garlic, crushed

Salt and pepper to taste

2 tablespoons balsamic vinegar (page 495)

GARNISH

Freshly shaved or grated Parmesan cheese

Soak the dried bread cubes in cold water for 1 minute. Drain and squeeze the water out. Place the bread in a large bowl and add the tomatoes, onion, cucumbers, parsley, capers, and basil.

Mix the ingredients for the dressing together and drizzle it over everything in the bowl and toss well. Allow to sit at room temperature, covered, for at least 1 hour.

MOZZARELLA, TOMATO, AND BASIL SALAD

SERVES 4–6

This is an oldie but a goodie. It is a common sight through-out Italy on both the antipasti buffets and the salad bars. Every sandwich counter has one of these ready for you if you prefer a heavy salad over a formal sandwich.

Be sure to use very ripe tomatoes.

3 medium-size ripe tomatoes	½ cup extra virgin olive oil
¾ pound fresh mozzarella cheese (not aged)	1 tablespoon lemon juice
1 bunch fresh basil	Salt and pepper to taste

Core and slice the tomatoes. Slice the fresh mozzarella. Shingle the slices of tomato and cheese onto a serving platter with fresh basil leaves in between the slices. Mix the olive oil, lemon juice, and salt and pepper together and pour over all. Allow to marinate at room temperature for at least 2 hours.

SALAD WITH LEMON OLIVE OIL

Toss fresh salad greens with Lemon Olive Oil (page 489), a little grated Parmesan cheese, and salt and freshly ground black pepper to taste. Don't use too much cheese or pepper because they will overpower the subtle oil.

ASPARAGUS AND MUSHROOM SALAD WITH EGG

SERVES 6 AS A SALAD COURSE OR MORE AS PART OF AN ANTIPASTI PLATE

This is rather rich, I will admit. However, everyone at your table will love this wonderful blending of two products of the earth. First, mushrooms that grow from the waste of the earth, and two, a form of grass that has reached the level of glory!

2 **pounds asparagus, medium thickness**	**THE DRESSING**
2 **tablespoons olive oil**	⅓ **cup extra virgin olive oil**
½ **cup thinly sliced white onion**	**Juice of ½ lemon**
1 **clove garlic, crushed**	**Salt and freshly ground black pepper to taste**
½ **pound mushrooms, sliced**	
2 **tablespoons freshly grated Parmesan cheese**	
3 **hard-boiled eggs, coarsely grated**	

Break off the tough woody ends of the asparagus and discard. Cut the asparagus on an angle into 1½-inch pieces. Bring a 3-quart pot of water to a boil and add a pinch of salt and 1 tablespoon of the olive oil. Blanch the asparagus a couple of minutes until barely tender. Drain and rinse with cold water to stop the cooking. Drain well and place in a bowl with the onion.

Heat a frying pan and add the remaining 1 tablespoon of oil, the garlic, and the mushrooms. Sauté 2 to 3 minutes until just tender, allow to cool, and add to the asparagus and onion. Add the cheese and the grated eggs.

Combine the ingredients for the dressing and add to the bowl. Toss together and serve.

GREEN SALAD BAGNA CAUDA

SERVES 4–6

I enjoy this salad just as much as I do a Caesar. It is very simple to prepare if you have leftover Bagna Cauda sauce, and you will certainly learn to make extra sauce after you have tasted this dressing. Simple and yummy!

½ cup Bagna Cauda (page 78), at room temperature	**GARNISH** **Freshly ground black pepper**
Juice of ½ lemon	
2 tablespoons good mayonnaise	
1 large head Romaine lettuce, cleaned and torn	

Blend together the Bagna Cauda, lemon juice, and mayonnaise. Toss with the cleaned lettuce and serve topped with freshly ground black pepper to taste.

BAGNA CAUDA POTATO SALAD

SERVES 6–8

I do not like potato salad with sweet relishes and pimentos. Potato salad is to speak of potatoes, not sweet relishes. However, this variation using the Bagna Cauda sauce makes a great deal of sense to me. Everyone who has tasted this is convinced of same. Please try it!

3 pounds russet potatoes, washed	1 cup mayonnaise
5 hard-boiled eggs, sliced	¼ cup olive oil
2 bunches green onions, chopped	Salt and pepper to taste
3 tablespoons chopped parsley	
½ cup Bagna Cauda (page 78), at room temperature	

Place the potatoes, skin on, in a 4-quart pot and cover with ample water. Bring to a boil and simmer, uncovered, about 30 minutes for large potatoes. Test the potatoes for doneness by inserting a table knife in the center of the potato. The knife should insert easily, but the potatoes should still be a bit firm. Carefully drain the potatoes and allow to cool completely.

Peel the potatoes by scraping the skin off with the back of a table knife. Dice the potatoes and place in a large bowl along with the eggs, green onions, and parsley.

In a small bowl, whisk together the Bagna Cauda and mayonnaise. Add the olive oil and whisk again. Add to the bowl of potatoes. Fold the salad together until evenly incorporated. Salt and pepper to taste.

WARM SPINACH SALAD WITH BAGNA CAUDA

SERVES 4–6

This is a blend of the Old World and the New. I love warm spinach salad with bacon, but this blending of a bit of mayonnaise with Bagna Cauda is my new favorite. It is rich, of course, so plan on light servings.

1½ pounds cleaned spinach leaves (no stems)	2 tablespoons good mayonnaise
1 bunch green onions, chopped	½ cup Bagna Cauda (page 78), barely warmed
Juice of ½ lemon	

Place the cleaned spinach and green onions in a bowl. Whisk the lemon juice and mayonnaise into the warm Bagna Cauda. Pour the dressing over the spinach and toss together. Serve immediately. You will not need salt or pepper.

MUSHROOM AND PARMIGIANO-REGGIANO CHEESE SALAD

MAKES 6 SALADS

If you are a mushroom fan, then this blending of mushrooms with Parmigiano-Reggiano cheese is for you.

Follow the recipe for Celery and Parmigiano-Reggiano Cheese Salad (page 110). Simply substitute thinly sliced fresh button mushrooms for the celery. You may want to sauté the mushrooms for just a moment with a bit of olive oil. Allow to cool before mixing the salad.

ITALIAN POTATO SALAD WITH GREEN BEANS AND RED ONION

SERVES 4–6

No, I really did not see this in Italy but in the Italian Market in Little Italy, New York City. It is a good idea and a bit different from the heavy mayonnaise salad that most of us know.

2 1-pound russet potatoes, skin on	**THE DRESSING**
¾ pound fresh green beans, trimmed and cut into 1-inch pieces	½ cup extra virgin olive oil
	¼ cup mayonnaise
	Juice of ½ lemon
2 tablespoons regular olive oil for blanching	1 tablespoon chopped fresh parsley
	Salt and pepper to taste
½ cup thinly sliced red onion	
2 hard-boiled eggs, grated	

Place the potatoes in a pot and cover with water. Bring to a boil uncovered. Simmer 30 to 40 minutes until very tender when pierced with a knife. Carefully drain and allow to cool. Peel and cut the potatoes into ½-inch dice.

Blanch the beans for 4 minutes in a pot of water with a pinch of salt and the 2 tablespoons olive oil. Drain and rinse the beans in cold water. Drain well again. Toss with the potatoes, onion, and eggs.

Prepare the dressing and toss the salad. Simple and delicious.

RUSSIAN SALAD

A description of this dish is all that you will need. You find it at all the luncheon bars in Northern Italy. The same dish is popular in Greece.

The name has something to do with the claim that the dish was invented in Russia by Olivier, chef to the czars.

Prepare your own favorite potato salad, omitting any mustard in the mayonnaise and any pimentos. Please don't overcook the potatoes. Add a bit of chopped dill pickle and a package of frozen mixed peas and diced carrots, completely defrosted. I like hard-boiled egg in mine.

Toss all together and add salt and pepper to taste. Then try to figure out how a Russian salad created by a French chef became so popular in Greece and why it is now so popular in Italy.

COLD VEGETABLE
SALAD MILANO

MAKES ENOUGH SALAD FOR 6–8

This is very colorful and great for a lighter lunch. In Milan lunch bars, the vegetables, meat, and cheese are arractively arranged on individual plates and they are ready for you when you go into the place.

½ pound
cauliflowerettes in
1-inch pieces

½ pound broccoli
flowerettes in 1-
inch pieces

½ pound carrots,
peeled and sliced
in ¼-inch pieces

2 cups fresh spinach
leaves, packed

⅓ pound mozzarella
cheese, julienned

⅛ pound prosciutto,
thinly sliced and
chopped

Regular olive oil
and salt for
blanching

THE DRESSING
Use your favorite,
or lemon juice
and extra virgin
olive oil

Salt and freshly
ground pepper to
taste

Blanch cauliflowerettes, broccoli, and carrots separately in boiling water with a bit of salt and a little olive oil. Cook each until just tender, then rinse in cold water. Drain very well.

Toss all ingredients together or arrange neatly on separate plates.

GRILLED VEGETABLE SALAD

MAKES 4 SALADS

In the fine coffee bars of Milan you will find the most lovely things as offerings for lunch. If you play around a little with the presentation on this one, it is an absolute knockout!

1 ½-pound eggplant, sliced ⅛ inch thick crosswise
2 teaspoons salt
1 ½-pound zucchini, sliced ⅛-inch thick lengthwise
4 ripe Roma tomatoes (¾ pound), sliced ¼ inch thick lengthwise
Olive oil for grilling
3 hard-boiled eggs, sliced

THE DRESSING

⅓ cup extra virgin olive oil
2 tablespoons fresh lemon juice
1 tablespoon chopped parsley
Salt and pepper to taste

Sprinkle the eggplant slices with the 2 teaspoons of salt and place in a colander in the sink. Allow the eggplant to drain for 45 minutes. Rinse the eggplant with fresh water and pat dry on paper towels.

Brush one side of all the vegetables with olive oil. Place

the vegetables, oiled side down, on a very hot grill. (Le Creuset stove-top grill, page 35, works great for this.) Do this in batches to keep the temperature of the grill up. Brush the top side of the vegetables with a little more oil. When the vegetables are nicely browned and done to your liking, flip and grill the other side. The vegetables should cook 2 to 3 minutes total on a good hot grill, a little longer for the eggplant. Remove the vegetables to a small sheet pan to cool.

Arrange the cooled vegetables on a serving platter in an attractive shingle pattern with the hard-boiled egg slices. Prepare the dressing and pour over all. Allow to marinate 1 hour at room temperature.

CELERY AND PARMIGIANO-REGGIANO CHEESE SALAD

SERVES 6

Typical of the salads you find in wonderful Milan, this one is easy to make and can be enjoyed year-round, of course.
I like crunchy salads that contain no lettuce whatsoever. Nothing but cheese and celery and oil and lemon. Delicious!

3 cups very thinly
   sliced fresh celery
¼ cup Parmigiano-
   Reggiano cheese
   shavings (use
   truffle cutter
   [page 36] or
   cheese plane
   [page 41])
⅓ cup extra virgin
   olive oil

Juice from one
   lemon, squeezed
   over the top
Salt and freshly
   ground black
   pepper to taste

Prepare six small salads using the above ingredients.

SOUPS AND STOCKS

I wish Americans could think of soup as the Italians do. In this country we generally see soup as a light meal in itself when nothing else seems to be readily available, and it usually comes from a can. Not so in Italy.

The Italians have a much longer food history than we, and certainly that helps explain their affection for wonderfully rib-sticking soups. While we cannot track down the first people to eat soup, we do know that soup has been popular in Italy as far back as we can record its history. The soups were made in early times with anything that was left over, or anything you could find. Lord knows what that means! Rome learned a lot about soup making from the Greeks, as did the French, but in our time Italian soups are superior to those you find in Greece. Italian cooks have always taken a good idea from another people and improved upon it.

The bread soups and the bean soups that you will find in this section point to hearty peasant stock . . . both the people and the soup stock itself. The people who till the earth seem to understand the concept of a sustaining soup much better than businesspeople. The earthy crowd would use anything in the soup pot, including bread. They still do!

Those of us who feel we don't have the time to prepare soup from scratch, let alone the time to eat it, are the losers.

You need a good 12-quart stockpot if you are going to run an Italian kitchen. With that you can prepare the necessary stocks and bases from which all else will come. The stocks freeze well, so don't think I am expecting you to start from scratch each day.

My favorite soups include the Bread Soup, Craig's Bean

Soup with Fried Escarole over Bruschetta, Fennel Soup with Fish Broth, Passatelli from Bologna, and Zuppe di Pesce from Venice. The Bread and Tomato Soup with Olive Oil is also very basic to the Italian understanding of the table. So take the time to prepare your own stocks, and then the production of great soups will be easy and rewarding.

In addition to the recipes included in this chapter you may also wish to see:

Pisarei (page 410)

    Bread and Tomato Soup with Olive Oil (page 122)

    Bean Soup with Fried Escarole over Bruschetta (page 409)

    Mushroom Soup (page 421)

    Zuppe di Pesce Venetian (page 446)

BEEF STOCK

MAKES ABOUT 5 QUARTS

I cannot run my kitchen without good beef stock. It is the basis of many sauces and soups, and it is so easy to prepare. I find it very necessary to my enjoyment of Italian foods since the product is far superior to those salty bouillon cubes. Try this once and you will never be without it!

5 pounds bare beef
  rendering bones,
  sawed into 2-inch
  pieces
1 bunch carrots,
  unpeeled and
  chopped

1 bunch celery,
  chopped
3 yellow onions,
  unpeeled and
  chopped

Tell your butcher that you need bare rendering bones. They should not have any meat on them at all, so they should be cheap. Have him saw them into 2-inch pieces.

Roast the bones in an uncovered pan at 400° for 2 hours. Be careful with this because your own oven may be a bit too hot. Watch the bones, which you want to be light toasty brown, not black.

Place the roasted bones, along with the fat, in a 20-quart soup pot and add 1 quart of water for each pound of bones. For 5 pounds of bones, add the carrots, celery, and onions. (The onion peel will give a lovely color to the stock.)

Bring to a simmer, uncovered, skimming off any foam, and cook for 12 hours. You may need to add water to keep the soup up to the same level. Do not salt the stock.

Strain the stock, and store in the refrigerator. Allow the fat to stay on the top of the stock when you refigerate it. The fat will seal the stock and allow you to keep it for several days.

Stock also keeps well in the freezer.

CHICKEN STOCK

MAKES ABOUT 3 QUARTS

I know you can buy canned chicken stock. Some of it is not bad . . . but I promise you your Italian kitchen will run much better if you make your own stocks. After refrigeration overnight the fat can be removed from the top of the stock. The flavor will be fresh and comforting, and your soups and sauces will be superb. Further, once you taste fresh pasta cooked in your fresh chicken stock, you will never go back to bouillon cubes.

3 pounds chicken
backs and necks
3 quarts cold water
4 ribs celery, coarsely
chopped
6 carrots, unpeeled,
thickly sliced

2 medium yellow
onions, peeled and
quartered
8 whole black
peppercorns

Place the chicken backs and necks in a 12-quart soup pot and rinse with very hot tap water. Drain and add the cold water to the pot, along with the other ingredients. Bring to a simmer, skimming off any foam, and cook for 2 hours. Be sure to skim off the froth that forms when the pot first comes to a simmer.

The stock will taste a bit flat to you since it has no salt. Salt will be added when you use the stock in the preparation of soups, sauces, pasta, or stews.

MOCK VEAL STOCK

MAKES ABOUT 4½ CUPS

Few of us are willing to pay the price for veal bones. We developed this Mock Veal Stock and we are quite pleased with it. The Chicken Stock softens the Beef Stock so that it really is close to a veal stock.

4 cups Chicken Stock
   (page 116)
4 cups Beef Stock
   (page 115)
1 cup dry white wine
1 tablespoon olive oil
2 cloves garlic,
   chopped

1 medium yellow
   onion, thinly sliced
4 sprigs parsley
   Salt and pepper to
   taste

Bring stocks and wine to a simmer in a 4-quart pot, uncovered.

Heat a medium-size frying pan and add the oil, garlic, and onion. Sauté until evenly browned and lightly caramelized. Do not burn. Do this over low heat, stirring frequently.

Add to the pot of stock along with the parsley and simmer uncovered until reduced by half, about 2 hours. Strain the reduced stock and season with salt and pepper to taste.

FISH STOCK

You really don't need a recipe for such a thing. It is so easy to make that you will read this once and never refer to it again, but I hope you make it often. It is great to have a fine fish stock in your refrigerator so that you can create soups, sauces, and fish stews without any pain at all. This will freeze well in 1-quart plastic containers.

Pick up fresh fish bones, skin, heads, and tails. Just tell your fishmonger what you are preparing and he will take good care of you. Be sure that everything is fresh.

Rinse the bones in fresh water and then place in a soup pot. Add 1 quart of water for each pound of bones and a few chopped carrots, yellow onions, celery ribs, and a bit of salt and pepper. Do not oversalt since you may wish to reduce the stock. Bring to a boil and then turn to a simmer. Cover and cook for 1 hour. Strain the stock and discard the solid material. Chill.

FENNEL SOUP WITH FISH BROTH

SERVES 8

Fresh fennel is now "in" here in America. It has always been popular in Italy, and this recipe will show you why. I love fennel in any form, but in a fish stock it is particularly good.

3 tablespoons olive oil	2½ quarts Fish Stock (page 117)
2 cloves garlic, crushed	½ cup dry white wine Salt and pepper to taste
1 medium yellow onion, peeled and thinly sliced	
	GARNISH
1¾ pounds fresh fennel, with tops attached	2 tablespoons chopped fresh parsley

Heat a large frying pan and add the oil, garlic, and onion. Sauté until just tender.

Cut off the tops of the fennel bulbs and chop the tops coarsely. Place the fennel tops in a 4-quart pot along with the stock and wine. Bring to a boil, covered, and simmer for 30 minutes.

Trim the bottom cores of the fennel bulbs and discard.

Julienne the fennel and add to the frying pan of onion. Sauté 5 minutes more.

Strain the stock, discarding the solids, and return it to the pot. Add the sautéed fennel and onion to the pot of stock. Simmer, covered, until the fennel is tender, about 10 to 15 minutes. Skim off the excess oil from the soup and discard. Add salt and pepper to taste. Garnish with parsley.

BREAD SOUP

SERVES 8–10

This is frugal. No waste, certainly not in terms of bread. We do not see bread as a basic expense in our culture but in the old days in Italy bread was quite expensive. Old bread was never thrown out but saved to be used in soups and even salads. Please do not hesitate to try this dish. Your kids will love it!

This dish is from Tuscany and the hills around beautiful Florence.

4 cups Chicken Stock
    (page 116)
4 cups Beef Stock
    (page 115)
½ cup white wine
4 tablespoons olive oil
3 cloves garlic
1 medium yellow
    onion, peeled and
    chopped
2 ribs of celery,
    chopped
3 medium tomatoes,
    chopped
1 bay leaf
⅛ teaspoon red pepper
    flakes
¼ cup chopped fresh
    basil

¼ cup chopped fresh
    parsley
½ pound Italian
    Peasant Bread
    (page 254) or
    crusty French
    bread, cut into 1-
    inch cubes, dried
    overnight on a
    sheet pan
Salt and pepper to
    taste

GARNISHES
Grated Parmesan
    cheese
Chopped parsley

Heat the Chicken Stock, Beef Stock, and wine in a 4- to 6-quart pot. Heat a large frying pan and add 2 tablespoons of the oil and the garlic, onion, and celery. Sauté for 5 minutes. Add the tomato and sauté 5 minutes more. Add to the pot of stock along with the bay leaf, red pepper flakes, basil, and parsley. Cover and simmer 1 hour.

Heat the frying pan again and add the remaining 2 tablespoons of oil. Add the dried bread cubes and toast them until light golden brown. Do not burn. Add to the pot. Add salt and pepper to taste. Simmer for 15 minutes and serve with grated Parmesan cheese and chopped parsley.

BREAD SOUP WITH RAGS

Serves 8–10

How can there be so many variations on bread soup? Well, the answer has something to do with the amount of leftover

bread in Italy, a land in which the kitchen values bread.
The addition of eggs, or "rags," to this dish is wonderful.
It will be a hit with your family, I promise.

2 tablespoons butter
¼ cup sliced and
    chopped
    pancetta
3 cloves garlic,
    crushed
1 medium yellow
    onion, chopped
8 cups Chicken
    Stock (page 116)
½ cup dry white wine
1½ tablespoons
    chopped fresh
    rosemary
1 tablespoon
    chopped parsley
Salt and black
    pepper to taste

¼ pound day-old
    bread cubes, cut
    into ½-inch
    squares (weigh
    out about ½
    pound of cubes
    and let dry
    overnight)
4 eggs
¼ cup grated
    Parmesan cheese

GARNISHES
Chopped parsley
Grated Parmesan
    cheese
Freshly ground
    black pepper

Heat a 4 to 6-quart pot and add the butter, pancetta, garlic, and onion. Sauté until the onion is tender, about 10 minutes. Add the Chicken Stock, wine, rosemary, and parsley. Bring to a boil and simmer, covered, 1 hour. Add salt and pepper to taste. Stir in the dried bread and simmer a few minutes until the bread softens and swells up.

Beat the eggs and the ¼ cup cheese together in a small bowl. Remove the soup from the burner and drizzle the beaten-egg mixture into the pot. Allow to stand covered for 2 minutes and then gently stir to create strands of egg or "rags." Adjust the salt if necessary. Serve in bowls with the garnishes to taste.

BREAD AND TOMATO SOUP
WITH OLIVE OIL

SERVES 12

I have never seen so much olive oil on the table as in Tuscany. We were served a dish similar to this one at the Machiavelli Inn. It must be fine extra virgin oil, and then you will be in Heaven!

½ pound Italian
Peasant Bread
(page 254) or a
good heavy
white bread,
dried overnight

8 cups Chicken
Stock (page 116)

1 medium yellow
onion, finely
chopped

2 cloves garlic,
crushed

1½ tablespoons
chopped fresh
sage

2 cups Fresh Tomato
Sauce Sicilian
(page 139)

1½ cups coarsely
chopped ripe
tomato

Salt and pepper to
taste

GARNISHES
Plenty of extra
virgin olive oil
(drizzle
liberally!)

Grated Parmesan
cheese

Cut the bread into 1-inch pieces and place on a sheet pan. Allow to dry overnight. Place the Chicken Stock, onion, and garlic in a 6-quart pot. Cover and simmer gently for 30 minutes. Add the sage, tomato sauce, chopped tomato, and the bread, which has been soaked in cold water to cover for 2 minutes, then drained and squeezed dry. Simmer, covered, gently for 20 minutes. Allow to stand covered 15 minutes so that the bread will continue to expand and absorb flavor. Reheat the soup to serving temperature and add salt and pepper to taste. Serve with the garnishes.

MINESTRONE SOUP

SERVES 10–12

There must be thousands of variations on this basic dish, because there are thousands of Italian grandmas. However, this version is as close as we can come to what you will find in Italy. Notice that we did not just make a vegetable soup with tomatoes and then dump in some pasta, a common sin found on Italian restaurant menus in America. Craig insisted on thickening this soup with beans, just as they do in Italy. We are proud of this version and of the variations that follow. Craig also reminded me that one can make a fine minestrone by simply cleaning out the refrigerator.

2 cups dried
   cannellini beans
   (page 22)
1 cup dried
   cranberry beans
   (page 401)
10 cups Chicken
   Stock (page 116)
½ pound pancetta
   (page 23), sliced
   and chopped
2 tablespoons olive
   oil
4 cloves garlic,
   crushed
2 medium carrots,
   peeled and diced
2 medium yellow
   onions, peeled
   and diced
1 cup thinly sliced
   celery
2½ cups chopped ripe
   tomato

2 cups peeled and
   diced potatoes
½ cup dry red wine
2 tablespoons
   chopped fresh
   parsley
1 teaspoon dried
   marjoram
1½ cups diced zucchini
1 pound kale
   (remove the
   stems and chop
   coarsely)
½ cup grated
   Parmesan cheese
Salt and pepper to
   taste

GARNISHES
Extra virgin olive
   oil to taste
Grated Parmesan
   cheese to taste

Place the cannellini beans and the cranberry beans in separate bowls. Cover each with at least 2 inches of cold water
and allow to soak overnight.

Drain the cannellini beans and place in a small pot along
with 5 cups of the Chicken Stock. Bring to a boil, cover,
and simmer 1 hour until the beans are tender. Strain the
liquid into an 8- to 10-quart pot and puree the cannellini
beans. You will have to use some of the liquid to puree the
beans smooth. Drain the soaked cranberry beans and add
to the pot along with the pureed cannellini.

Heat a large frying pan and add the pancetta. Brown the
pancetta until almost crisp and discard the fat. Add the pancetta to the pot. Heat the frying pan again and add the oil,

garlic, carrots, onions, and celery. Sauté until tender and add to the pot.

Add the tomato, potatoes, red wine, parsley, marjoram, and the remaining 5 cups of Chicken Stock. Bring to a simmer and cook, covered, for 1 hour, stirring often. Add the zucchini, kale, and ½ cup of Parmesan cheese. Simmer gently 30 minutes more or until the soup is nice and thick. Stir the soup often to prevent scorching. Add salt and pepper to taste. Garnish with extra virgin olive oil and grated cheese.

MINESTRONE BREAD SOUP

This is the Tuscan's solution to the use of bread in soup. When you finish preparing this soup, have someone help you carry it to the table. Heavy, yes. Delicious, yes. We first tasted this in Florence.

Cut 1 pound of good Italian bread into cubes and allow to dry overnight on the countertop. Place the dried bread in a large bowl and cover it with cold water. Soak the bread for 1 minute, then drain it and squeeze it dry. Add to a batch of finished Minestrone Soup (page 123) and simmer 15 minutes. Stir the soup often to prevent scorching. Turn off the heat and allow the soup to stand covered for 15 minutes more. Adjust the salt and pepper if necessary. Serve the soup with a drizzle of extra virgin olive oil.

MINESTRONE SOUP WITH PESTO

For a nice variation on regular Minestrone try this one, which has a lovely but heavy flavor of fresh basil.

Prepare a batch of Minestrone Soup (page 123) and add pesto sauce (page 23) to taste when the soup is finished.

Make your own pesto sauce or buy a frozen sauce from a good Italian delicatessen. Do not use bottled or canned pesto sauces as they don't have the bright fresh flavor that you want for this soup.

MUSSEL SOUP WITH SAFFRON

Serves 6

Craig must receive full credit for this one. In Venice mussels show up in all sorts of dishes, and this version that he developed is better than any we had in Italy. Yes, it is rich!

2¾ pounds mussels (the small Penn Cove type are best)
2 teaspoons olive oil
2 cloves garlic, crushed
½ cup dry vermouth
1 medium yellow onion, diced
1 cup thinly sliced celery
2 tablespoons butter
1 pint whipping cream, milk, or half-and-half
1½ cups Chicken Stock (page 116)
½ cup bottled clam juice
¼ teaspoon saffron threads
2 green onions, thinly sliced
1 tablespoon chopped parsley
¼ cup dry sherry
Salt and pepper to taste

Remove the beards from the mussels. A pair of pliers works well for this. Just pull the beard off and rinse the mussels well.

Heat a 6-quart pot with the oil and garlic and sauté a few seconds. Do not burn the garlic. Add the cleaned mussels and the vermouth. Cook, covered, over medium-high heat. Steam the mussels open, about 3 to 4 minutes, stirring once. Strain the mussels in a colander, reserving the broth or nectar. Pour the mussels out onto a sheet pan to cool.

Return the pot to the stove and sauté the onion and celery in the butter until clear; do not brown. Add the cream, Chicken Stock, clam juice, and saffron. Heat to a gentle simmer and cook, covered, for 15 minutes.

Remove the meat from the mussels and discard the shells. Add the green onions and parsley to the pot and simmer 2 minutes more. Add the mussel meat along with any juices and the sherry. Restore the heat but don't over-cook the mussels. Add salt and pepper to taste and serve immediately.

GREEN SOUP WITH RAGS AND CHEESE

MAKES ABOUT 3 QUARTS

This hearty peasant soup will become a favorite in your house. It is found in many regions in Italy and even in the better restaurants.

The rags, Stracciatelle in Italian, are simple to make and act as a sort of quick-made egg noodle in this delicious green broth.

THE SOUP

- 2 tablespoons olive oil
- 2 cloves garlic, chopped
- 1 cup thinly slice yellow onion
- 1 pound Swiss chard (1 bunch large, trimmed and thinly sliced)
- 1 pound spinach (no stems, cleaned and thinly sliced)
- 8 cups Chicken Stock (page 116)

  Salt and pepper to taste

THE "RAGS"

- 3 eggs, beaten
- 4 tablespoons semolina flour (page 24) or regular flour
- 4 tablespoons freshly grated Parmesan cheese
- 1 teaspoon finely grated lemon peel

  Pinch of salt

GARNISH

Extra freshly grated Parmesan cheese

Place the olive oil, garlic, and onion in a 6-quart stockpot and sauté for a few minutes. Add the greens and Chicken Stock. Cover and simmer gently 1 hour and 15 minutes. Salt and pepper to taste.

Beat the eggs, flour, and cheese together. Add the lemon peel and salt and ¼ cup of the mixed soup stock.

Move the simmering pot from the heat and pour the rag batter into the soup in a thin stream, pouring carefully all over the surface of the soup. Return to the heat and stir with a wooden spoon as the tatters and rags cook. Simmer for about 2 minutes. Garnish with extra Parmesan cheese.

ESCAROLE SOUP WITH
TINY MEATBALLS

SERVES 6–8

This is a meal in itself, though it is still usually served as a part of a special Italian family dinner. Our driver in Boston, David Stewart, has become a good friend through the years and he is strictly Boston Italian. That is a special blend of person, I promise.

We had a soup close to this one in a Boston restaurant and David leaned over and said, "Nope." Nope what! "She didn't sauté the escarole before she added the chicken stock. My grandmother always sautéed the escarole first!" God bless everybody's Italian grandma.

THE MEATBALLS
½ cup milk
½ cup bread crumbs
½ pound pork, finely ground
½ pound beef, finely ground
1 egg, beaten
2 teaspoons finely chopped fresh sage
¼ teaspoon grated lemon zest
2 tablespoons grated Parmesan cheese
Salt and white pepper to taste
2 cloves garlic, crushed
1 tablespoon olive oil

THE SOUP
2 tablespoons olive oil
4 cloves garlic, thinly sliced
1 1-pound head of escarole, washed and coarsely chopped
8 cups Chicken Stock (page 116)
Salt and pepper to taste

GARNISH
Grated Parmesan cheese

Mix the milk and bread crumbs together in a small bowl and allow to soak for 5 minutes. Combine the remaining ingredients for the meatballs in a large bowl along with the soaked bread crumbs. Mix together very well with your hands. Form tablespoon-size balls with the meat mixture and place them on a sheet pan. Keep your hands a little moist with cold water to prevent the meatballs from sticking to your hands.

Heat a 4- to 6-quart pot and add the 2 tablespoons oil and the sliced garlic. Sauté for 30 seconds, being sure not to burn the garlic. Add the escarole and sauté for 5 minutes, or until it collapses. Be careful not to burn this. Add the Chicken Stock and simmer gently, covered, for 30 minutes. Add salt and pepper to taste. Carefully drop the meatballs into the simmering soup but do not stir. After 1 minute, when the meatballs have held their form, carefully stir the meatballs. Poach the meatballs for another 6 to 7 minutes but do not boil the soup heavily. Serve in shallow bowls with lots of grated cheese.

EGG AND ASPARAGUS SOUP

SERVES 6

*The affection the Italians have for asparagus goes back to
ancient Rome. During the first century Apicius offered instructions for cooking the tender grass and we use his
methods to this day. The only problem is that Italians have
a tendency to overcook many vegetables, at least by contemporary American standards. This is a great recipe, but
you must not overcook the asparagus.*

1 pound medium asparagus	Salt and black pepper to taste
1 tablespoon olive oil	4 eggs
2 cloves garlic, crushed	1 tablespoon fresh lemon juice
1 medium yellow onion, peeled and chopped	**GARNISHES**
6 cups Chicken Stock (page 116)	Chopped parsley Freshly grated Parmesan cheese
½ cup dry white wine	

Break the tough woody ends of the asparagus off and discard. Wash the asparagus and cut it diagonally into ½-inch
pieces; set aside.

Heat a 4-quart pot and add the oil, garlic, and onion.
Sauté until the onion is clear. Do not brown. Add the

Chicken Stock and wine and simmer, covered, for 40 minutes. Add the asparagus and simmer 5 minutes. Add salt and pepper to taste.

Beat the eggs and lemon juice together and drizzle into the simmering soup. Stir and cook the eggs for 1 minute. Serve in bowls with the garnishes.

PASSATELLI

SERVES 6-8

I had never heard of this soup, though I had been in Bologna before. During this last trip, however, I went to the Leonida Restaurant several times just for this dish. Noodles made from bread crumbs and egg. That's it. Amazing results. I really think this is one of the best recipes in this book.

6½ cups Chicken Stock (page 116)
1½ cups fine bread crumbs (unseasoned!)
1 cup semolina flour (page 24)
¼ cup freshly, finely grated Parmesan cheese
2 teaspoons baking powder
1 teaspoon salt
Pinch of ground white pepper

½ teaspoon grated lemon zest
4 eggs, beaten
1 chicken bouillon cube
2 tablespoons butter, melted

GARNISHES
Chopped parsley
Freshly grated Parmesan cheese

In a 4- to 6-quart pot bring the Chicken Stock to a gentle simmer.

Combine the bread crumbs, semolina, Parmesan cheese, baking powder, salt, white pepper, and lemon zest in a bowl. Stir everything together well.

Beat the eggs in a small bowl. Dissolve the bouillon cube in a water glass with the hot ½ cup of the Chicken Stock. Add the bouillon to the dry ingredients along with the beaten eggs and the melted butter. Stir together and knead with your hands to form a smooth dough. Cover the dough and allow to rest 10 minutes.

Season the simmering stock with salt to taste. Place some of the dough in a spaetzle press (page 34). Squeeze the dough directly into the simmering stock.

(You can also make these noodles by simply pressing the dough into the pot, through the backside of a coarse potato grater, the old-fashioned box grater.)

Stir the noodles very gently to separate.

Poach the noodles 1 minute or until they float and are very tender. Do not overcook or they will fall apart. Using a skimmer, transfer to a tureen or large bowl. Repeat with the remaining dough. When all the noodles are cooked, pour the hot broth into the tureen.

Garnish with chopped parsley and freshly grated Parmesan cheese.

SAUCES

The current increasing interest in regional Italian cooking has taught Americans a very important lesson. Italian cuisine does *not* necessarily mean tomato sauce. The types of sauces vary from region to region, just like everything else in the country's kitchens.

Tomato sauce is popular, however, in the South. Naples claims that the popular condiment originated there, perhaps as early as the sixteenth century. By the eighteenth century it was common in the South, but to this day it is much less popular in the Northern regions, where it is used with a very light hand. The famous ragù of Bologna, for instance, has only a touch of tomato, and in Venice you rarely see a "red" dish.

I love a good freshly prepared tomato sauce, but I prefer it in the Italian way. In America we serve pastas absolutely swimming in sauce. I suppose we feel that this makes a more expensive and satisfying dish. Actually, too much sauce will ruin the pasta dish. Just a touch, and then the cheese, and perhaps some fine olive oil.

The Northerners would just as soon have a pasta with oil and garlic. Period! And the young chefs are coming up with creative and rather unusual sauces, such as the Sweet and Sour with Fruit and the Brown Butter with Sage and Parmesan Cheese. You will also enjoy the Gorgonzola Sauce and the heavy but delicious Fonduta cheese sauce.

Use all of these sauces sparingly so that the food that is sauced can be tasted and raised, not covered. In addition to the recipes in this chapter you may also wish to see:

Fonduta (page 80)
Lemon Olive Oil (page 489)

MUSHROOM SAUCE FOR PASTA AND POLENTA

MAKES ABOUT 3 CUPS

You can use this wonderful sauce on almost anything but the kids. I love it on pasta and polenta but it is also grand on rice, gnocchi, soups, and sandwiches, and on pork or beef dishes. Do not forget those chicken thighs!

1 ounce dried porcini mushrooms (These are expensive. You may wish to purchase a less expensive dried mushroom from South America. Still very good but a tenth of the price.)
1 cup hot water
2 cups Mock Veal Stock (page 116)

2 tablespoons butter
4 tablespoons flour
2 cloves garlic, crushed
1 tablespoon olive oil
½ pound fresh morel mushrooms or white meadow mushrooms
¼ cup dry white wine
Salt and pepper to taste

Soak the porcini in 1 cup hot water for 45 minutes.

Heat the stock in a small saucepan. Heat a small frying pan and cook the butter and flour together to form a roux. Whisk the roux into the hot stock and simmer and stir until smooth and slightly thickened. Return the frying pan to the burner and add the garlic and oil.

Drain and chop the porcini and sauté in oil with morels or meadow mushrooms, cover, and sweat. Deglaze the pan with wine and add to sauce. Simmer 5 minutes. Salt and pepper to taste.

FRESH TOMATO SAUCE SICILIAN

MAKES ABOUT 5 QUARTS

In Sicily a good tomato sauce is considered an absolute basic in the kitchen. This is not a meat sauce or a "spaghetti" sauce. It is much more versatile than that. We use it throughout the book and we thank Criniti's Restaurant, in Philadelphia, for teaching us that you do not necessarily need meat in a tomato sauce. This is rich and good, meat or not.

While we do use both canned tomatoes and fresh tomatoes, we call the whole "Fresh" because it has a very clean and bright flavor. Please don't try to get away with using generic canned tomatoes. Use a good brand such as plum tomatoes from Italy or one of the better American packers such as Contadina.

¼ cup olive oil
4 cloves garlic, crushed
1 medium yellow onion, finely chopped
9 cups cored and chopped very ripe fresh tomatoes
4 28-ounce cans whole tomatoes, crushed with juice

¼ cup chopped parsley
½ cup dry white wine
1 cup Chicken Stock (page 116)
1 teaspoon dried marjoram
1 teaspoon dried rosemary
6 tablespoons butter
Salt and freshly ground black pepper to taste

Heat an 8- to 10-quart heavy-bottom pot and add the oil, garlic, and onion. Sauté until the onion is clear. Add the remaining ingredients except the butter and salt and pepper. Bring to a simmer and gently cook, uncovered, for 4 hours, stirring often. Stir in the butter and salt and pepper to taste.

TOMATO WITH LEMON OLIVE
OIL QUICKIE SAUCE

SERVES 4 AS A PASTA COURSE

I have included the pasta with this recipe since they love each other! The sauce is made from your previous preparatory recipes, so it can be one of the quick dishes that you throw together at the last moment . . . providing you have the stuff of this recipe in your refrigerator, already prepared. It is also worth your while to make this for an evening meal or for weekend guests.

¾ pound pasta
    (spaghetti,
    penne, or what-
    ever you like)
Salt to taste

1¼ cups Fresh Tomato
    Sauce Sicilian
    (page 139)
⅓ cup Lemon Olive
    Oil (page 489)

Cook the pasta in ample water with salt to taste until al dente. Heat the fresh tomato sauce with the Lemon Olive Oil to a light simmer. Do not boil the sauce, just bring to a simmer. Drain the pasta well and return to the pot. Add the sauce and toss together.

I prefer mine without any grated cheese so that I can taste the tomato and the brightness of the oil. However, if you wish to add good Parma cheese, so be it.

ITALIAN GRAVY

MAKES 3 QUARTS

In Southern Italy one can find a thousand variations of this gravy. It is not used widely in classic cooking in the Northern regions. Make a good batch and keep it sealed and refrigerated. It will keep for a good week and one can prepare dozens of dishes with this basic "gravy." While the sauce is typical of the cooking of Naples, you will find all sorts of uses for this blend other than on pasta. It is great on polenta, pizza, and toast and works well for cooking meats and sausages. Try chicken in Italian Gravy. The gravy keeps well in the freezer, so make a large batch and freeze it in small containers.

2 28-ounce cans tomato puree
1 6-ounce can tomato paste
1 quart Chicken Stock (page 116) or Beef Stock (page 115)
2 cups dry red wine
¼ cup olive oil
2 yellow onions, peeled and minced
6 large garlic cloves, chopped
2 ribs celery with leaves, minced
1 carrot, grated
½ cup chopped parsley
½ pound fresh mushrooms, chopped (optional)

½ teaspoon crushed red pepper flakes
1 tablespoon crushed oregano
1 teaspoon dried rosemary
2 bay leaves
1 tablespoon dried basil or 2 tablespoons fresh
2 whole cloves (optional)
½ tablespoon freshly ground black pepper
2 tablespoons salt, or to taste
1 teaspoon sugar
1 pound pork neck bones or chicken backs and necks

In a large pot, place the tomato puree, tomato paste, Chicken or Beef Stock, and wine. Heat a large frying pan and add the olive oil. Sauté the onions, garlic, celery, and carrot until they just begin to brown a bit. Add to the pot along with the remaining ingredients. Bring to a light boil and then turn down to a simmer. Simmer for 2 hours, partly covered, stirring often. Remove the bones and discard or make a private lunch of them. Skim the fat from the top and discard.

Store in the refrigerator covered, in either glass, plastic, or stainless steel. It will keep for a week. Use for pasta topping or for any other dish calling for Italian tomato sauce or "gravy." This freezes very well.

BOLOGNESE SAUCE

MAKES ABOUT 7 CUPS

This is that very rich beef sauce that will turn a plate of pasta into a bit of glory. Or you can use this for fillings for cannelloni, a frittata, or a quick little meat pie. Very good! Note that the beef is not ground but simply cooked until it falls apart. Such a sauce!

1 **pound boneless beef chuck**	1 **cup Chicken Stock (page 116)**
Salt and pepper to taste	⅓ **cup grated Parmesan cheese**
1 **tablespoon olive oil**	½ **cup cream**
¾ **cup water**	**Salt and pepper to taste**
⅓ **cup dry red wine**	
2 **cloves garlic, crushed**	
2½ **cups Fresh Tomato Sauce Sicilian (page 139)**	

Season the meat with salt and pepper to taste. Brown well in a frying pan with the olive oil. Place the meat in a small heavy saucepan and add the water, red wine, and garlic. Bring to a boil and simmer gently, covered, for 2 hours. If the pan begins to dry out, add a little more water to prevent burning. Allow to cool in the pot with the lid on until you can handle it.

Shred the meat and place it in a 4-quart pot along with its cooking juices. Add the remaining ingredients except the Parmesan cheese, cream, and salt and pepper to taste. Cover and simmer gently for 45 minutes, stirring often. Add the cheese and cream and simmer 15 minutes more. Salt and pepper to taste.

TONNATO SAUCE

MAKES 1½ CUPS

Traditionally this tuna sauce has been served with very rare cold veal slices. Now I realize that this wonderful sauce has many uses. I put it on vegetables, salads, meats, even pasta, and every time it is a hit. This is a sort of tuna mayonnaise. It is even great on sandwiches.

1 7-ounce can tuna packed in water, drained	¼ cup fresh lemon juice
8 canned flat anchovies, drained on a paper towel	2 tablespoons brandy
	¾ cup olive oil, at room temperature
	1 tablespoon capers

Place the tuna, anchovies, and lemon juice in a food blender. Blend for a few moments and add the brandy. Slowly pour in the olive oil as the machine runs. Remove the sauce from the container and stir in the capers. Serve over meats, vegetables, pasta, or salads.

LIGHT TOMATO CREAM SAUCE

MAKES 2½ CUPS

If you do not like to use half-and-half in this creamed to-mato sauce, then you can certainly use milk. I'll stick with the half-and-half.

This is a very refreshing sauce, though a little heavy with butterfat.

2 cups Fresh Tomato **Sauce Sicilian** **(page 139)**	**½ cup half-and-half**

Heat both ingredients together and toss with your favorite pasta, or serve as an elegant sauce over sautéed meats. You may wish to garnish the dish with grated Parmesan cheese and chopped parsley.

RAGÙ

MAKES ABOUT 3 QUARTS

This is not to be confused with the canned product offered on the American market. That is not ragù sauce at all!

Ragù is a simple sauce made almost entirely with meat, and it is common throughout the Emilia-Romagna region— well, all of Northern Italy for that matter. There are as many recipes for this dish as there are grandmas in the area. Tambaurini, one of the finest food stores in Bologna, makes something like the following. However, in a very famous restaurant in Parma, the chef uses little else than veal and butter. So enjoy, but this dish makes anything on which you put it into an entire meal.

½ cup olive oil
6 cloves garlic
1 rib celery, finely chopped
1 medium carrot, peeled and finely chopped
1 medium yellow onion, finely chopped
½ pound pancetta (page 23), coarsely ground
2 pounds veal, coarsely ground
2 pounds pork butt, coarsely ground

¼ cup chopped parsley
2½ cups Chicken Stock (page 116)
½ cup dry white wine
1 6-ounce can tomato paste
6 tablespoons butter
¼ cup whipping cream
2 teaspoons chopped fresh sage
⅔ cup freshly grated Parmesan cheese
Salt and pepper to taste

Heat a 10- to 12-quart heavy-bottom stainless-steel kettle, and add the oil, garlic, celery, carrot, and onion. Sauté until the onion is transparent, about 10 to 15 minutes. Add the pancetta and sauté 5 minutes. Add the veal and pork and brown until crumbly, about 5 minutes. Add the parsley, Chicken Stock, white wine, and tomato paste. Bring to a boil and simmer gently, partly covered, for 2 hours. Add the butter, cream, sage, and cheese and simmer gently for 5 minutes. Skim the fat from the top of the sauce. Salt and pepper to taste.

GREEN SAUCE WITH PICKLED
RED CHERRY PEPPERS

MAKES 2¼ CUPS

We tasted this sauce in Piedmont. It is much more lively than the normal green sauce that is served with boiled meats in Bologna, and I see many uses for this brightly flavored sauce. A pot roast would come alive with this sauce, and a boiled tongue would be in Heaven. Why not? Try it before you wonder about me. Nice, rare roast beef could use the kick that this sauce will offer.

3 cups finely chopped Italian parsley	2½ tablespoons white wine vinegar
½ cup minced yellow onion	1 tablespoon lemon juice
2 cloves garlic, crushed	½ cup seeded and chopped pickled red cherry peppers
1 stalk celery, minced	Salt and pepper to taste
½ lemon peel, grated	
1½ cups olive oil	

Place all ingredients in a food processor and process just until all is a bit coarse. This should not be a smooth sauce.

Great! A bit hot for the timid, but great on most meats and sausages.

GREEN SAUCE FOR MEATS

Green sauce is common in Italy, particularly in Bologna, where boiled meat dishes are so popular. When eating at Leonida, one of our favorite restaurants in Bologna, I tasted the green sauce that was being offered along with a wonderful sausage called coteghino. I was surprised by a special difference in this excellent sauce and I asked Craig what he thought. "They use the oil from the tuna cans in this dish." He was right, I am sure. In any case this is the best green sauce that I have ever tasted.

Follow the recipe for Green Sauce with Pickled Red Cherry Peppers (page 146) but omit the cherry peppers. Drain the oil from two 7-ounce cans of tuna packed in olive oil. Stir tuna oil into the sauce. Save drained tuna for other dishes.

PINZIMONIO

Craig calls this the original Tuscan relish tray. He was raised in Chicago in the days when every decent restaurant offered a relish tray, and this one is superior to the old pickle plates that Craig remembers.

This dish goes back hundreds of years and it must be served with very good oil.

Extra virgin olive oil   Pepper
Salt

Mix on a plate or in a little bowl. Dip raw vegetables into the pinzimonio. With a glass of white wine you can have a whole meal of vegetables such as celery, fresh fennel bulb, carrots, green onions, red bell pepper, endive, or romaine lettuce leaves. Pinzimonio is generally used as a course all its own.

GORGONZOLA SAUCE

MAKES ABOUT 2¼ CUPS

*Now we talk rich! This wonderful sauce will appeal to those
of us who love a truly rich cheese flavor, and Gorgonzola,
the blue cheese of Italy, has it.*

*I use this often in my Italian kitchen on everything from
pasta and ravioli to vegetables and toast. It is very simple
and really an Italian gourmet's treat.*

2 tablespoons butter	1 cup milk

2 tablespoons all-
  purpose flour
	½ pound Gorgonzola,
	  crumbled

Heat the butter in a 2-quart saucepan. Add the flour and
cook together to form a roux. Do not brown! Add the milk
and whisk together until smooth. Bring to a simmer, stirring
regularly until thickened. Add the Gorgonzola and stir until
all is incorporated but still a bit lumpy.

SWEET AND SOUR SAUCE
WITH FRUIT
(Agrodolce)

MAKES ABOUT 3½ CUPS, ENOUGH FOR 6–8 SERVINGS

*Chef John Chikulas is something. I met him when I did my
first show in Chicago in 1983. He was very young and was
the sauce chef at Avanzare's, a fine Chicago Italian res-*

taurant. Soon he was the executive chef; now he is executive at Scoozie's, another fine Italian eating house . . . and he is Greek! A Greek chef can learn about any cuisine. After all, the Greeks were some of the first fine cooks.

Get ready for some very contemporary Italian cooking.

1 cup packed mango
  or papaya (cut in
  ½-inch dice)
2 cups packed diced
  fresh plum
  tomatoes, seeds
  removed
¼ cup tiny capers,
  without juice
¼ cup peeled,
  chopped, and
  rinsed red onion
¼ cup extra virgin
  olive oil

1 tablespoon red wine
  vinegar or cider
  vinegar
Salt and freshly
  ground black
  pepper to taste

GARNISH
1 small ripe avocado,
  pitted, peeled, and
  sliced

Mix all the ingredients. Let the sauce marinate for 30 minutes to 1 hour. Mix again and serve with sea scallops or grilled fish. Drizzle extra virgin olive oil over the top of the seafood. Garnish with avocado.

BROWN BUTTER WITH
SAGE SAUCE

MAKES ENOUGH FOR 4 SERVINGS

Please do not read this recipe and decide that since it is not complicated it must be inferior. I think that kind of thinking has done great damage to creative cooking in our time.

Chef Bobby Estanzo, of Prego's in San Francisco, gave us this quickie, which is actually quite profound. He served

*it over broiled chicken thighs, but it is equally good with
steaks, pork, and certainly vegetables.*

Please try this!!

½ **stick (4 tablespoons) unsalted butter**	**Parmesan cheese, freshly grated, over the entrée**
4 **fresh sage leaves**	
Salt to taste	

Melt the butter in a small frying pan. Add the fresh sage
leaves and allow the butter to brown. Do not burn!

Salt the entrée (four servings) and top with the freshly
grated cheese.

When the butter is lightly browned, pour over the cheese
on the entrée, giving each serving one sage leaf. The hot
butter should have a sort of sizzling effect on the cheese.

Serve hot.

This is one of the most delicious sauces I know. Thanks,
Bobby!

PASTA

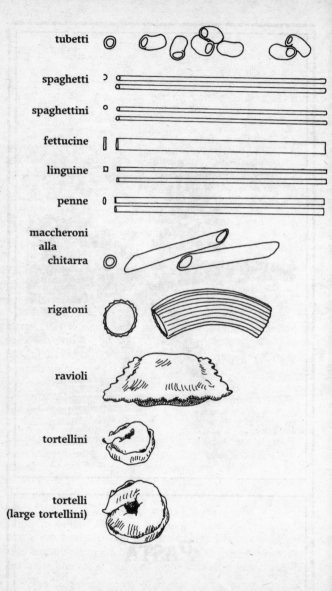

tubetti

spaghetti

spaghettini

fettucine

linguine

penne

maccheroni
alla
chitarra

rigatoni

ravioli

tortellini

tortelli
(large tortellini)

There are more than fifty recipes for pasta in this section. That number will not impress any Italian, particularly those from the South, as every Southerner's grandmother knows of at least twice that many dishes.

Pasta is not considered a side dish or even an extra course in Italy. It is considered a regular necessity. While in earlier times it was eaten because it was not as expensive as meat, it is eaten in our time because it is loved and enjoyed, sometimes twice a day, seven days a week.

The old argument over who created pasta, the Chinese or the Italians, no longer interests me. It is true that Marco Polo traveled to China and returned to his beloved Venice with noodles from the Imperial Court. But it is also true that prior to Mr. Polo's trip, from 1271 through 1295, pasta was quite common in the South. Venetians had not seen pasta so they were fascinated. The Southerners had had pasta for many years before Polo, the idea probably coming into Italy from the Arabs and, even later, the Greeks.

So it is best to say that the Chinese and the Italians discovered pasta quite independently of one another. End of argument!

We must also observe a very serious difference between what the Italians do with pasta over against the Chinese. The Chinese make noodles from all kinds of food products, from wheat to rice to mung beans to yams to tapioca to buckwheat. But everything is made into one form, the noodle. The Italians, on the other hand, use primarily wheat and then turn it into a hundred different shapes of pasta, everything from spaghetti to hats and ties and bows and nests and rice shapes and wheels and cockscombs and ears and sheets and rolls and angel hair and tubes and stars and elbows and rings and shells and flowers and quills and twists and wide noodles and thin noodles and fat noodles and pillows and belly buttons!

Further, the Italian never sees the noodle as the basis of the whole meal, as do the Chinese, but rather as one integral part of the meal, a course in its own right.

I expect that you will have fun with these dishes. My favorites include Spaghetti Vodka, Pasta Carbonara with Saffron, Pasta with Eggplant Sicilian, Pappardelle with Duck Ragù—in short, I love it. Pasta is for me and, I hope, for you.

One more word or two. Do not overcook pasta as it should be both firm and tender at the same time, never soggy. And I do not think that you always need to make your own pasta from scratch, though that is delicious. There are many fine dried pastas on the market such as De Cecco from Italy and Primo from Canada. Don't let the pasta swim in sauce but rather allow it to be flavored by the sauce. Then it is Italian.

In addition to the recipes in this chapter you may also wish to see:

Crepes with Porcini and Mushrooms (page 418)

SPAGHETTINI TONNATO

SERVES 6 AS A PASTA COURSE

I love tonnato or tuna sauce. It is normally served with cold sliced veal, but I enjoy it with chicken and pork as well. In this recipe we simply tried it on pasta. Works great!

THE SAUCE

- 1 7-ounce can tuna in water, drained
- 8 flat anchovies, drained on a paper towel
- ¼ cup fresh lemon juice
- 2 tablespoons brandy
- ¾ cup olive oil, at room temperature
- 1 tablespoon capers, drained

THE PASTA

- 1 teaspoon salt
- 1 pound spaghettini

GARNISHES

Freshly ground black pepper to taste

Grated Parmesan cheese

Chopped parsley

Shred the tuna with your hands and place in a food blender with the anchovies and lemon juice. Blend for a few moments and add the brandy. Slowly pour in the olive oil as the machine runs. Blend until smooth. Remove the sauce to a small bowl and stir in the capers.

Bring to a boil a 12-quart pot two thirds full with water. Add the salt and boil the spaghettini until al dente. Drain very well and return the pasta to the pot.

Add the sauce and toss together. Top with the garnishes and serve immediately.

SPAGHETTINI CAPONATA

SERVES 4–6

The eggplant relish that is so popular in Sicily is anxious to do other things. Normally it is served with crackers or dried bread. But this stuff is so versatile that we should try it on many foods. My friend Carlo Middione, a chef in San Francisco, offers it on eggplant. I enjoyed that and then tried the relish on cold shrimp. Terrific! Now, try it on pasta. The flavors of the Caponata are released as you warm the relish with the pasta. Such a wedding!

2 tablespoons olive oil	¾ pound spaghettini
2 cloves garlic, crushed	**GARNISHES**
1½ cups Caponata (page 64)	**Chopped parsley**
¼ cup dry white wine	**Freshly grated**
Salt and freshly ground black pepper to taste	**Parmesan cheese**

Heat a frying pan and add the oil and garlic. Sauté 1 minute and add the Caponata and the wine. Simmer the sauce a few minutes and adjust salt and pepper if necessary. Boil the pasta in lightly salted water until al dente. Drain well and return to the pot. Add the sauce and toss together. Top with the garnishes.

SPAGHETTINI WITH PEPPERS
AND SAND

SERVES 4

The whole concept behind this recipe is a gift from a wonderful Italian chef who is Palestinian. Yes, you read it correctly. His name is Saleh and he runs a fine restaurant in Seattle called Saleh al Lago, or Saleh by the Lake. He is in the Greenlake region of my beloved Seattle and you must stop by and dine with him.

I added a few peppers to his fine Spaghettini and Sand recipe and we offered this to Julia Child on her eightieth birthday. Good dish, great birthday, the most beautiful woman!

- **6 tablespoons good olive oil**
- **1 medium red bell pepper, cored, seeded, and julienned**
- **4 cloves garlic, crushed**
- **½ cup fresh bread crumbs, not too fine**
- **¼ teaspoon dried red pepper flakes**
- **½ pound spaghettini Salt and pepper to taste (very little if any)**

Place a 12-quart pot of water on to boil for the pasta. Lightly salt the water. Heat a large frying pan and add 2 tablespoons of the oil. Add the peppers and sauté over high heat 2 minutes. The peppers should remain a bit crisp. Remove from the pan and set aside uncovered.

Heat the frying pan again and add the remaining oil and the garlic. Sauté a few seconds and add the bread crumbs and red pepper flakes. Gently toast the bread crumbs, stirring often, until very lightly browned.

Boil the pasta until al dente and drain well. Return to the pot and toss with the red bell pepper and the bread crumbs. Adjust salt and pepper if needed.

SPAGHETTI VODKA

SERVES 4–6 AS A PASTA COURSE OR 4 AS A MAIN DISH

This sounds like something invented in this country, but my cooking friends in Italy also know of this dish, so I am stumped as to where it originated. Contemporary Italian chefs are always at work on new dishes, and this one cannot be very old. It is delicious!

Please understand that you cannot use really fine vodka for this dish as the expensive stuff lacks the flavor that you need. Go for a popular brand like Smirnoff.

2 tablespoons olive oil	Salt and pepper to taste
2 cloves garlic, crushed	
½ cup dry white wine	¾ pound spaghettini
1 cup whipping cream	½ cup vodka
¼ cup grated Romano cheese	
¼ cup thinly sliced and chopped prosciutto	**GARNISHES** Chopped parsley Additional freshly ground pepper

Heat a medium-size frying pan, add the oil and garlic, and sauté for 30 seconds. Add the wine and simmer for 2 minutes. Add the cream and simmer for 2 minutes more. Add the cheese and prosciutto and heat until smooth. Salt and pepper to taste.

Cook the pasta until al dente in lightly salted water. Drain well.

Bring the sauce to a simmer again and add the vodka. Simmer for 30 seconds to burn off some of the alcohol. Toss with the pasta and serve with chopped parsley and additional black pepper.

CHEESE FILLING FOR RAVIOLI

MAKES ABOUT 3 CUPS

The cheese-filled ravioli is an invention that no one else can claim, only the Italians. While it takes a bit of time to make your own ravioli from scratch, you will feel good at the end of the day . . . and probably a bit tired. However, you will find simple instructions for ravioli on page 183. Just use this filling as a variation.

1 pound ricotta cheese
½ cup grated Romano cheese
¼ pound provolone cheese, grated
¼ cup chopped parsley
Freshly ground black pepper to taste (no salt needed)

Combine all ingredients in a bowl and mix well.

CARLO'S MACARONI WITH ARUGULA AND FRESH TOMATOES

SERVES 6

It is always a joy to be in Carlo Middione's kitchen, either at his home or at his highly respected restaurant, Vivande Porta Via, on Fillmore in San Francisco.

He is the author of The Food of Southern Italy, *an unusually good cookbook. He demonstrated this pasta dish on our Italian series. The recipe appears in his book.*

¼ cup virgin olive oil
1 small yellow onion,
   peeled and very
   finely chopped
2 garlic cloves,
   peeled and well
   crushed
2 pounds fresh
   tomatoes, cored,
   peeled, and well
   crushed

1 pound short pasta
   such as *penne*,
   small *rigatoni*,
   fusilli, etc.
1 bunch
   (approximately 2
   cups) arugula,
   washed and cut
   into 4-inch
   pieces
1⅓ cups grated
   pecorino cheese

Heat the olive oil in a large frying pan until it is quite hot, add the onion, and cook it until it is just transparent. Add the garlic, and fry it until it is golden and fragrant. Add the tomatoes, and stir the mixture well. Cook the tomato sauce for about 30 minutes or so.

Boil about 6 quarts of salted water in a large pot. Add the pasta, and after about 2 minutes, add the arugula. When the pasta is *al dente,* pour it through a colander. Put the pasta and arugula mixture on hot plates, and ladle on some tomato sauce. Sprinkle plenty of the grated *pecorino* cheese on the pasta, and serve it immediately, very hot.

TORTELLINI AND PANNA
WITH PROSCIUTTO, PEAS,
AND MUSHROOMS

SERVES 4 AS A VERY RICH PASTA COURSE

In Bologna they display fresh tortellini in the windows of the best shops, just as they display diamonds on Fifth Avenue in New York. The Bolognese are very serious about this dish. No, I do not make my own. It is just too much work. However, you can find very good tortellini in freezers and very often fresh.

1 tablespoon olive oil
1 clove garlic, crushed
¼ pound mushrooms,
   sliced
1 cup frozen baby
   peas, thawed
½ cup thinly sliced
   and chopped
   prosciutto

¾ cup whipping cream
   or half-and-half
1 pound fresh or
   frozen cheese
   tortellini
¼ cup freshly grated
   Parmesan cheese
Salt and pepper to
   taste

Heat a medium-size frying pan and add the oil, garlic, and mushrooms. Sauté over medium-high heat for 3 minutes until the mushrooms are just tender. Add the peas and prosciutto and sauté for 2 minutes. Add the cream and simmer 2 minutes more.

Boil the tortellini in a pot of lightly salted water until tender and drain well. Return the tortellini to the pot and add the cheese. Toss all together and add salt and pepper to taste.

VARIATION: Another version of this dish omits the peas and mushrooms: Cream and Prosciutto with Tortellini. Simple and delicious.

TORTELLINI WITH PROSCIUTTO AND PEAS

SERVES 6–8 AS A SOUP OR PASTA COURSE

This dish falls between a soup and a pasta dish, but it is very typical of the wonderful food found in Bologna. On a cold winter's day this will warm your Italian soul . . . and I am convinced that we all have one.

1 tablespoon olive oil
2 tablespoons butter
2 cloves garlic, crushed
1 cup diced yellow onion
1 tablespoon chopped parsley
¾ cup Fresh Tomato Sauce Sicilian (page 139)
1¾ cups Chicken Stock (page 116)
¼ cup dry white wine
½ cup thinly sliced and chopped prosciutto

1 10-ounce box frozen baby green peas, thawed
Salt and pepper to taste (not too much)
1 pound fresh or fresh frozen cheese tortellini

GARNISH
Freshly grated Parmesan cheese to taste

Bring a 12-quart pot of water to a boil to cook the tortellini.

Heat a 4- to 6-quart pot and add the oil, butter, garlic, and onion. Sauté until the onion is clear. Add the parsley, tomato sauce, Chicken Stock, and wine. Simmer, covered, for 5 minutes. Add the prosciutto and the peas and simmer a few minutes until the peas are cooked but not discolored. Add salt and pepper to taste if needed.

Boil the tortellini until just tender and drain well. Add the tortellini to the pot of sauce. Serve in bowls garnished with grated cheese.

TORTELLINI WITH GORGONZOLA SAUCE

SERVES 4 AS A PASTA COURSE

If there is such a thing as double happiness, and the Chinese claim that there is, this is it for me!

1 pound meat-filled
  tortellini (buy
  fresh or frozen in
  a good Italian
  delicatessen)
¾ cup Gorgonzola
  Sauce (page 148),
  hot

GARNISH
Chopped parsley

Cook the tortellini as instructed on the package. Drain and toss with the sauce. Garnish with parsley.

TORTELLINI WITH TOMATO SAUCE

SERVES 4 AS A PASTA COURSE

What a simple and quick dish, providing you have taken our advice and have fresh tomato sauce in the refrigerator or freezer.

1 pound cheese-filled tortellini (buy fresh or frozen in a good Italian delicatessen)	**GARNISHES** Grated Parmesan cheese Chopped parsley
1 cup Fresh Tomato Sauce Sicilian (page 139), hot	

Cook the tortellini as instructed on the package and drain well. Toss with the sauce and top with the garnish.

TORTELLINI IN BRODO CON PESTO

SERVES 6–8

You may be able to think up more variations on tortellini than we, but this one is especially good. It should prove to

*you that "belly buttons" are good with just about anything.
Brodo means "broth."*

8 cups Chicken Stock (page 116) Salt and pepper to taste 1 pound fresh or frozen tortellini (meat or cheese filled)	Pesto sauce (page 23) to taste (make your own or buy frozen or fresh from a good Italian delicatessen)

Heat the stock in 4-quart pot and season lightly with salt and pepper to taste. Cook the tortellini in the stock until just tender and add pesto sauce to taste.

LINGUINE WITH WHITE CLAM SAUCE

SERVES 6-8

I prefer this classic pasta dish made with fresh clams, but I am realistic enough to know that you are not going to cook it very often if you use only the fresh mollusks. Also, please note that we do not use cheese on this dish since cheese and seafood do not mix for the Italian taste buds. Further, little black pepper should be used so that the dish can stand on its own clean clam and vermouth flavors. Taste the sauce before adding any additional salt since canned clams are already salty enough.

3 tablespoons butter
1 tablespoon olive oil
3 cloves garlic, minced
1 medium yellow
  onion, in ¼-inch
  dice
2 tablespoons flour
½ cup dry vermouth
1 cup bottled clam
  juice
1 tablespoon lemon
  juice
½ cup cream
1 teaspoon dried
  marjoram
5 green onions,
  chopped
2 tablespoons chopped
  parsley
¾ pound linguine
3 6½-ounce cans
  chopped clams
  (Gorton's is a
  good brand)
Salt and pepper to
  taste (not too
  much)

Heat a large frying pan and add the butter, oil, garlic, and onion. Sauté over low heat until the onion is tender and clear. Add the flour and cook together for 1 minute. Add the vermouth, clam juice, and lemon juice. Simmer until slightly thickened and add the cream and marjoram. Add the green onions and parsley. Simmer the sauce uncovered for 3 minutes to reduce and thicken. Cook the pasta until al dente in lightly salted water. Drain well. When pasta is almost done, add the clams with their juice to the sauce and heat to a simmer. Add salt and pepper to taste (not too much). Toss the drained pasta with the sauce and serve.

SPAGHETTI WITH ANCHOVY AND TOMATO

SERVES 6 AS A PASTA DISH

I love this dish, but now and then I find people who do not like canned anchovies. I make no apologies. If you like anchovies and tomato, this dish is for you. Since the anchovies are first soaked in milk for a few minutes, the harsh flavor is gone. Trust me on this one! It is great.

12 flat canned anchovy
    fillets
½ cup milk
3 tablespoons olive oil
3 cloves garlic,
    crushed
1 medium yellow
    onion, chopped
½ cup Chicken Stock
    (page 116)
3 medium ripe
    tomatoes, or 6
    plum tomatoes,
    coarsely chopped

3 tablespoons chopped
    parsley
½ cup dry vermouth
¼ teaspoon red pepper
    flakes
Salt and pepper to
    taste
1 pound spaghetti

GARNISH
Grated Parmesan
cheese

Soak the anchovies in the milk for 15 minutes and then drain well. Heat a large frying pan and add the oil, garlic, and onion. Chop the anchovies coarsely and add to the pan. Sauté until the onion is clear. Add the Chicken Stock, tomatoes, parsley, vermouth, and red pepper flakes. Cover and simmer gently for 25 minutes until the tomatoes collapse and form a sauce. Add salt and pepper to taste.

Cook the pasta in lightly salted water until al dente. Toss with the sauce and serve with grated cheese.

PASTA WITH WALNUTS

SERVES 6

We have a wonderful new friend by the name of Father Giuseppe Orsini. He is a priest in New Jersey and the author of some basic and creative Italian cookbooks. One is called Papa Bear's Cookbook *because the youngsters in his parish and in his family call him Papa Bear. The name Orsini in Italian means "little bear." So now you understand.*

The good father offered us this dish one day after explaining that it is perfect for Christmas Eve, a time when Roman Catholics abstain from meat. So, even though we have taken a few liberties with his recipe, here is a great dish for Christmas Eve or any other night when it is dark and cold and you are hungry!

2 cloves garlic, crushed
⅓ cup olive oil
½ cup thinly sliced yellow onions
⅛ teaspoon dried red pepper flakes
¾ cup finely chopped walnuts
1 tablespoon chopped fresh parsley

Salt and pepper to taste
¾ pound dry penne pasta

GARNISH
Freshly grated Parmesan cheese

In a medium skillet, sauté the garlic and onions in oil until clear. Add the red pepper flakes, walnuts, parsley, and salt and pepper to taste. Sauté for 1 minute.

Boil the pasta until al dente in lightly salted water. Drain the pasta and return it to the pot. Add the walnut mixture and toss together. Garnish with the cheese and serve.

VARIATION: Papa Bear mixes a few bread crumbs with the cheese before he garnishes the dish. It really is a good addition.

PASTA MADE WITH
FRESH PARSLEY

SERVES 4–6

Fresh pasta is fun to make since you can mix in different herbs or spices to suit your mood and menu. This version is easy to do, but you must remember to chop the herbs finely so that they will go through your pasta cutter.

1¾ cups unbleached flour	½ teaspoon salt
1 cup semolina flour	1 tablespoon water, more if needed
3 eggs, beaten	
¼ cup finely chopped fresh parsley	

Place both flours in a bowl and form a well in the center. Add the remaining ingredients to the well and stir together with a wooden spoon. Pinch the dough together with your hands and knead a smooth ball. Allow the dough to rest on the countertop, covered with the bowl, for 30 minutes. Roll the dough out and cut into the desired pasta shape. While working with one portion of pasta, keep the remaining covered under the bowl.

VARIATION: Try this with finely chopped fresh basil or even sage. Fresh rosemary is just terrific.

TRUFFLE OIL OVER PASTA

I admit that truffle oil (page 424) is expensive, but it is to be used like a perfume, a condiment, a light garnish. The fifteen dollars you invest in a small bottle of this stuff will give you more than fifteen dollars' worth of pleasure.

Cook any fresh pasta you wish in Chicken Stock (page 116). Drain, reserving the used stock for another use. Add a bit of butter and perhaps some salt to the pasta. Toss and add a few drizzles of truffle oil.

Nothing else is needed for this unusually delicious dish.

PENNE WITH LEMON OLIVE OIL
AND GARLIC

SERVES 6 AS A PASTA COURSE

Sometimes the simple things are the best, especially in terms of food. This simple dish is what pasta is all about!

½ cup Lemon Olive
    Oil (page 489)
3 cloves garlic,
    crushed
Salt and freshly
    ground black
    pepper to taste

1 pound dry penne
    pasta
3 tablespoons chopped
    parsley
¼ cup freshly grated
    Parmesan cheese

Heat the Lemon Olive Oil and garlic together in a small frying pan. Do not burn! Add salt and pepper to taste.

Boil the pasta in lightly salted water until al dente. Drain well and return to the pot. Add the oil mixture, parsley, and cheese. Toss together and serve.

PASTA WITH MUSSELS IN WHITE WINE SAUCE

SERVES 4–6

I remember the days of my childhood in the Seattle area when we would not eat mussels. They were too much work, and besides, only the Italian immigrants would gather mussels on the beach. Just too much work!

Today mussels are one of my favorite seafoods, and they are farmed here in the Pacific Northwest for distribution all over the country. Now I have to pay plenty for what used to be free . . . and they are still a bit of work.

This dish is just filled with garlic and vermouth, and the mussels seem to be quite happy about it.

2 pounds fresh mussels in the shell	¼ cup whipping cream
	2 tablespoons chopped parsley
1 tablespoon olive oil	Salt to taste (not too much)
6 cloves garlic, thickly sliced	¾ pound spaghetti or spaghettini
¼ cup dry vermouth	
1 tablespoon butter	2 tablespoons fine bread crumbs
½ cup bottled clam juice	

Bring a kettle of lightly salted water to a boil for the pasta.

Wash the mussels and remove their beards. Use a kitchen towel to grab hold of the beard and just pull it off. Heat a 4- to 6-quart pot and add the oil, garlic, mussels, and vermouth. Cover and simmer 3 to 5 minutes until the mussels open. Drain the mussels through a strainer, reserving the broth. Place the mussels in their shells back into the pot and cover to keep warm.

Place the broth in a medium-size frying pan. Add the butter, clam juice, cream, and parsley to the strained broth. Bring to a simmer and reduce the sauce for 2 to 3 minutes. Adjust the salt to taste.

Boil the spaghetti until al dente in the salted water and drain well. Place the pasta on plates and arrange the warm mussels attractively on top.

Add the bread crumbs to the sauce and simmer for 30 seconds. This will not be a thick sauce but the bread crumbs will add a little consistency to the sauce. Pour the sauce over the pasta and mussels.

No cheese is needed for a shellfish dish.

PASTA WITH EGGPLANT SICILIAN

SERVES 6–8 AS A PASTA COURSE

Philadelphia is filled with wonderful Sicilians. The Italian restaurants in this great American city generally serve the food of the South of Italy.

We found a little place through the guidance of our dear friend and driver, Big Dennis. He took us to Criniti's Restaurant after a bad experience at a well-known and arrogant joint where we had dined the night before. For lunch the next day he promised a delight. Criniti's is a delight.

In this recipe, which is as close as we can come to his, Criniti displays the love that the people of Sicily have for the eggplant. A pasta dish without meat but with tons of flavor!

1 1-pound eggplant
1½ tablespoons salt
2 eggs
½ cup milk
2 cups fine bread crumbs
½ cup or more olive oil for frying
2½ cups Fresh Tomato Sauce Sicilian (page 139)

¾ pound dry spaghetti

GARNISH
Grated Parmesan cheese (optional)

Slice the eggplant ⅛ inch thick. Sprinkle each slice of eggplant with a bit of the 1½ tablespoons salt and place the slices in a colander. Allow to drain for 30 minutes. Rinse each slice with cold water and pat dry with a towel.

Beat the eggs and milk together in a medium-size bowl.

Bread the eggplant slices by dipping into the egg wash and then into the bread crumbs. Pat off excess crumbs and place on a sheet pan.

Heat a large frying pan and pan-fry the slices in batches, using some of the oil each time. Fry the eggplant in plenty of oil until golden brown on each side. Remove to drain on paper towels. Cut the fried eggplant into ¼-inch-wide strips and keep warm.

Heat the tomato sauce to a simmer and bring a large pot of water to a boil for the pasta. Lightly salt the water and boil the pasta until al dente. Drain very well and place the hot pasta on plates. Top with the fried eggplant and the tomato sauce. Garnish with optional cheese.

LINGUINE WITH DUCK, PORCINI, AND SUN-DRIED TOMATOES

SERVES 8 AS A PASTA COURSE

When it comes to duck I am smart enough to step aside in the kitchen and let Craig do his stuff. He loves duck so much that I think he talks to them before he cooks them. In any case, we had a dish very close to this one at Carmine's Il Terrazzo Restaurant, in Seattle. Craig assured me that he could produce a similar dish and you must taste his success. This is rich and unusually good.

**FOR THE ROAST
DUCK**
1 4-pound duck,
   frozen and fully
   defrosted
Salt and pepper to
   taste
1 bunch fresh
   rosemary

THE SAUCE
½ ounce dried porcini
   mushrooms
   (page 415)
½ ounce sun-dried
   tomatoes
1½ cups hot tap water
2 tablespoons olive
   oil
1 medium yellow
   onion, peeled
   and thinly sliced

2 tablespoons butter
4 cloves garlic, sliced
1½ cups Mock Veal
   Stock (page 116)
2 tablespoons
   chopped parsley
2 tablespoons dry
   Marsala
1½ cups roasted duck
   meat, julienned
Salt and pepper to
   taste

1 pound dry linguine

GARNISH
Grated Parmesan
   cheese

Remove the excess fat from the duck and save for another use. Salt and pepper the duck inside and out to taste. Place the rosemary inside the duck. Place the duck on a roasting rack inside a roasting pan. Bake in a preheated 400° oven for 20 minutes. Reduce the heat to 325° and roast for 1 hour. Remove and allow to cool. Remove the skin and discard. Debone the meat and julienne into 1½-inch by ¼-inch pieces. Set aside. Use any leftover duck meat for Polenta with Duck and Mushroom Sauce (page 227). Or make a salad out of it.

Place the dried porcini and the dried tomatoes in two separate water glasses. Add ¾ cup hot tap water to each glass to reconstitute. Allow to stand 45 minutes. Drain each, chop coarsely, and set aside.

Heat a medium-size frying pan and add the oil and onion.

Sauté over medium heat, covered, until very tender and browned. Toss and stir the onion until caramelized but not burned. Remove the caramelized onion and set aside.

Heat the pan again and add the butter, garlic, and reserved porcini and tomatoes. Sauté 2 minutes, add the Mock Veal Stock, parsley, and Marsala, and bring to a simmer. Reduce the sauce by one third and set aside.

Bring a large kettle of water to a boil with a pinch of salt. Cook the pasta until al dente and drain well.

Return the sauce to a simmer and add the duck meat. Add salt and pepper to taste. Place the drained pasta in a large bowl and add the hot duck sauce and reserved onions. Toss all together and serve. Garnish with grated cheese.

SPAGHETTI BAGNA CAUDA

SERVES 6 AS A PASTA COURSE

I do not know why I didn't think of this before because I really do love Bagna Cauda. It makes a great pasta dressing and it is simple to prepare . . . providing you have some Bagna Cauda just sitting around in your refrigerator.

Remember, this stuff is rich, so keep that in mind when planning the rest of the menu.

¾ **pound spaghettini**
¾ **cup Bagna Cauda**
   (page 78), warm

GARNISHES
Grated Parmesan
   cheese
Chopped parsley

Boil the pasta in lightly salted water until al dente. Drain well and toss with warm Bagna Cauda. Top with cheese and parsley.

PASTA WITH
MUSHROOM SAUCE

Prepare Mushroom Sauce for Pasta and Polenta (page 138). Cook your favorite pasta al dente and toss with the desired amount of the sauce. Garnish with fresh grated Parmesan cheese. Very rich and delicious!

LOW-CHOLESTEROL PASTA

SERVES 4–6

I admit that I do not spend a lot of time trying to think up low-cholesterol recipes as I think the whole food-fear thing is getting to be blown out of shape. However, for those of you placed on a restricted diet, this pasta will become a favorite. The idea was given us by one of our fans, and with a lot of fooling around we got it to work beautifully.

1½ cups unbleached bread flour	3 egg whites
1 cup semolina flour (page 24)	2 tablespoons olive oil
½ teaspoon salt	5 tablespoons cold water

Place the dry ingredients in a large bowl and stir together. Form a well in the center and add the remaining ingredients to the well. Stir with a fork and press together with your fingers. Knead the dough until smooth and elastic. Place the dough on the counter and cover it with the mixing bowl. Let the dough rest for ½ hour. Knead the dough again briefly and you're ready to make pasta.

To make spaghetti, use an Atlas pasta machine.

Divide the pasta dough into 6 equal parts. When working with one portion of the dough, keep the remainder covered. Run a portion of the dough through the pasta-rolling machine on the widest setting (#1). Turn the setting to #2 and run the dough through again. Turn the setting to #3 and run through once more. Continue adjusting the machine to higher settings until you reach #5. Run the sheet of dough through the spaghetti-cutting roller.

Use the same process for making fettucine, but roll the dough out on the #6 setting and then cut the sheet on the fettucine cutter.

FRESH PASTA DOUGH

MAKES ENOUGH FOR 6–8 SERVINGS FOR A PASTA COURSE

Fresh homemade pasta is a great gift to your family, and certain dishes simply cannot be pulled off with dried pasta. However, while this is a fine recipe that Craig developed, neither of us wants you to think that we do not like dried pasta as well. Different pastas for different uses.

This one is actually very easy and it will hold up well as you cook it.

1½ cups unbleached white flour (use bread flour, not all-purpose)	½ teaspoon salt
	3 large eggs
	1 tablespoon olive oil
	1 tablespoon water,
1 cup semolina flour (page 24)	or more as needed

Place the flours and salt in a large bowl. Mix well and form a well in the center. Add the remaining ingredients and pinch all together with your fingers to form a dough. Knead for a few minutes until the dough is smooth and elastic. Place the dough on the counter and cover with the bowl. Let rest ½ hour. Knead again briefly and form into any shape desired.

Remember to allow your pasta to dry on a counter in a cool place for about an hour before cooking. Or, most pasta freezes well. Dry a bit first and then freeze on covered trays or in boxes.

PENNE FONDUTA

What more needs to be said? The recipe for the Fonduta is on page 80 and it is one of the richest cheese sauces that you have ever tasted. The rest of the recipe is simple.

Cook the penne al dente and toss with Fonduta. Garnish with black pepper and chopped parsley. Great!

Remember that when you serve this, everyone is going to tell you that it is very rich. So keep the servings down to 1 pound of dried pasta for 6 people. You will not need more than 1 cup of Fonduta to dress the pasta.

No other garnish will be necessary.

MACCHERONI ALLA
CHITARRA RAGÙ

My favorite method of serving this firm and delightful pasta is with Ragù sauce. It is also a popular version offered in the Abruzzi region. The firm texture of the noodles and the heavy meatiness of the Ragù make for a superb dish that I doubt you have ever tasted in this country.

Prepare a batch of Maccheroni alla Chitarra (page 180). Heat a couple of cups of Ragù (page 144) and toss all together. Add a few tablespoons of butter and top with freshly grated Parmesan cheese.

So good!

MACCHERONI ALLA CHITARRA

SERVES 6–10 AS A PASTA COURSE

The name of this dish should sound like "guitar." In the old days it was cut on a frame that had a whole series of wire strings on it, much like a guitar. Since Italians love different shapes of pasta, this one became a jewel of the Abruzzi region. (See illustration on page 152.) The pasta is rolled to the thickness of the distance between the wires on the press. The dough is pressed through the wires and the result is a firm and wonderful noodle that is square in shape, not round.

One day when we were in L'Aquila, a major city in this region, we went to the most famous restaurant in town and ordered Maccheroni alla Chitarra. The menu stated that it was "made in the old-fashioned way on the old-fashioned machine typical of our exceptional region. It is made in house!" When the owner and chef could not produce a working chitarra, I realized that he bought the pasta from some guy down the street who cranks it out on a metal roller and cutter, typical of our time. It was a good dish, but a menu should never lie!

I have done it on a wire press and on a metal hand roller and cutter. The mechanized version is easier; the old-fashioned version has a better texture.

1½ cups unbleached bread flour	½ teaspoon salt
1 cup semolina flour (page 24)	3 eggs, beaten
	3 tablespoons water

Place the flours and salt in a large bowl. Stir together and
form a well in the center. Add the remaining ingredients to
the well and pinch all together with your fingers to form a
dough. Knead for a few minutes until the dough is smooth
and elastic. Place the dough on the counter and cover with
the bowl. Allow to rest ½ hour.

Cut the dough into 6 equal parts. Set up an Atlas pasta
rolling machine (page 38), with the "chitarra" attachment,
on the counter or cutting board. Lightly flour the machine
and the countertop. Flatten a portion of dough with your
hand and run it through the machine on the #1 setting.
Leave the remaining dough covered while working with
each piece.

Adjust the setting to #3 and run the dough through again.
Adjust the setting to #5 and run the dough through once
more. Continue with the remaining dough. Lay the sheets
of pasta out on a lightly floured surface and allow to dry
for 10 minutes.

Use a real chitarra cutter to cut the special noodles: Lay
a sheet of pasta on top of the strings and run a rolling pin
over the dough firmly. You may have to use the edge of
the rolling pin to work the pasta through the strings. You
can also strum the strings to help the pasta fall through.
Lightly flour the cut pasta and dry on the countertop for 15
minutes.

Boil the desired number of portions in lightly salted
water 2 to 3 minutes until al dente. This won't take long—
don't overcook! Serve with melted butter and grated Parmesan cheese or your favorite sauce.

You can find the old-fashioned chitarra cutter in Italian
specialty shops.

Chitarra

PASTA CARBONARA
WITH SAFFRON

SERVES 4–6 AS A PASTA COURSE

I have tasted, tested, and written more Pasta Carbonara recipes than I can remember. It is a classic dish that refers to coal miners, or roasting the bacon over coal, or just peasant food, depending on which story you care to believe. Whatever the background, the dish is basic and this version was offered us in L'Aquila, in the Abruzzi region. Wonderful little city in the hills, with good food and kind people. They do love their saffron!

¼ pound pancetta,
    thinly sliced
6 tablespoons butter
2 cloves garlic,
    crushed
1 cup milk
1 tablespoon wine
    vinegar
¼ teaspoon saffron
¾ pound tubetti pasta
    (page 152)

1 egg, beaten
¼ cup grated
    Parmesan cheese
Salt and pepper to
    taste

GARNISH
Chopped parsley

Chop the sliced pancetta coarsely and sauté in butter with the garlic until transparent. Simmer the milk gently in a small saucepan along with the sautéed pancetta and butter, for 4 minutes. Add the vinegar. This will turn the milk to cheese. Simmer, stirring, for about 15 minutes, or until the sauce cooks smooth. Stir in the saffron.

Boil the tubetti in a large pot of lightly salted water until al dente. Drain well and return to the pot. Immediately throw in the hot milk mixture, beaten egg, and Parmesan cheese. Toss together quickly and adjust the salt and pepper to taste. Garnish with chopped parsley.

RAVIOLI WITH CHEESE, POTATO, AND SPINACH FILLING

MAKES 3 DOZEN

Other cultures have dumplings, but I do not think anyone can touch the creativity of the Italians when it comes to little pasta pillows filled with goodies. This is a good recipe, and you will be surprised by the supportive presence of the potato. This sort of thing is common and loved in the Reggio-Emilia region.

THE FILLING

1 1-pound russet potato
1 recipe Fresh Pasta Dough (page 178)
½ cup frozen chopped spinach, thawed and squeezed dry
½ cup grated Parmesan cheese
1 cup ricotta cheese
Salt and pepper to taste
1 egg yolk

Boil the potato in the skin about 35 minutes or until tender when a knife is inserted. Drain and allow to cool.

Prepare the pasta dough and allow to rest, covered, on the counter.

Peel the potato using the back of a table knife. Run the potato through a potato ricer into a mixing bowl. Squeeze the thawed spinach dry and add to the bowl along with the remaining ingredients for the filling. Mix together well.

Divide the pasta dough into 6 equal parts. When working with one portion of the dough, keep the remainder covered. Run a portion of the dough through an Atlas pasta-rolling machine on the widest setting #1. Turn the setting to #2 and run the dough through again. Turn the setting to #3 and run through once more. Continue adjusting the machine to higher settings, until you reach #5. Lay the sheet of pasta across a lightly floured Ravioli Chef (page 48) ravioli former, or some other brand. Place about 1½ teaspoons of filling in each compartment on the press and even it out. Using a small artist's paintbrush, paint a light line of water along the edges of each of the ravioli. Place another sheet of pasta on top and pat it down lightly to seal, being careful to press out any air bubbles. Run a rolling pin over the press to cut the ravioli. Remove the ravioli and continue the procedure with the remaining dough. Save any leftover filling for another use.

Boil the ravioli in lightly salted water about 3 minutes (fresh pasta cooks quickly!) or until the filling is hot and the pasta is tender. Serve with Fresh Tomato Sauce Sicilian (page 139) or melted butter and fresh grated Parmesan cheese.

CREPES WITH PORCINI AND ASPARAGUS

Asparagus and mushrooms seem to belong together. Both are rather strange in terms of their background, one being a fungus that grows from waste, and the other being the highest form of grass that we know, but both are delicious. This is a fine marriage of the two.

Follow the recipe for Crepes with Porcini and Mushrooms (page 418) and add the asparagus below to the mushroom filling in that recipe. Fold the mushroom and asparagus filling into the crepes and bake as usual.

½ **cup cooked asparagus (Cut the asparagus into ½-inch pieces and blanch just until tender. Drain very well and combine with the usual filling.)**

CARBONARA (LIGHTER VERSION)

SERVES 3–4 AS A PASTA COURSE

This version is a bit lighter than the classic Carbonara since it uses ham instead of bacon. We tasted it in a tiny restaurant in the Italian section of Boston, a fine little place called Piccola Venezia. When you go to Boston you must go to the old Italian neighborhood, called the North End. You will have a great time.

1 tablespoon olive oil	2 egg yolks, beaten
3 tablespoons butter	¼ cup freshly grated
¾ cup milk	Parmesan cheese
¼ cup sliced and chopped prosciutto	Salt and pepper to taste
1 tablespoon white wine vinegar	**GARNISH**
½ pound dry penne pasta	Additional freshly grated Parmesan cheese

Bring a kettle of water to boil for the pasta, adding a bit of salt.

Heat a 1-quart saucepan and simmer the oil, butter, milk, and prosciutto. Then add the vinegar and continue to simmer for about 5 more minutes.

While the sauce simmers, cook the pasta al dente, drain, and place in a mixing bowl. If the sauce has cooled during the cooking of the pasta, quickly reheat it. Add the sauce, the beaten egg yolks, and cheese to the pasta. Quickly toss the mixture and check for salt and pepper.

Garnish with the additional cheese.

FOUR-CHEESE LASAGNA

SERVES 6–8

Often fans will stop me on the street and ask me to do a vegetarian cookbook. I point out to them that every book we have ever done contains recipes for the vegetarian. This is one of them. No meat whatsoever, but it is loaded with good cheeses, so there is certainly no lack of flavor. I really enjoy this version of the classic and you must be prepared for a much moister dish than that firm and highly heaped edition that is so common in restaurants in this country.

½ pound lasagna noodles, maybe a hair less (You will need 9 unbroken noodles. Standard size is about 9¾ inches by 2 inches. Wow! What details!)

1½ cups riccotta cheese

¼ cup grated Parmesan cheese

1 egg, beaten

Salt and pepper to taste

2 cups Fresh Tomato Sauce Sicilian (page 139)

½ pound aged mozzarella, thinly sliced

½ pound provolone, thinly sliced

Additional grated Parmesan cheese for topping

Bring a large kettle of water to a boil and lightly salt it. Cook the noodles until al dente, making sure they separate in the water. Carefully drain the noodles and rinse in cold water. Drain very well and lay the noodles out flat. Mix the riccotta, ¼ cup Parmesan cheese, egg, and salt and pepper to taste together.

Lightly oil a 13×9×2-inch baking pan and spread ½ cup of the tomato sauce on the bottom of the pan. Lay three of the cooked noodles lengthwise in the pan. Spread ⅓ of the total quantity of the riccotta mixture on top of the first layer of noodles. Top with ⅓ of the mozzarella and ⅓ of the provolone. Top with another ½ cup of the tomato sauce and add another layer of noodles. Spread another ⅓ of the ricotta on top of the noodles and another layer of mozzarella and provolone. Top with another ½ cup of the sauce and the remaining three lasagna noodles. Spread the remaining ricotta on the noodles and spread the remaining sauce over the ricotta. Top with the mozzarella and provolone, and sprinkle with additional grated Parmesan cheese.

Bake in a preheated 375° oven for 40 minutes until bubbly and the cheese lightly browns. Allow the lasagna to cool and set up a bit before cutting.

PENNE ALLA VODKA WITH TOMATO AND ONIONS

SERVES 4–6 AS A PASTA COURSE

This version is from Philadelphia, and it features crunchy, barely cooked onions in the sauce. I like the marriage of onions and garlic, but a friend who is a great authority on Italian cooking told me that she uses only onions in this dish, never mixed with garlic. Her name is Anna Teresa Callen, and I am sure you have seen her books and her fine articles in the fancy food magazines. Well, Anna, I tried it both ways and I still love my garlic . . . along with the onions, of course.

2 tablespoons olive oil
1 medium yellow
   onion, thinly
   sliced
2 cloves garlic,
   crushed
½ cup dry white wine
1 cup whipping cream
⅓ cup Fresh Tomato
   Sauce Sicilian
   (page 139)
¼ cup grated
   Parmesan cheese
   Salt and pepper to
   taste

¾ pound dry penne
   pasta
½ cup vodka (Don't
   use an expensive
   brand of vodka
   for this dish as
   you will not have
   the flavor. Go
   ahead and choose
   a popular brand
   like Smirnoff.)

GARNISH
Chopped parsley

Heat a medium-size frying pan and add 1 tablespoon of the oil and the onion. Sauté until almost tender—the onion should still be a little bit fresh and crunchy and not at all browned. Remove and set aside.

Heat the pan again and add the remaining 1 tablespoon of oil and the garlic. Sauté for 30 seconds and add the wine. Simmer the wine and garlic for 2 minutes and add the cream, tomato sauce, and cheese. Simmer and stir together until smooth. Add salt and pepper to taste and keep the sauce covered at a very gentle simmer while the pasta cooks.

Cook the pasta until al dente in lightly salted water and drain well. Add the vodka to the sauce and just bring to a simmer. Don't cook the vodka out! Toss the pasta, reserved onions, and sauce together and garnish with parsley. Let stand for a few minutes so the pasta can absorb the sauce.

CANNELLONI STUFFED
WITH RAGÙ

SERVES 4 AS A MAIN COURSE

*With a little advance preparation—meaning that the sauces
and crepes and fillings are made a day or two ahead—this
is one of those dishes that you can throw together at the
last minute. The only way you can do this sort of cooking
on a working schedule is to cook ahead, and I mean cook
seriously one day a week.*

*This dish is just delicious, and it is typical of the kind of
food that you will find in Bologna.*

1 recipe Basic
   Cannelloni
   Crepes (page
   207) (You will
   need 8 good
   crepes.)
3 cups Ragù sauce
   (page 144), at
   room
   temperature
1 tablespoon butter
   for greasing 4
   individual
   oblong baking
   dishes

2 cups Fresh Tomato
   Sauce Sicilian
   (page 139)
⅓ cup whipping
   cream
1½ cups grated
   mozzarella
   cheese
¼ cup grated
   Parmesan cheese

Lay the crepes out on a clean counter and divide the ragù
filling between them in a line down the center. Butter the
individual baking dishes. Roll the filled crepes up and place
2 in each buttered dish seam side down. Combine the tomato sauce with the cream and pour over the filled crepes.
Top each dish with the mozzarella and sprinkle with the
Parmesan cheese. Bake in a preheated 375° oven for 15 to
20 minutes or until bubbly and the cheese starts to brown.

VARIATION: This recipe can also be prepared as a first
course with each person receiving one filled crepe instead
of two.

PAPPARDELLE RAGÙ DA BRUNO

SERVES 6–8 AS A PASTA COURSE

*While it takes a few minutes to roll out fresh-made pap-
pardelle, you must understand that there is no way around
this . . . unless you live in an Italian community where you
can buy this freshly made. Dried pappardelle is much too
thick, and you want something that is thin and tender.*

*This is a great recipe and very close to that which is
served in one of our favorite restaurants in Milan, Da
Bruno.*

Take the time to make this. It will delight the entire table.

¼ ounce dried porcini
    mushrooms
    (page 415)
¾ cup warm water
2 tablespoons olive
    oil
2 cloves garlic,
    crushed
½ pound veal,
    coarsely ground
1¼ cup Fresh Tomato
    Sauce Sicilian
    (page 139)

½ cup dry white wine
½ cup whipping
    cream
2 tablespoons grated
    Parmesan cheese
Salt and pepper to
    taste
1 recipe Fresh Pasta
    Dough (page
    178)

GARNISH
Grated Parmesan
cheese

Place the porcini in a small glass and add ¾ cup warm
water. Allow the porcini to soak for 45 minutes. Drain and
discard the liquid. Rinse the porcini to be sure it contains
no sand and chop coarsely. Heat a frying pan and add the
oil, garlic, and chopped porcini. Sauté for 2 minutes and

add the ground veal. Brown the meat until crumbly and add the tomato sauce and wine. Simmer, covered, for 5 minutes and add the cream and Parmesan cheese. Continue simmering gently for 20 minutes, stirring often, until the sauce reduces and thickens a bit. Add salt and pepper to taste.

Prepare the pasta dough and divide it into 8 equal parts. Flatten a portion with your hands. Flour and lightly run it through an Atlas or Marcato pasta machine (page 38). Run the flattened dough through on the #2 setting first and then adjust the machine to setting #5. Run the dough through again and change the setting to #7. Run the sheet of pasta through three times to create very thin sheets. Lightly flour the pasta and cut the sheets lengthwise with a knife into 1-inch-wide ribbons. Allow to dry for 15 minutes.

Bring a large pot of lightly salted water to a boil and cook the pasta for about 1½ minutes and drain well (this particular type of pasta will cook very quickly). Toss with the sauce and serve with grated cheese.

PENNE WITH LIGHT CREAM SAUCE AND FRESH SPINACH

SERVES 8–10 AS A PASTA COURSE

This is a fine dish that contains no meat but a great deal of flavor. It is typical of the cooking in the North, and I think we saw something like this in Milan. In any case it is a refreshing dish. Not too heavy. Please note that the spinach is added to the pasta raw, which means you will have a nice fresh flavor here.

2 tablespoons butter
2 tablespoons flour
1½ cups milk
Salt and pepper to taste
1 tablespoon olive oil
2 cloves garlic, crushed
1 1-pound bunch spinach, washed and drained well, stems removed, and chopped coarsely

1 pound dry penne pasta

GARNISH
Freshly grated Parmesan cheese to taste

Bring 8 quarts of water to a boil so that you will be ready to cook the pasta.

Melt the butter in a small frying pan and add the flour. Stir together and cook over low heat a few minutes to form a roux. Do not brown the roux! Heat the milk to a simmer and whisk the roux into the milk. Simmer for 3 minutes, whisking until smooth and slightly thickened. Add salt and pepper to taste.

Heat another small frying pan with the oil and sauté the garlic for 30 seconds, making sure not to burn it.

Boil the pasta in lightly salted water until al dente. Drain well and return the pasta to the pot. Add the garlic oil, the raw chopped spinach, and the thickened milk. Toss together and serve with the garnish. You may want to warm this on the stove for a moment while the spinach collapses. Do not overcook.

PASTA AL PESTO WITH CREAM, GREEN BEANS, AND POTATOES

SERVES 4–6 AS A PASTA COURSE

We found this dish in a little trattoria in Milan. Rough neighborhoods sometimes offer some very creative and rather inexpensive food, at least by Italian standards. While the basic dish certainly originated in Genoa, the variations offered in this workers' restaurant in Milan are very good.

2 teaspoons salt
3 tablespoons olive oil
¼ pound green beans, trimmed and cut into 1-inch pieces
½ pound small red potatoes
2 cloves garlic, crushed
⅓ cup pesto sauce (Buy a good one from an Italian market, best frozen or in glass. Avoid the cans!)

½ cup cream
½ pound dry penne pasta
Salt and pepper to taste

GARNISH
Grated Parmesan cheese

Bring 4 quarts of water to a boil with the salt and 1 tablespoon of the oil. Parboil the cut green beans 2 minutes and remove with a skimmer to cool on a plate. Place the potatoes with the peel on in the pot of water and boil 10 to 15 minutes until just tender. Drain the potatoes, cool, and slice ¼ inch thick.

Heat a frying pan and add the remaining 2 tablespoons of the oil and the garlic. Sauté 30 seconds and add the potatoes and green beans. Sauté 3 to 5 minutes until the vegetables are tender.

Mix the pesto sauce with the cream and set aside. Boil the pasta in lightly salted water until al dente. Drain well and return to the pot. Add the sautéed beans and potatoes and the pesto cream. Toss all together and add salt and pepper to taste if needed. Serve with grated Parmesan cheese.

LINGUINE WITH ZUCCHINI, TOMATO, AND GRILLED SHRIMP

SERVES 6

The flavors of zucchini and shrimp go together beautifully. The result is a light and pleasing dish, in terms of both taste and color. If you have that fresh tomato sauce already made and in the refrigerator, this recipe is a snap to whip up after a working day.

Vegetable and seafood pastas are common throughout Italy.

½ pound fresh
   medium shrimp,
   peeled
Salt and pepper to
   taste
3 tablespoons olive oil
2 cloves garlic,
   chopped
½ pound green
   zucchini,
   julienned (2
   inches by ¼ inch)

1 cup Fresh Tomato
   Sauce Sicilian
   (page 139)
¾ pound dried
   linguine

GARNISH
Freshly grated
Parmesan cheese
to taste

Heat a large pot of lightly salted water to a boil for the pasta.

Place the peeled shrimp in a small bowl and season with salt and pepper to taste and 1 tablespoon of the oil. Grill the shrimp over high heat about 1 minute per side or until opaque and lightly charred. (The Le Creuset stove-top grill [page 35] works great for this or grill the shrimp on the barbecue.) Don't overcook; set aside.

Heat a medium-size frying pan and add the remaining 2 tablespoons of oil, the garlic, and the zucchini. Sauté until the zucchini is just tender. Add the tomato sauce and bring to a simmer. Adjust salt and pepper to taste if needed. Cook the pasta until al dente, drain, and return to the pot. Add the grilled shrimp to the simmering sauce and cook gently for 1 minute. Add to the drained pasta and toss together. Serve with grated Parmesan cheese.

PASTA CARBONARA ANTICO TORRE

SERVES 4–6 AS A PASTA COURSE

This is an interesting variation on the old classic in that it contains caramelized onions in the sauce. The onions give it a sweet flavor, due to their natural sugar. We had a dish very much like this one in Venice, at Antico Torre.

¼ pound pancetta, chopped
1 tablespoon butter
1 tablespoon olive oil
1 medium yellow onion, sliced
¾ pound penne pasta
4 eggs, beaten
⅓ cup freshly grated Parmesan cheese

Salt and black pepper to taste

GARNISHES
Chopped parsley
Additional grated cheese

Brown the pancetta in a frying pan. In another pan heat the butter and oil. Add the onion and sauté for 2 minutes. Turn down the heat to very low and cover the pan. Cook very slowly for 15 to 20 minutes. Stir occasionally to caramelize. Cook the pasta al dente and drain.

Return the pasta to the pot and add the pancetta sauce, the eggs, and the cheese. Toss quickly; check for salt and pepper.

Garnish with chopped parsley and grated cheese and serve. Some guests may want additional black pepper.

GREEN RAVIOLI WITH FONDUTA

SERVES 2–4

This is just a suggestion that will turn you on to other sauces that are great with ravioli. Please remember that this Fonduta cheese sauce is very rich. Tread lightly!

1 pound fresh or frozen spinach ravioli (meat- or cheese-filled)

¾ cup Fonduta (page 80), hot

Cook the ravioli as instructed on the package and drain. Toss with the Fonduta and serve.

PASTA E CECI

SERVES 6–8

Pasta and chick-peas—or garbanzo beans, or ceci—*sounds like it will be too starchy. This dish is a double starch, of course, but the* ceci *give it a great flavor and between the flavor and the body your kids will be delighted.*

1½ cups dried
    garbanzo beans
5 cups cold water
6 cups Chicken
    Stock (page 116)
2 tablespoons olive
    oil
½ cup thinly sliced
    celery
1 cup yellow onion,
    chopped
½ cup diced tomato
2 tablespoons
    chopped parsley
½ cup dry white wine

¾ cup dry tubetti
    pasta
Salt and pepper to
    taste
2 cloves garlic,
    peeled and thinly
    sliced

GARNISHES
Chopped parsley to
    taste
Freshly grated
    Parmesan cheese
    to taste

Place the garbanzos and the water in a bowl and allow to soak overnight. Drain the soaked beans and place in a 4- to 6-quart pot along with the Chicken Stock. Bring to a boil, cover, and simmer 1 hour and 25 minutes or until the garbanzos are very tender but not mushy.

Heat a medium-size frying pan and add 1 tablespoon of the oil, the celery, and the onion. Sauté until tender and add the tomato and parsley. Sauté a few minutes more and set aside.

Remove half the garbanzos and puree with some of the broth in a food processor or food blender. Return to the pot along with the sautéed vegetables. Add the wine and the uncooked pasta. Bring to a simmer and cook, covered, 20 minutes more, or until the pasta is very tender and the soup thickens slightly. Stir the soup often while simmering to prevent sticking. Add salt and pepper to taste.

Sauté the sliced garlic for 30 seconds in the remaining 1 tablespoon of olive oil. Pour the garlic oil over the soup and top with the garnishes.

SPAGHETTINI WITH BLACK TRUFFLE PASTE

Serves 4 as a pasta course

Get ready! This is a wonderful but expensive Italian treat. Do it once in a while, maybe at your seventy-fifth wedding anniversary.

½ pound dry spaghettini	1 1-ounce can black truffle paste
2 quarts Chicken Stock (page 116)	2 tablespoons butter Salt to taste

Cook the spaghettini in the Chicken Stock until al dente. Drain, reserving the Chicken Stock for another use, and toss the pasta with the butter and the small can of black truffle paste. Nothing else need be done to this dish as the truffle paste needs nothing to support it. The pasta will do it. Expensive and yummy. This is the sort of thing that you save for a family holiday, and what a holiday it will be!

FRESH TAGLIATELLE DI PARMA

SERVES 4-6

The joy offered in this recipe stems from the fact that the old lady of Parma, chef at Trattoria Vecchio Molinetto, not only makes her own fresh tagliatelle but then cooks it in chicken broth, not water. What a delicious dish! Cheese and butter, of course.

PREPARING THE PASTA

Prepare the pasta dough as in the recipe for Maccheroni Alla Chitarra (page 179). Divide the dough into 6 equal pieces. Keep the dough covered with a bowl while you work. Make the noodles by flattening a portion of the dough with your hands and running it through an Atlas or Marcato pasta machine. Roll the pasta out on the #2 setting first, then adjust the machine to the #4 setting. Run the pasta through again and adjust to the #5 setting. Run the sheet of pasta through a third time and lightly flour it. Continue with the remaining dough. Roll each pasta sheet up like a jelly roll and cut crosswise by hand with a sharp knife into ⅛-inch-wide coils. Unroll the coils and allow the noodles to dry for 15 minutes.

  (Note: If you have a different brand of pasta machine from the ones above, the settings will most likely be different. The idea is to end up with fresh pasta that is about the same width and thickness as fettucini.)

COOKING THE PASTA

6 to 8 quarts Chicken Stock (page 116)

1 stick butter, melted
⅓ cup freshly grated Parmesan cheese
Black pepper to taste

Boil the pasta in the Chicken Stock 2 to 3 minutes and drain well, reserving the stock for another use. Toss with the melted butter, cheese, and black pepper to taste.

PASTA CARBONARA WITH PANCETTA CRACKLINGS

SERVES 6–8 AS A PASTA COURSE

This favorite pasta dish is terribly simple to make. We have several versions in this book, and I am sure there are many more.

There are many stories behind the name, but the most common has something to do with coal miners thinking of creative ways to use the cured and dried meats that they had at hand. Where they would have gotten the butter and eggs and the fresh milk is beyond me.

In any case, this is a terrific version. Just remember to be patient while the sauce cooks smooth. It will. Just stir for a few more minutes.

⅓ pound pancetta, in one piece
¼ pound butter
1 cup milk
2 tablespoons white wine vinegar
1 pound dry pasta

2 eggs, whipped
⅓ cup grated Parmesan or Romano cheese
Salt and pepper to taste

Cut the pancetta into little pieces ¼ inch square and sauté in a small frying pan with the butter until the pancetta barely begins to brown. It should be a bit crunchy but not dry. Heat the milk in a small saucepan and add the bacon and butter. Add the vinegar; this will turn the milk to cheese. Simmer gently for about 15 minutes, or until the sauce cooks smooth.

Boil your favorite pasta al dente. Drain and return to the pan. Immediately throw in the eggs, the bacon sauce, and the grated cheese. Add salt and pepper to taste, toss, and serve immediately.

PASTA WITH EGGPLANT RAGÙ

SERVES 6–8 AS A PASTA COURSE

Normally the term "ragù" refers to a very heavy and rich meat sauce from Bologna. However, when we tasted this dish in Bologna we decided that we had to learn to make it. The addition of the eggplant and fresh peppers is just a terrific idea.

1 ¾-pound eggplant, sliced ¼ inch thick
1½ tablespoons salt
4 tablespoons olive oil
2 cloves garlic
½ cup finely chopped yellow onion
½ cup seeded and diced mild fresh Anaheim or Cubanelle peppers
½ pound veal, coarsely ground

1¼ cups Fresh Tomato Sauce Sicilian (page 139)
½ cup Chicken Stock (page 116)
Salt and pepper to taste
1 pound dry penne pasta

GARNISH
Freshly grated Parmesan cheese

Sprinkle both sides of the eggplant slices with the 1½ tablespoons of salt. Allow the slices to drain in a colander for 45 minutes. Rinse the eggplant with cold water and pat dry with paper towels. Heat a large frying pan and fry the eggplant in batches until lightly browned, using 3 tablespoons of the oil, more if needed. Chop the fried eggplant coarsely and set aside.

Heat the frying pan again and add the remaining 1 tablespoon of oil, the garlic, onion, and peppers. Sauté until the onion is clear. Add the ground veal and sauté for 10 minutes until crumbly. Add the tomato sauce, Chicken Stock, and fried eggplant and simmer gently, covered, for 30 minutes. Add salt and pepper to taste.

Boil the pasta in lightly salted water until al dente. Drain well and toss with the sauce. Garnish with grated cheese.

PAPPARDELLE WITH DUCK RAGÙ

SERVES 6–8 AS A PASTA COURSE

This dish was inspired by one we tasted in Florence. The cook simply placed cooked duck pieces on top of a plate of fresh pappardelle dressed with veal ragù. When Craig, our culinary whiz, tasted the dish, he could not help but think of a sauce in which the duck is incorporated rather than sitting on top. The result is further proof of Craig's ability to make a duck talk, and I mean really speak!

¾ pound cooked,
boneless duck
meat (Prepare
the roasted duck
as in the recipe
for Linguine
with Duck,
Porcini, and
Sun-Dried
Tomatoes [page
174]. Debone the
roasted duck
and tear the
meat into coarse
pieces. Set aside.
Save any
remaining duck
meat for another
dish.)

1 recipe fresh
pappardelle
pasta (page 190)

2 tablespoons olive
oil
3 cloves garlic,
crushed
¼ cup finely chopped
celery
¼ cup finely chopped
carrot
¼ cup finely chopped
yellow onion
2 tablespoons parsley
¼ cup dry white wine
1½ cups Chicken
Stock (page 116)
1¼ cup Fresh Tomato
Sauce Sicilian
(page 139)
Salt and pepper to
taste

GARNISH
Freshly grated
Parmesan cheese

Heat a 4-quart pot and add the oil, garlic, celery, carrot, and onion. Sauté for 10 minutes until the onion is clear. Add the parsley, white wine, Chicken Stock, and tomato sauce. Cover and simmer for 1 hour and add salt and pepper to taste. Add the ¾ pound of boneless duck meat and simmer gently for 5 minutes. Cook the pappardelle in lightly salted water for 1 to 2 minutes and drain well. Toss with the Duck Ragù and garnish with grated cheese.

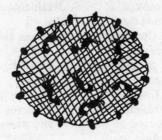

PASTA WITH RAGÙ AND SHRIMP

SERVES 4 AS A PASTA COURSE

Shrimp in a meat sauce sounds a bit strange at first but it works very well. This sort of thing is common throughout Northern Italy and it probably came from the South, so it can be found throughout the nation. Remember that since the country is so long and narrow, no matter where you live, you are not far from the sea.

½ **pound fresh medium shrimp, peeled**	½ **pound penne pasta**
	2 tablespoons olive oil
Salt and pepper to taste	**2 cloves garlic, chopped**
1 cup Ragù (page 144)	**GARNISH**
¼ **cup dry white wine**	**Chopped parsley**

Season the peeled shrimp lightly with salt and pepper to taste. Simmer the Ragù and the wine in a small pan for 5 minutes. Set aside and keep hot.

Bring a kettle of lightly salted water to a boil and cook the pasta until al dente and drain well.

While the pasta finishes cooking, sauté the shrimp in the oil and garlic for 1 minute. Don't overcook! Toss the drained pasta with the hot sauce. Serve with the sautéed shrimp on top of the pasta and garnish with parsley.

PASTA WITH GARLIC OIL
AND GINGER

SERVES 4–6 AS A PASTA COURSE

This is a bit strange, at least for my taste. But if you like ginger, this may be your cup of pasta. It is a dish from the city of Perugia, in Umbria, where ginger is to be found in special dishes. Ginger is not common in much of the rest of Italy, but you might find some enjoyment in this very simple-to-prepare recipe.

¾ pound spaghettini
½ cup olive oil
4 cloves garlic,
   crushed
¾ teaspoon dry
   ground ginger
1 tablespoon chopped
   parsley

Salt and pepper to
   taste

GARNISH
Freshly grated
Parmesan cheese

Bring a large pot of lightly salted water to a boil and cook the pasta until al dente. While the pasta is cooking heat a medium-size frying pan and add the oil, garlic, and ginger and sauté for 30 seconds. Don't burn the garlic! Drain the pasta well and return it to the pot. Add the parsley, the oil mixture, and salt and pepper to taste. Toss together and serve with grated cheese.

FANTASIA DI FARFALLE

SERVES 4

This is delicious! Saleh, a chef of Arabian blood who studied medicine in Italy, decided that he was more interested in food than he was in medicine. What's the difference? Healing is healing!

He runs a first class restaurant in Seattle called Saleh al Lago, Saleh's by the Lake. Wonderful. He did a show with us, and while he is a rather quiet and calm man, he runs a first-class kitchen.

8 ounces Brie cheese
1 cup olive oil
1½ cups diced ripe tomato
2 teaspoons finely chopped garlic
1 tablespoon chopped parsley
4 large basil leaves, chopped
1½ tablespoons toasted pine nuts (toast the pine nuts in a small frying pan over low heat for a few minutes with no oil until golden brown)

Salt and pepper to taste
12 ounces farfalle pasta (bow ties—the Italians like to call this type of pasta "butterflies")

GARNISHES
Parsley sprigs or basil leaves
Freshly grated Parmesan cheese (optional)

Bring a large pot of water to a boil for cooking the pasta.

Trim the rind off the Brie and discard; set the cheese aside. Heat the olive oil in a large frying pan and add the tomato, garlic, parsley, and basil. Sauté for 1 minute and add the Brie and the toasted pine nuts. Toss together over low heat for two minutes to melt the cheese. Add salt and pepper to taste. Set the frying pan aside in a warm place while the pasta cooks.

Lightly salt the boiling water and cook the pasta until al dente. Drain and return to the pot along with the warm sauce and toss together. Serve immediately with the garnishes.

RIGATONI BOLOGNESE

SERVE 4 AS A PASTA COURSE

This is a common dish throughout the Emilia-Romagna region. Since the sauce keeps well in the refrigerator or freezer, you can prepare this quickly after work. This dish is certainly heavy enough for a single-dish lunch or dinner. A green salad dressed with Lemon Olive Oil (page 489) and a good dry red wine and you will be happy and satisfied. A true classic from Bologna.

½ pound dry rigatoni
    pasta
1½ cups Bolognese
    Sauce (page 142)

GARNISH
Grated Parmesan
    cheese to taste

Heat the sauce in a small frying pan. Boil the pasta in lightly salted water until al dente. Drain well and toss with the heated sauce.

BASIC CANNELLONI CREPES

MAKES 8–10 CREPES

These are easy to make and far superior to any frozen variety. Useful for many forms of stuffed pasta, as you will find with just a little imagination. Note that you cook these only on one side, but the top must dry completely.

3 eggs
1 cup water
1 cup all-purpose flour

Pinch of salt
Peanut oil

Place the eggs in a blender. Add the water, flour, and salt. Blend until smooth. Scrape down the sides of the container and blend again. Heat a 10-inch nonstick frying pan and lightly oil the pan, using a paper towel. Ladle ¼ cup of the batter into the pan and quickly turn the pan to evenly coat the bottom with batter. Cook on one side only until dry on the top, about one minute. These should be only very lightly browned and not too dry, so the pan should not be too hot. Lightly oil the pan before cooking each crepe. Separate the crepes with wax paper until ready to use. The noodles can be refrigerated overnight if you seal them in a plastic bag.

GNOCCHI

One of the three most important foods to come to Italy from the Americas was the potato, the other two being the tomato and corn. In this country we don't do much with potatoes other than the deep-fried version, the mashed version, and the Methodist Church Potluck Supper Scalloped Version, the last of which I deplore.

The gift of the potato from the New World to the Old resulted in potato gnocchi, dumplings that serve as pasta and are used with any number of wonderful sauces. The best gnocchi are made from scratch at home, and they are allowed to dry for a short time before being simmered in salted water. Since they must be made by hand the dish takes some time. Oh, I know that there is a machine on the market that will crank them out, but even the importer of this device admits that much more flour must be used in the machine version than in the one made by hand, thus resulting in a heavier dumpling. Fresh-made is best.

I have discovered an imported product from Italy that is quite inexpensive and really very good. It consists of a sealed plastic tray of just a bit more than a pound of potato gnocchi, nicely formed and in a container that needs no refrigeration. I am always very suspicious of such packaging and products, but this one is excellant. I was directed to it by my friends at Panelli Brothers Italian Delicatessen in Little Italy in San Francisco. It is produced by Emilia Foods in Italy. Gnocchi for under three dollars a pound and that needs no refrigeration is a deal! It takes a lot of work to produce homemade gnocchi and this one is almost as good as the homemade. It is imported by Ital Foods in San Francisco and I am sure that you can find it on the East Coast as well.

Whether you make it from scratch or buy it frozen or use the prepared batch from Italy, I know that your family will love this dish. It raises potatoes to a whole new level of enjoyment.

I have also included a recipe for Semolina Gnocchi, a recipe that I consider an Italian national treasure.

POTATO GNOCCHI

SERVES 6

This recipe is from our dear friend Lidia Bastianich, chef at Felidia's in New York and author of a fine cookbook bearing recipes from her childhood in Istria, on the border between Italy and what used to be called Yugoslavia. As a child she used to spend part of her Sunday afternoon rolling these in preparation for dinner. All of the kids in the family were involved, and when I heard her story I assumed that the kids were probably bored with the task. ''Not so,'' said Lidia, ''because handmade gnocchi is so delicous that we looked forward to the meal. Besides, if we each didn't roll enough dumplings, we wouldn't have enough to eat at the table!''

This is a great dish, even though it will take a few minutes to talk the kids into participating. Once they catch on you are set!

6 **large Idaho or russet
  potatoes**
2 **tablespoons plus 1
  teaspoon salt**
  **Dash of freshly
  ground white
  pepper**

2 **eggs, beaten**
4 **cups unbleached
  flour**
  **Grated Parmigiano
  for serving**

Boil the potatoes in their skins about 40 minutes, until easily pierced with a skewer. When cool enough to handle, peel and rice the potatoes, and set them aside to cool *completely,* spreading them loosely to expose as much surface as possible to air. (The reason for this is to allow as much evaporation of moisture as possible, to avoid heaviness when the flour is worked into the dough.)

Before proceeding further, bring 6 quarts water and 2 tablespoons of the salt to the boil.

On a cool, preferably marble work surface, gather the cold riced potatoes into a mound, forming a well in the center. Stir the remaining 1 teaspoon salt and the white pepper into the beaten eggs and pour the mixture into the well. Work the potatoes and eggs together with both hands, gradually adding 3 cups of the flour and scraping the dough up from the work surface with a knife as often as necessary. (Incorporation of the ingredients should take no longer than 10 minutes. The longer the dough is worked, the more flour it will require and the heavier it will become.)

Dust the dough, your hands, and the work surface lightly with flour and cut the dough into six equal parts. Continue to dust dough, hands, and surface as long as the dough feels sticky.

Using both hands, roll each piece of dough into a rope ½" thick, then slice the ropes at ½" intervals. Indent each dumpling with a thumb, or use the tines of a fork to produce a ribbed effect. (This facilitates adhesion of the sauce. As a child, I'd sometimes lightly press the dough against a cheese grater, to produce a different pattern.)

Drop the gnocchi into boiling water a few at a time, stirring gently and continuously with a wooden spoon, and

cook 2 to 3 minutes, until they rise to the surface. Remove
the gnocchi from the water with a slotted spoon or skimmer, transfer them to a warm platter, adding a little sauce
of choice, and boil the remaining pieces in batches until all
are done. Sauce as desired, add freshly ground white pepper
to taste and, if appropriate, grated cheese, and serve immediately.

POTATO GNOCCHI WITH
GARLIC BUTTER AND
DRIED RICOTTA CHEESE

SERVES 6

*While gnocchi is common throughout the Northern regions,
this version was offered us by a friend in Boston. It is delicious. Be sure that you buy your dried ricotta from an
Italian deli, and buy it whole, never pre-grated.*

1 recipe Potato Gnocchi (page 212)	1½ tablespoons chopped fresh basil
3 tablespoons olive oil	½ cup grated dried ricotta cheese (page 469)
4 tablespoons butter	Salt and pepper to taste
3 cloves garlic, thinly sliced	
⅛ teaspoon red pepper flakes	

Heat a medium-size frying pan and add the oil, butter, garlic, and red pepper flakes. Sauté for 1 minute but don't burn
the garlic. Cook the gnocchi as instructed, drain, and place
in a bowl. Add the garlic butter and remaining ingredients
and toss together.

POTATO GNOCCHI WITH GORGONZOLA SAUCE

Are you ready for something rich? Baked potatoes with cheese and butter have nothing on the cheese and potato dumpling recipe. So good, if you like blue cheese. Gorgonzola is even better.

Prepare a batch of Potato Gnocchi (page 212). Toss it with Gorgonzola Sauce (page 148). Garnish with chopped parsley.

POTATO GNOCCHI WITH TRUFFLE OIL

SERVES 8–10

We had a similar dish at the absolutely wonderful Alla Pasina restaurant in Treviso, in the Veneto region. Have mercy upon us, it is so rich and good. You have to try this.

1 recipe Potato Gnocchi (page 212)	2 tablespoons truffle oil (page 424)
2 tablespoons butter	
¾ cup plain cream or half-and-half	**GARNISH** Chopped parsley (very little)
½ cup grated Asiago cheese	

Heat the butter and cream in a small saucepan. Add the cheese and heat until melted and smooth. Do not boil. Cook the gnocchi as instructed and drain well. Place in a bowl and add the cream mixture. Toss together and drizzle with truffle oil. Garnish with chopped parsley.

GNOCCHI BAGNA CAUDA

SERVES 8–10

You have already figured it out! We expect you to have several good Italian sauces sitting around in your refrigerator. That is the only way you can relax and enjoy the Italian kitchen. Try anchovy sauce with potato gnocchi. Those who like anchovies will adore you. Those who do not will ask you to move from the neighborhood. There seems to be no middle ground on this issue.

Prepare a batch of Potato Gnocchi (page 212) and a batch of Bagna Cauda (page 78). Boil the gnocchi as instructed in the recipe and toss with ½ cup of warm Bagna Cauda sauce or more to taste. Garnish with grated Parmesan cheese and chopped parsley.

POTATO GNOCCHI WITH PORCINI SAUCE

SERVES 8–10

Now you see how versatile is the gnocchi. This is a dish of potatoes and mushrooms brought to a new understanding, I promise.

Prepare a batch of Potato Gnocchi (page 212) and a batch of Mushroom Sauce for Pasta and Polenta (page 138). Cook the gnocchi and drain well. Toss with the sauce and garnish with freshly grated Parmesan cheese and chopped parsley.

POTATO GNOCCHI WITH
ASPARAGUS AND CREAM SAUCE
SERVES 8–10

Craig thought up this one. It made so much sense to him that he had to try it. A grand success! Don't bother to try this with frozen asparagus, just fresh.

1 recipe Potato
  Gnocchi (page
  212)
1½ cups milk
2 tablespoons butter
2 tablespoons flour
2 tablespoons freshly
  grated Parmesan
  cheese
Salt and pepper to
  taste
½ pound fresh thin
  asparagus (break
  the tough woody
  ends of the
  asparagus off
  and cut into 1-
  inch pieces)

GARNISH
Additional freshly
  grated Parmesan
  cheese

Bring a large pot of lightly salted water to a boil for blanching the asparagus and cooking the gnocchi.

Heat the milk in a small saucepan. In another small saucepan, melt the butter. Add the flour and cook together to make a roux. Do not brown. Stir the roux into the hot milk and whisk until smooth. Stir in the 2 tablespoons grated cheese and simmer a few minutes until slightly thickened. Add salt and pepper to taste.

Blanch the cut asparagus in the boiling water for 2 minutes and remove to drain. Boil the gnocchi in the same water for 2 to 3 minutes until they float. Drain the pot and return the gnocchi to the pot along with the blanched asparagus and the cream sauce. Toss together and garnish with additional cheese.

POTATO GNOCCHI WITH TOMATO AND CHEESE, BROILED

SERVES 6–8

This is the way it is done in Bologna and Milan. Good tomato sauce, good cheese, and then all is placed under the broiler. If you use that packaged gnocchi from Italy that I mentioned above (page 211) you can have dinner ready in just a few minutes.

1 recipe Potato
    Gnocchi (page
    212)
1½ cups Fresh Tomato
    Sauce Sicilian
    (page 139)

½ pound aged
    mozzarella,
    grated
¼ cup freshly grated
    Parmesan cheese

Boil the gnocchi as instructed, drain well and place in 6 or 8 individual baking dishes. Top with the tomato sauce and the grated mozzarella and Parmesan cheese. Broil a few minutes under high heat until bubbly and slightly browned.

SEMOLINA GNOCCHI

SERVES 8 AS A PASTA COURSE

I first tasted something similar to this wonderful dish in Venice, on an island called Torcello. There is a Cipriani restaurant there run by a member of the same clan that is behind the famous Harry's Bar of Venice. This simple dish is just one of the most delicious pasta dishes that you can serve. It is also a very old dish. Similar baked grain dishes go back to ancient Rome.

1 **cup water**	**THE TOPPING**
3 **cups milk**	¼ **pound butter,**
1¼ **teaspoons salt**	**melted**
1 **cup semolina flour**	½ **cup freshly grated**
(page 24)	**Parmesan cheese**
2 **tablespoons butter**	
2 **egg yolks**	**GARNISH**
¼ **cup freshly grated**	Chopped parsley
Parmesan cheese	
2 **tablespoons**	
additional butter	
for greasing	
baking dishes	

Place the water, milk, and salt in a small saucepan. Bring to a gentle simmer and add the semolina slowly, stirring all the time. Cook the semolina for 30 minutes, stirring often, until thickened. Remove from the heat and stir in the 2 tablespoons butter, the egg yolks, and ¼ cup Parmesan cheese.

Clean a space of smooth countertop and dampen it with

cold water. Use a wet towel for this procedure. Pour the mixture onto the smooth damp counter and spread the mixture out to a ⅜-inch thickness. Use a wet spatula to do this. Allow to cool completely and cut into 1½-inch circles using a cookie cutter. If you have some fancy cutters you can make whatever shapes you like.

Lightly butter 8 small individual baking dishes and shingle the cut semolina in the dishes. Drizzle with melted butter and sprinkle with Parmesan cheese. Bake in a preheated 375° oven for 10 to 15 minutes until the top begins to brown. Garnish with parsley.

POLENTA

Most of us in the Americas do not realize that we have given Italy some of its most famous foods, namely the tomato, the potato, and a beauty, corn.

In the old days of Rome, pulses, types of mush, were made from many kinds of grain. Everything was used, from chestnut flour to chick-pea flour to early forms of wheat. These pulses were taken with the troops wherever they went in conquest for glorious Rome. Mush, cooked and cooled a bit, and then served sliced or even browned in a pan, was a common and basic food. When corn arrived in Italy from the New World, polenta became the inexpensive and delicious favorite of pulses.

Tom Jefferson was reared in Virginia. He certainly knew the basic American dish called "cornmeal mush." When he represented us in the Italian court he fell in love with the Italian method of cooking cornmeal, polenta. Cooked with cheese, or baked with sauces, in either case Jefferson was amazed. He came back to his beloved Monticello and began serving Italian-style polenta at official state functions.

So the international exchange of food products goes. I still contend that the Italians have always been able to take on a good idea, when it comes to food, and make it better.

You will appreciate all of the dishes in this section but the Polenta Lasagna will stop traffic in your house. We can thank our chef, Craig, for this one. We found it in Florence and Craig made great improvements upon the dish that we tasted there.

Don't pass this section by. Polenta is an Old World wonder!

THREE-CHEESE SOFT POLENTA

SERVES 6, AT LEAST!

In the polenta world there are two creatures . . . one being soft and the other being hard. Actually, hard polenta is just a bit more firm than the following very rich version, which will run just a tiny bit on your plate. This is my favorite polenta, ever.

2½ cups water
2 cups milk
½ teaspoon salt
1 cup polenta
2 cloves garlic, minced
2 tablespoons butter
2 tablespoons freshly grated Parmesan cheese
½ cup imported Italian Fontina cheese (page 468), diced into small pieces
½ cup Mascarpone cheese (page 469)
Freshly ground black pepper to taste

In a 3- to 4-quart preferably heavy-bottomed pot heat water, milk, and salt to a simmer. Add the polenta and garlic and simmer, covered, for 30 minutes, stirring regularly. Stir in the cheeses and black pepper to taste. Serve as it is, soft and warm, or pack into a greased mold and chill until firm. Slice and pan-fry.

HARD POLENTA

SERVES 6

This is basic to the Italian kitchen, just as are pasta and oil and cheese. Note that we have included thyme in this particular version but you may wish to omit the herb depending on how you are going to serve the grain.

3 cups water
2 cups milk
1½ teaspoons salt
1¼ cups polenta,
    medium grain
1 teaspoon thyme
    (optional)
⅛ teaspoon freshly
    ground black
    pepper

½ cup grated
    Parmesan cheese
2 teaspoons olive oil

GARNISH
Freshly grated
Parmesan cheese

In a 2-quart saucepan place 2½ cups of the water, the milk, and the salt. Bring to a simmer, being careful that the pot doesn't boil over. Place the polenta in a small bowl and stir in the remaining ½ cup water. Slowly stir the polenta into the boiling milk and water. Stir regularly until it begins to thicken, about 3 minutes. Reduce the heat and simmer the polenta, uncovered, for 30 minutes, stirring regularly, until very thick. Stir in the remaining ingredients except the oil.

Oil a 9½ × 5½-inch loaf pan and fill with the warm polenta. Smooth the polenta out evenly with a rubber spatula. Cover the pan and refrigerate several hours or overnight until completely cooled and firm. To serve, pop the polenta out of the pan and slice about ⅜ inch thick. Pan-fry the slices in olive oil until golden brown on both sides. Or place on an oiled sheet pan and sprinkle with grated Parmesan cheese. Broil until hot and lightly browned.

THREE-CHEESE POLENTA TOPPED
WITH PORCINI SAUCE

If you want to serve a smashing dinner party, try this course. It is so rich and delicious that you may not have to serve anything else! I am kidding, but this is really good.

Serve small dishes of Three-Cheese Soft Polenta (page 224) and top each with the Mushroom Sauce for Pasta and Polenta (page 138). Cheese, perhaps, but not much. You should need no other garnish than perhaps a bit of chopped parsley.

SAUSAGE POLENTA

SERVES 6–8

Here we offer a favorite item for a single-plate dinner. This is rich and filling and since so little pork is used for 6 to 8 people, it contains relatively little fat.

½ **pound mild Italian sausage**

1 **recipe Hard Polenta (page 225)**

Squeeze the sausage out of the casings if necessary. Brown the sausage in a frying pan until cooked through and crumbly. Drain and discard the fat. Prepare the polenta and stir in the cooked sausage while it is still soft. Pack the mixture into a well-oiled 9 × 5-inch loaf pan. Cover and refrigerate.

Slice the molded polenta ⅜ inch thick and fry in a nonstick frying pan using a little olive oil.

POLENTA WITH DUCK AND MUSHROOM SAUCE

SERVES 6

This dish needs nothing but an explanation, since it refers to all kinds of other good things among the recipes. I suppose Craig and I thought this up when the refrigerator was full of leftovers, but I promise you this is a grand way of cleaning out your Italian refrigerator. Just grand!

1 recipe Mushroom
    Sauce for Pasta
    and Polenta (page
    138)
1 recipe Hard Polenta
    (page 225) or
    Three-Cheese Soft
    Polenta (page
    224)
¾ cup boneless cooked
    duck meat, in
    coarse pieces (If
    you don't have
    any leftover duck
    meat in your
    refrigerator,
    follow the
    instructions for
    roasting the duck
    in the recipe for
    Linguine with
    Duck, Porcini,
    and Sun-Dried
    Tomatoes on page
    174.)

GARNISHES
Chopped parsley
Freshly grated
    Parmesan cheese

Heat the boneless duck meat in the Mushroom Sauce. Serve over pan-fried Hard Polenta slices or Soft Polenta.

FRIED CHEESE POLENTA WITH TRUFFLE OIL

SERVES 4–6, AT LEAST!

This is just a description of a very nice dish that will be almost too much for a starch course. I enjoy it very much, but I do not offer this to my friends who are dieting.

1 **recipe Three-Cheese**   **Truffle oil (page 424)**
   Soft Polenta (page   **to taste**
   224)
Olive oil for pan-
   frying

Prepare the polenta as instructed on page 224. Pour the hot polenta into a well-greased 9 × 5-inch loaf pan. Cover and refrigerate overnight. Slice the polenta ⅜ inch thick and fry in a nonstick frying pan using a little olive oil. Be careful when turning the polenta as it can be very tender. Serve with a drizzle of truffle oil to taste.

FRIED CHEESE POLENTA WITH LEMON OLIVE OIL

SERVES 4–6, AT LEAST!

A very fresh marriage . . . if you believe in those things. The Lemon Olive Oil tends to lighten the three cheeses in the polenta, and we are left with a very refreshing course.

1 **recipe Three-Cheese**   **Lemon Olive Oil**
   Soft Polenta (page   **(page 489) to taste**
   224)
Olive oil for pan-   **GARNISH**
   frying   **Chopped parsley**

Prepare the polenta as instructed on page 224. Pour the hot polenta into a well-greased 9 × 5-inch loaf pan.

Cover and refrigerate overnight. Slice the polenta ⅜ inch thick and fry in a nonstick frying pan using a little olive oil. Be careful when turning the polenta as it can be very tender. Serve with a drizzle of Lemon Olive Oil and garnish with parsley.

POLENTA WITH LEMON OLIVE OIL AND TOMATO

SERVES 4–6, MORE LIKE 6!

Since you can have the polenta sitting in the refrigerator overnight, and since you made the fresh tomato sauce earlier in the week, what is to prevent you from serving this nice dish with comfort—I mean on your part?

1 recipe Hard Polenta (page 225)	**Lemon Olive Oil (page 489) to taste**
Fresh Tomato Sauce Sicilian (page 139) to taste	**GARNISH** **Chopped parsley**

Pan-fry the sliced polenta in a little olive oil as instructed. Top with fresh tomato sauce, warmed, and drizzle with Lemon Olive Oil. Garnish with chopped parsley.

SAUSAGE POLENTA WITH SAGE BUTTER

SERVES 6–8

This is a great way to brighten up the flavor of polenta when you serve it the second time. The fresh sage absolutely changes the whole dish. It is excellent!

½ cup butter
2 tablespoons chopped
   fresh sage
   Freshly ground
   black pepper to
   taste

1 recipe Sausage
   Polenta (page
   227)

Melt the butter in a small frying pan and add the sage. Simmer the sage in the butter for about a minute or until the butter is frothy. Add black pepper to taste. Fry the polenta slices as instructed on page 227 and top with the sage butter.

POLENTA BROILED WITH GORGONZOLA

SERVES 6, AT LEAST!

In the Northern regions polenta is used as a base for just about any kind of sauce. This version is particularly good because it uses my favorite Italian cheese. I hope it is your favorite as well. Be careful with the rest of the menu when you serve this dish as the pasta course since the dish is so rich your guests or family might just eat this and quit! I think it is wonderful.

1 recipe Hard
   Polenta (page
   225), chilled in a
   loaf pan
½ cup Gorgonzola
   Sauce (page 148)

½ cup additional
   crumbled
   Gorgonzola
   cheese
1 tablespoon
   chopped parsley

Slice the polenta ⅜ inch thick and place on a lightly oiled sheet pan. Combine the Gorgonzola Sauce, the additional Gorgonzola, and the chopped parsley. Top each slice of the polenta with the Gorgonzola mixture and place under a broiler on high. Broil until hot and bubbly. Serve hot or at room temperature.

FRIED POLENTA WITH
BLACK OLIVE PASTE

SERVES 4

So unusual. I served this one night at a formal buffet and it was a real hit. This dish does not look very attractive, but once a guest tries it, the word will pass and the dish will be gone! This is a must for your Italian kitchen. Very legit!

1 recipe Hard Polenta (page 225), chilled in a loaf pan	**GARNISH**
2 tablespoons olive oil	**Chopped parsley**
½ cup Black Olive Paste (page 490)	

Cut 8 slices of the Hard Polenta into ⅜-inch-thick pieces. Pan-fry the polenta in the oil until golden brown on both sides. Arrange 2 slices of the fried polenta on a plate and top with about 1½ tablespoons of the olive paste. Garnish with parsley.

POLENTA LASAGNA

SERVES 6

I know that you think of pasta noodles when you think of lasagna. I always have as well. This dish, which is really a jewel, could only have come from the corn-loving Northern regions. I am afraid that the South would not be attracted to one of the best pasta dishes that I have ever eaten.

Craig's adaptation of this dish that we tasted in . . . in . . . well, I can't remember where, but it was in the North, and his rendering of this dish is just outstanding. It really is much easier to prepare than the similar dish with thin lasagna noodles. And it is much more sensible. Try it.

1 recipe Hard
 Polenta (page
 225), chilled in a
 loaf pan
1½ cups Fresh Tomato
 Sauce Sicilian
 (page 139)
⅔ pound ricotta
 cheese (about 1¼
 cups), at room
 temperature

1 cup Ragù (page
 144), at room
 temperature
⅔ pound mozzarella
 cheese, grated
3 tablespoons grated
 Parmesan cheese

Slice the cold polenta ³⁄₁₆ inch thick. Spread out ¾ cup of the tomato sauce in the bottom of a 9 × 13 × 2-inch baking pan. Place a layer of sliced polenta on top of the sauce. Spread half of the ricotta cheese on the polenta in the pan. Spoon half the Ragù on top of the ricotta. Top with half of the mozzarella cheese. Place another layer of sliced polenta on top and spread with the remaining ricotta cheese, Ragù, and tomato sauce, and finally the remaining mozzarella. Sprinkle with the grated Parmesan cheese and bake in a preheated 375° oven for 45 minutes.

POACHED POLENTA CUBES

This is a rather clever trick that we learned from the dear lady who cooks at Piccola Venezia in Boston's Little Italy. She cuts cold Hard Polenta (page 225) into one-inch cubes. When ready to serve polenta with any kind of sauce she puts a few servings of polenta cubes into a strainer basket and lightly simmers them in water for 2 or 3 minutes. That is all it will take to heat them up. Do not overcook or they will begin to fall apart and get mushy. This is a really good idea, as far as I am concerned.

SAUSAGE AND SPINACH POLENTA

SERVES 6–8 AS A PASTA COURSE

Fresh spinach would be best in this dish but I am never reluctant to use the frozen product. Spinach freezes quite well and it adds a lovely color and flavor to this dish.

Completely defrost a 10-ounce box of chopped spinach and squeeze out most of the water. Or, quickly blanch a bunch of fresh spinach and chop it up. Drain very well.

Prepare a batch of Sausage Polenta (page 227) and stir in the spinach as a last step. Mold and cool. Slice and pan-fry in a little olive oil.

RICE AND RISOTTO

Unless they have been to Italy most Americans do not think of rice as being particularly Italian. The starch we think of as being Italian is pasta, of course. But rice has been known in Italy since Roman times, though it did not become really popular until the 1400s, and today Italy produces more rice than any other country in Europe. Only Russia exceeds Italy's rice production.*

Who eats all this rice? It is popular primarily in the Northern regions, and for some reason, which I do not understand, it has never gained real popularity in the South, where pasta still reigns as king of the starches. The North enjoys both pasta and rice, and you will often find menus in Florence or Milan that offer as many rice dishes as they do pasta plates.

The most common varieties used in Italy are a long-grain, similar to the one we know, and superfino, a short-grain rice that cooks up into those beautiful creamy risotto dishes. Arborio is the most common form of superfino rice exported to this country. While arborio costs a bit more than American rice, do not even think of substituting American for the necessary arborio in risotto. The dish will simply be mush. Arborio has the wonderful quality of cooking up in a sort of self-made creamy sauce, yet it still maintains a bit of firmness or crunchiness if cooked properly.

While it is true that we have exported some major food products to Italy, such as corn, tomatoes, beans, and peppers, all products of the New World, we certainly cannot claim rice. Our rice was inferior to that grown in Italy until the wise Thomas Jefferson pulled a quick one on the Ital-

*Anna Del Conte. *The Gastronomy of Italy* (New York: Prentice-Hall, 1988), p. 282.

ians. The British had pretty much wiped out our rice crops in the Colonies during the Revolutionary War. Following the war, Big Tom, with his gorgeous red hair and his burgundy velvet coats, was representing us in Italy and he realized that the Italians grew rice of a much better quality than our own. Ours had come to this country with the first of the English immigrants, and it had never been top quality. So, even though the Italian government declared it illegal to export their rice, deserving of the death penalty, Tom took it upon himself to smuggle out a few bags for the New World. This thief was the author of the Declaration of Independence! In just a few years rice was growing beautifully in the Carolinas, an unoffered gift from the Italians.

If you have never prepared risotto it may take you one or two times to get it right. But please understand that this is one of the great rice dishes of the world and you will be very pleased with your success, I know. You will also enjoy Risi e Bisi and the Rice and Tomato Timbale with Bolognese Sauce.

In addition to the recipes in this chapter you may also wish to see:

Risotto with White Truffles (page 425)
Risotto with Sweetbreads and Mushrooms (page 364)

BASIC RISOTTO

SERVES 6–8 AS SIDE DISH

*Rice is very common in the North of Italy and rather un-
common in the South where pasta demands full attention.
The dishes in this section are easy to prepare and they will
certainly help you understand why risotto is served as a
separate course in such wonderful cities as Milan.*

*Please note that good risotto takes a bit of time and
patience . . . and you must use arborio rice. The results will
please you very much.*

7 cups Chicken Stock   2 cups arborio rice
   (page 116)   (page 237)
3 tablespoons olive   Salt and pepper to
   oil   taste

In a small saucepan bring the stock to a gentle simmer.
Heat a 4-quart heavy-bottomed pot and add the oil. Add
the arborio and toast the rice a few minutes but do not burn.
Ladle in 1½ cups of the simmering stock initially, stirring
the rice constantly. Cook the rice over medium-low heat.
When the liquid has almost been absorbed by the rice, add
another ½ cup of hot stock. Continue stirring and adding
the remaining stock ½ cup at a time as the stock is absorbed. This should take about 30 minutes to cook and the
arborio should be tender but a bit firm to the tooth when
done. Add salt and pepper to taste.

RISOTTO WITH SAFFRON

SERVES 6–8

This is one of the most colorful of the risottos, the saffron giving the dish that gorgeous yellow-orange hue and that certain lovely bitterness.

While this dish is particularly popular in Milan it is also popular in Abruzzi where saffron is grown.

This dish will help you prepare a truly attractive plate.

7 cups Chicken Stock (page 116)	1 medium onion, diced
1 cup dry white wine	2 cups arborio rice (page 237)
Good pinch saffron threads (page 24)	Salt and pepper to taste
2 tablespoons olive oil	1 tablespoon chopped parsley
2 cloves garlic, crushed	

Bring the Chicken Stock, wine, and saffron to a gentle simmer in a 4-quart pot. Heat another 4- to 6-quart pot and add the oil, garlic, and onion. Sauté for 3 minutes and add the arborio. Sauté over low heat for 5 to 7 minutes to lightly toast the rice.

Add 1 cup of the simmering stock to the toasted rice and cook over medium-low heat, stirring all the time until the rice absorbs the liquid. Begin adding the remaining simmering stock ½ cup at a time, allowing the rice to absorb the liquid each time. Cook for about 30 minutes until all the stock has been used. Add salt and pepper to taste and stir in the parsley.

RISOTTO WITH MOCK VEAL STOCK

SERVES 6–8

This is a very rich dish, particularly if you use your own homemade beef stock. The recipe assumes this is what you will do, and therefore we have thinned down the homemade

*stock with a bit of water. IF YOU USE CANNED BEEF
STOCK, OMIT THE WATER AND INCREASE THE BEEF
STOCK TO 5½ CUPS.*

3½ cups Beef Stock
    (page 115)
2 cups water
½ cup dry white wine
2 tablespoons olive
    oil
2 cloves garlic,
    crushed
1 medium yellow
    onion, chopped
2 cups arborio rice
    (page 237)

1 cup Mock Veal
    Stock (page 116)
    (heated in a
    separate small
    saucepan)
½ cup freshly grated
    Parmesan cheese
¼ cup chopped
    parsley
Salt and pepper to
    taste

Bring the Beef Stock, water, and wine to a gentle simmer
in a 4-quart pot. Heat another 4- to 6-quart pot and add the
oil, garlic, and onion. Sauté for 3 minutes and add the arborio. Cook over medium-low heat for 5 to 7 minutes to
lightly toast the rice.

Add 1 cup of the simmering stock and cook over
medium-low until the liquid is absorbed. Begin adding the
remaining simmering stock ½ cup at a time, allowing the
rice to absorb the liquid each time. Cook for 20 to 25
minutes until all the stock has been used. Add the Mock
Veal Stock and cook 5 minutes more. Stir in the grated
Parmesan, parsley, and salt and pepper to taste.

RISOTTO WITH FENNEL

SERVES 8 AS A SIDE DISH

*I am so glad that fresh fennel can now be purchased year-
round. Any large American city with a significant Italian
population will have supermarkets that offer vegetables we*

considered quite exotic only a few years ago. The fennel makes this rice dish just delightful.

3 tablespoons butter	**Salt and pepper to**
2 cloves garlic	**taste**
1 cup diced yellow	
onion	
3 cups julienned fresh	**GARNISH**
fennel bulb	2 tablespoons grated
1 recipe Basic Risotto	Parmesan cheese
(page 239)	2 tablespoons chopped
	parsley

Heat a large frying pan and sauté the butter, garlic, and onion until the onion is almost clear. Add the julienned fennel and sauté until the fennel is tender, about 7 to 10 minutes. Prepare the recipe for Basic Risotto. When the risotto is 5 minutes from being finished, stir in the sautéed fennel mixture. Add salt and pepper to taste and garnish with the grated cheese and the parsley.

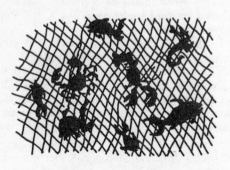

SEAFOOD RISOTTO

SERVES 8–10

The glorious colors of the seafood heaped upon the yellow saffron risotto create one of the most beautiful and delicious seafood dishes that I know. You can find this all over the Northern regions and we even found it in Naples, an area where rice is not that popular. This dish will be popular in your house, even if it does take a bit of time to prepare. Get everyone in on the act!

FOR STEAMING THE CLAMS
1 tablespoon olive oil
1½ pounds Manila clams
¼ cup dry white wine

FOR SAUTÉING THE SEAFOOD
3 tablespoons olive oil
½ pound medium prawns, peeled
½ pound swordfish, cubed into ½-inch pieces
¼ pound scallops (cut the scallops in half if they are large ones)

1 recipe Risotto with Saffron (page 240) (Prepare the risotto incorporating the reserved clam broth into the total quantity of stock [see below].)
Salt and pepper to taste

GARNISH
Chopped parsley

Heat a 4- to 6-quart pot and add the oil and clams. Stir together and add the wine. Cook, covered, over medium-high heat for 5 to 7 minutes until clams just open. Stir the clams once while cooking. Drain the clams, reserving the broth to make the risotto. Allow to cool and remove the clam meat, discarding the shells. Set the clam meat aside covered.

Heat a medium-size frying pan and add 1 tablespoon of the olive oil. Sauté each seafood individually in one tablespoon of the oil each time. Sauté quickly over high heat and remove from the pan to cool.

Measure out the reserved clam broth. Combine the clam broth with enough Chicken Stock to make up the 7 cups stock required for the Risotto with Saffron.

Prepare the risotto and stir in all the reserved seafood as the risotto is finishing. Heat throughout and add salt and pepper to taste. Garnish with chopped parsley.

FRIED RISOTTO MILANO

MAKES 2 FRIED RISOTTO CAKES

I was surprised to see such a dish in Milan, but then I should have known there was a better way to serve leftover risotto than to try to heat it up in a steamer. Won't work. This is delicious.

1 recipe Risotto with Saffron (page 240), at room temperature	**4 tablespoons olive oil**

Heat a 10-inch nonstick frying pan and add 1 tablespoon of the oil. Press half of the risotto into the pan and fry over medium heat about 4 minutes until golden brown. Remove from the heat and place a heavy plate that is larger than the pan on top of the frying pan. Carefully flip the fried risotto onto the plate. (Do this over the stove or counter and remember the pan is very hot.)

Return the pan to the burner and add another 1 tablespoon of oil. Push the uncooked side of the risotto into the pan and fry another 4 minutes or until golden brown. Cut into wedges and serve hot or cooled. Prepare another batch with the remaining risotto and oil.

RISOTTO MILANESE WITH BEEF MARROW

SERVES 6-8

The marrow from the bones gives this dish a very rich, dark and deep flavor. It is a favorite among the people of Milan, a people who have tastes much more akin to the rest of Western Europe than to the South of Italy.

1½ pounds beef
    marrow bones
    (sawed into ½-
    inch pieces)
1 recipe Risotto with
    Mock Veal Stock
    (page 240)

¼ cup half-and-half
1 tablespoon
    chopped parsley
Salt and pepper to
    taste

Dig the soft marrow out of the center of the bones. (A chopstick can be helpful for this.) Save the bones for making stock. You will need ½ cup of marrow. Heat a medium-size frying pan and add the marrow. Sauté for 5 minutes until melted and browned. Stir into the risotto as the rice is finishing. Add the half-and-half, parsley, and salt and pepper to taste.

RISOTTO WITH MUSHROOMS

SERVES 6–8

A common dish throughout most of Northern Italy, this can be served with just about anything. Meats and fish and sausages simmered in tomato sauce all would welcome these supportive and rich flavors. Remember that you can find dried porcini mushrooms from South America that are much cheaper than the real Italian variety.

½ ounce dried porcini
(page 415)

¾ cup hot water

2 tablespoons olive
oil

2 cloves garlic,
crushed

½ pound fresh
mushrooms,
sliced

6½ cups Chicken
Stock (page 116)

2 cups arborio rice
(page 237)

1 tablespoon
chopped parsley

¼ cup whipping
cream

2 tablespoons butter

Salt and pepper to
taste

Place the dried porcini in a water glass and add ¾ cup hot water. Allow to soak for 45 minutes and drain, reserving the liquid. Rinse the soaked porcini to be sure they contain no sand and chop coarsely. Heat a medium-size frying pan and add 1 tablespoon of the oil, the garlic, and the chopped soaked porcini. Sauté for 3 minutes and add the fresh mushrooms. Sauté until the mushrooms are just tender; set aside.

Bring the stock and ¼ cup of the reserved liquid from the porcini to a simmer in a small pot.

Heat a 4- to 6-quart pot and add the remaining 1 tablespoon of oil and the arborio. Sauté the rice over low heat 5 to 7 minutes to lightly toast the rice. Add 1½ cups of the simmering stock, stirring constantly, and simmer until the liquid is absorbed. Add the remaining stock ½ cup at a time as the rice absorbs the liquid. This will take about 30 minutes total time. Add the parsley, cream, butter, and reserved mushroom mixture when the rice is almost done. Add salt and pepper to taste.

RISOTTO WITH GORGONZOLA

SERVES 6–8

Yes, this is rich. No, you should not cook much else for dinner. Yes, you can substitute bleu cheese. No, it will not be as good.

Follow the recipe for Basic Risotto (page 239) and stir in the following ingredients when the rice is done.

¹⁄₃ **pound (5 ounces)**
    Gorgonzola,
    crumbled
¹⁄₃ **cup whipping cream**

GARNISH
Chopped parsley

RICE AND TOMATO TIMBALE
WITH BOLOGNESE SAUCE

SERVES 8 AS A SIDE DISH

If your Italian kitchen is well stocked and your refrigerator contains the prepared sauces, you can put this recipe together in nothing flat. It can serve as a main course or a pasta side dish.

We saw this dish in the deli cabinet of a very fancy take-out place in Parma. Oh, what gorgeous food, and what wild prices!

1 **cup Uncle Ben's**
    converted rice
2 **cups water**
1 **teaspoon salt**
2 **tablespoons butter**
¹⁄₂ **cup finely chopped**
    yellow onion
1 **tablespoon finely**
    chopped fresh
    parsley
¹⁄₄ **cup freshly grated**
    Parmesan cheese

1 **egg, beaten**
1¹⁄₄ **cups Fresh Tomato**
    Sauce Sicilian
    (page 139)
Salt and pepper to
    taste
Olive oil for
    greasing 8
    4-ounce timbale
    molds
1 **cup Bolognese**
    Sauce (page 142)

Place the rice in a small saucepan and add the water and the salt. Bring to a boil and simmer, covered, for 15 minutes. Pour the rice out onto a sheet pan and allow to cool completely.

Heat a frying pan and add the butter and the onion. Sauté until the onion is clear and then remove to a mixing bowl. Add the cooled rice and the parsley, cheese, egg, tomato sauce, and salt and pepper to taste. Stir together until all is incorporated.

Grease the 8 timbale molds with a little olive oil and lightly pack the rice mixture into the molds. Even the top of the molds out and cover each mold with foil. Place them in a baking pan. Fill the pan with enough hot water to come ¼ of the way up the sides of the molds. Place the pan in a preheated 350° oven for 40 minutes.

Take the pan out of the oven and remove the molds from the water to cool to lukewarm (be careful; these are hot!). Remove the foil and carefully run the back of a table knife around the inside edge of each mold and invert onto a platter or indivdual plates. Heat the Bolognese Sauce and top each rice mold with the sauce.

RISI E BISI

SERVES 8–10

This is favorite dish in Northern Italy, particularly in Venice. It is a sort of cross between a soup and a pasta dish, and it will work well for you as a first course.

- 2 tablespoons olive oil
- 4 cloves garlic, chopped
- 1 medium yellow onion, chopped
- ¼ cup thinly sliced and chopped pancetta
- 2 cups long-grain rice
- 5 cups Chicken Stock (page 116)
- ½ cup dry white wine
- 2 tablespoons chopped parsley
- 2 10-ounce boxes frozen baby peas, thawed ("early peas," not in butter sauce)
- ¼ cup butter
- ¼ cup grated Parmesan cheese
- Salt and pepper to taste

Heat a 4- to 6-quart pot and add the oil, garlic, onion, and pancetta. Sauté until the onion and pancetta are clear. Add the rice, stock, wine, and parsley. Bring to a boil, cover and simmer gently for 10 minutes. Stir in the thawed peas, cover, and cook 5 minutes more. Stir in the remaining ingredients.

BREADS

BREADS

The breads that you will find in Italy, for the most part, are just outstanding. Like everything else in the food field in Italy, the breads differ greatly from region to region. I dislike the sort of cracker-dough roll that is popular in Venice, but I am crazy about the heavy crusted loaves of Tuscany and Piedmont.

Bread baking goes back to very early times. The Roman bakers probably learned to make raised bread from the Egyptians, who had learned it from the Jews during the sojourn of Joseph and the tribes. When the Romans took on Greek bakers as slaves around 170 B.C. Roman bread began to have new and wonderful flavors. The Greeks taught the Roman bakers how to put all kinds of seeds and honey and dried fruits in the bread. Certainly this bread was the symbol of life, as it has been in so many cultures, but what wonderful improvements!

It is interesting to speculate on the Fall of Rome. Potters believe that the fact that the wealthy and well-educated drank wine from amphoras that contained lead in the glaze led to the demise of the intelligentsia. However, the bakers believe that when the government rented the farming lands to the already wealthy, a serious mistake was made. Rather than growing grains for bread, the aristocrats decided to increase their fortunes by growing more valuable crops such as grapes and olives. The grain farmers were forced off the land and a grain shortage resulted that caused starvation. The end of the Roman wheat supply coincided almost precisely with the fall of the empire. Certainly both factors, the lead in the good wine and the lack of bread for the common man, added to the demise.

In our time you can bake wonderful Italian-style bread

at home. This section includes a very old method of baking, a method I have only recently discovered. You will enjoy making your own breadsticks and bruschetta. Craig's Filled Rolled Bread will delight the kids and hot rolls for Italian sandwiches should become a regular in your home.

When you bake a batch of Italian bread, do not throw out the leftovers. If left uncut the loaves will last a few days and then they are to be cut for croutons, bread soup, bread salad, and more. That is the Italian way. Frugal!

ITALIAN PEASANT BREAD

MAKES 2 OR 3 LOAVES

Please do not be confused by this title. One of the major points we are trying to make in this book is that Italian peasant cooking is among the best cooking in the world.

I have learned a great deal about Italian bread baking since I gave you my last bread recipe. I have always allowed the dough to rise the first two times under plastic wrap or under a large bowl. So far so good. Then we traveled to Philadelphia and met the Lanci family and watched them bake some of the most wonderful bread that I have ever eaten.

They let the dough rise a couple of times and then they form loaves, just as I have done. But they do not use pans or metal baking sheets for the final raising. They put the formed loaves on floured flour sacks . . . and cover them with more flour sacks. When the bread is ready for baking they remove the loaf very carefully from the flour sack and place it upside down on a wooden paddle. Into the oven it goes . . . upside down! I saw them do the same thing in Italy and I now realize that the crust is much crunchier due to this Old World process. Grandma was right! Let the dough rise under floured towels. Such a crust. With that I offer this recipe. It works really well.

2 packages fast-rising dry yeast
2½ cups tepid water (about 110°)
2 pounds and 3 ounces good-quality unbleached white bread flour (about 6½ cups) (do not use all-purpose flour)

1 teaspoon salt dissolved in 1 teaspoon water
Cornmeal (optional, but necessary if you are using a wooden board or "peel" for sliding the dough onto hot bricks or a pizza stone)

Dissolve the yeast in the water. Let stand 5 minutes. Stir to dissolve.

Using a small paper sack on your scale, weigh out a total of 2 pounds and 3 ounces of flour.

Make a batter of the water and yeast, together with 4 cups of the weighed-out flour. Beat for 10 minutes with the paddle of an electric mixer. It will pull away from the sides of the mixing bowl.

Add the salted water. Add the remaining flour and knead for 5 minutes in a good machine, using a dough hook, or 15 minutes by hand. You may need to add more water to get a moist elastic dough.

Place the dough on a plastic counter, or on a piece of plastic wrap, and cover with a large metal bowl. Let rise for 1 to 2 hours or until doubled in bulk. Punch down, and let rise for 1½ hours.

Punch down again, and mold into 2 or 3 loaves. Don't worry too much about the shape. It does not matter. Place the loaves on a large floured cotton flour sack towel, or simply buy cotton muslin from the fabric shop. I prefer the towels. Sprinkle the loaves with additional flour and cover them with an additional towel or fabric.

Preheat the oven to 450°. Important: Place a pan of hot water on the bottom shelf. This will assure you of a great crust. When the loaves have risen to double their original bulk, place them UPSIDE DOWN in the upper one third of the oven. You can use either baking sheets (page 44), pizza stones, or bread bricks, available in any gourmet shop.

Bake in the oven for about 25 minutes, or until the bread is nicely browned and the loaves sound hollow when you thump their bottoms with your finger. Cool on a rack.

This bread is so rich that you need not put butter on it. The Italians rarely eat butter on bread. And if you wish to eliminate both salt and butter, simply cut down on the amount of salt in the recipe. It is tasty without. Further, do not forget the old Italian trick of dipping your bread in wine, just as with doughnuts and coffee. Delicious!

FILLED ROLLED BREAD

SERVES 6–8

I know that the instructions look long enough to be from one of those cooking encylopaedias. Really, it is not that bad. Craig developed this and he is just being a bit detailed. Read the recipe through and you will be comfortable. Besides, when you make this fine loaf your kids will think you are a genius. Maybe you will think the same.

THE DOUGH
1 package fast-rising dry yeast
1 cup tepid water (about 110°)
2 teaspoons sugar
2 tablespoons olive oil
¼ cup salad oil
½ teaspoon salt
2¾ cups unbleached flour

THE FILLING
⅓ pound mild Italian sausage (bulk or removed from casings)
2 tablespoons oil
3 cloves garlic, chopped
1 medium yellow onion, chopped
1 large red bell pepper, cored and sliced into ½-inch strips
3 tablespoons chopped parsley
1¾ cups canned plum tomatoes, crushed with juice
1 teaspoon dried oregano
⅓ pound Wine Cured Hard Italian salami, sliced ⅛ inch thick and chopped
1½ cups grated aged mozzarella cheese
⅓ freshly grated Parmesan cheese
Pinch of red pepper flakes
Salt and pepper to taste

Dissolve the yeast in a mixing bowl with the tepid water. Add the sugar, olive oil, salad oil, and salt. Mix in 1½ cups of the flour and whip until a batter has formed and begins to pull away from the sides of the bowl, about 10 minutes. Stir in the remaining flour and knead until a smooth dough is achieved. Allow the dough to rise twice right in the bowl and punch down after each rising.

Heat a large frying pan and brown the sausage until crumbley. Remove and drain the excess fat and discard. Set the cooked sausage aside. Heat the frying pan again and add the oil, garlic, onion, and bell pepper. Sauté for 5 minutes and add the parsley, crushed tomatoes, cooked sausage, and oregano. Simmer uncovered for 20 minutes more until all is tender, thickened, and some of the liquid has evaporated. Stir in the remaining ingredients for the filling. Allow the mixture to cool completely.

Press the dough out into a 18 × 13-inch lightly oiled nonstick sheet pan. Spread half the pepper mixture lengthwise down the center of the pan of pressed-out dough. Fold one layer of dough over the pepper mixture. Spread the remaining filling on top of the fold. Fold the remaining dough over the top of the pepper mixture. Bake in preheated 375° oven for about 50 minutes or until golden brown. Allow to cool until warm. Slice and serve.

DRIED OLIVE, BLACK PEPPER, AND SAGE BREAD

MAKES 2 LARGE LOAVES

The combined flavors of the oil-cured black olives and the black pepper make this a very unusual loaf. Further, the fresh sage points to the fact that the Italians have been having great fun combining flavors in bread since the old days in which the captured Greek bakers taught the Romans how to bake properly. This is another example of how the Italians can borrow a good idea and vastly improve upon it.

1 recipe Italian
   Peasant Bread
   (page 254)
1 teaspoon salt
   dissolved with 1
   teaspoon hot
   water
1 cup oil-cured Italian
   olives, pitted and
   chopped (Hint:
   Use a cherry
   pitter)

½ cup chopped fresh
   sage
1 tablespoon freshly
   ground black
   pepper
Cornmeal for
   baking

Use the Italian Peasant Bread recipe. After the batter is
achieved, knead in the other ingredients (except the cornmeal) along with the remaining weighed-out flour. The
dried olives will stain the dough but it will be delicious.

When the dough has been kneaded smooth, place on the
counter and cover it with a large bowl. Allow the dough to
rise until double in bulk, about 2 hours. Punch the dough
down and allow it to rise a second time under the bowl,
about 1½ hours. Sprinkle a sheet pan with a little cornmeal.
Form 2 oblong loaves out of the dough and place on the
sheet pan. Cover and allow the dough to rise 30 minutes
more. Bake in a preheated 450° oven for 30 minutes or
until the bread sounds hollow when the bottom is tapped.
Remove the loaves and place directly on a cooling rack.

BREADSTICKS WITH CHEESE

MAKES ABOUT 2½ DOZEN

Prepare a batch of Italian Peasant Bread (page 254). After the dough has risen twice, divide it into 4 parts. One fourth of the dough will make a couple of dozen breadsticks, so you can use the remaining dough to make bread.

Additional flour for rolling dough	**1 tablespoon freshly grated Parmesan cheese**

Roll the dough out to a little more than ⅛ inch thick with additional flour if needed. Using a roller/chopper (page 36) cut thin breadsticks about 12 inches long. Place the cut dough spaced apart on a nonstick sheet pan. Bake at 400° in the center of the oven for 12 to 14 minutes until lightly browned (be careful about burning). Remove from the oven and gather the sticks together in one layer on the pan and sprinkle with cheese. Allow to cool on the pan. Put the breadsticks upright in a water glass for serving.

REAL CROUTONS

Every now and then I eat in a restaurant and wind up pushing the salad to the side because it has commercially prepared croutons on it. You can even taste the chemicals and the staleness. Please understand that real croutons are

very simple to make and they will keep for a good week.
Your salads will be much improved.

I suggest that you use our Italian Peasant Bread recipe
(page 254) for these. Whenever you have leftover bread,
cube it up as instructed below and place it in a plastic
container in the freezer. When you have enough for a batch
of croutons, remove from the freezer, defrost, and allow to
dry out. And away we go. Very frugal, no waste.

3 tablespoons olive oil	Salt and pepper to
¾ pound dried bread	taste
cubes (Use	⅛ teaspoon paprika
leftover fresh	2 cloves garlic,
baked bread and	crushed
cut it into	1 tablespoon finely
¾-inch cubes.	chopped parsley
Place on a sheet	2 tablespoons grated
pan and allow to	Parmesan cheese
dry overnight on	
the counter.)	

Heat a large frying pan and add 1 tablespoon of the oil.
Add the dried bread cubes and drizzle with the remaining
oil. Sauté and toss over medium heat a few minutes until
lightly browned. Sprinkle with the remaining ingredients
except the cheese and continue cooking. Toss together until
the seasonings are evenly coated and the croutons are
golden brown. Remove to a large bowl and sprinkle with
the cheese. Toss together again and allow to cool. Use as
a garnish for soups and salads. Store the croutons in a
sealed container.

BRUSCHETTA WITH OIL AND
GARLIC MACHIAVELLI

Traditionally, this wonderful toast is cooked over coals. It
goes back to ancient times when it was called "crustulum,"
crusty toast. Certainly no one owned an electric toaster, so
a grill in the fireplace or kitchen was used, and the flavor

imparted to the bread from the fire is very important. I still enjoy doing this dish over the backyard charcoal barbecue.

When they make this in the hills of Tuscany, a real wood-fired grill is used. Then the toast is brought to you just after it has been rubbed with an entire clove of fresh garlic. The garlic is scrubbed onto the bread as if the bread were a washboard! A little extra virgin olive oil is sprinkled on the bread and it is placed in your hands.

Toast sounds like such a simple thing in our culture . . . because it is. But in Italy it can become a meal, all because of the glories of garlic and olive oil and bread.

If you are using an outside grill, toast both sides of the bread very carefully and then rub with garlic and drizzle on the oil. If you are using a stove-top grill over a gas burner, follow the same instructions. If you are using an electric toaster, the dish will still be good, but will not have the flavor of a real fire.

BREAD FOR NEW YORK SANDWICHES

MAKES 10 SANDWICH LOAVES

New York City boasts a fine Italian community. One of the stars of the place is a joint called The Italian Food Center.

They bake the bread for their "New York Special" right on the premises . . . and a sandwich like they make, served on their warm bread, is a delight! People march out of the place with several under their arms. The recipe for the sandwich is found on page 285.

Use our Italian Peasant Bread recipe (page 254) to make your own loaves.

Follow all of the steps up to the molding of the loaves. Divide the dough into 10 equal pieces and form into loaves. I find that this is easy to do if you simply mold into a single loaf about 20 inches long and 5 inches wide. Cut this up lengthwise into 10 small loaves and place on the floured cotton towels or muslin. Proceed with the rest of the recipe.

PIZZA AND FOCACCIA

While it is probably true that the Greeks were the first to enjoy relishes and toppings on a flat piece of bread (they called it an "Edible Plate"), the dish was greatly improved when it arrived in Italy. The Etruscans were already eating flat doughs that they baked on the stones of the household hearth. These were flavored with oil and herbs. They called the dish *focaccia*, which in Latin means "from the floor of the fireplace," and certainly it was the forerunner of what we now call pizza.

As Americans we can take credit for the tomato sauce, tomatoes being delivered to Italy from the Americas during the 1500s. Naples seems to remain the capital of tomato-topped pies, though you can now find them throughout Italy. When you are in Naples have some pizza at Brandi. The staff is rather rude but the pizzas are fine.

We have done pizza dough recipes for you before in other books but I think this new one is our best.

We are proud of these recipes. I think you will particularly like the Covered Filled Focaccia and the Radicchio, Porcini, and Onion Pizza.

PIZZA DOUGH

MAKES DOUGH FOR 3 14-INCH PIZZAS

We have stood about in our kitchens and tried more pizza dough recipes. We developed one that is close to that served at Brandi, a famous pizza house in Naples. Craig then got this idea and we like it even better. No problem to make and it is far superior to any commercial dough or preparation on the market. This one you will use.

1¼ cups tepid water (about 110°)
1 package fast-rising dry yeast
½ teaspoon salt
1 tablespoon olive oil

1 pound and 2 ounces unbleached flour (about 3¼ cups) (weighed out on a good scale)
¼ cup cornmeal

Place the tepid water in a mixing bowl. Dissolve the yeast and salt in the water. Add the oil, 1½ cups of the weighed-out flour, and the cornmeal. Beat together for 5 to 10 minutes to form a sticky batter. Knead in the remaining flour until you have a smooth dough. Place on a clean counter and cover with the bowl. Allow to rise until double in bulk, about 1 hour. Punch the dough down and divide into 3 equal parts.

To make a pizza, roll a portion of the dough on a lightly floured surface to a 14-inch diameter. Place the rolled dough on a lightly oiled Wilton Pizza Pan (page 39). We really do like those the best. Follow any of the recipes in this section for toppings and baking instructions.

This dough recipe makes enough for 3 14-inch pizzas. The recipes that follow for the different toppings are designed for 1 or 2 pizzas, so make a variety of pizzas and come up with your own toppings to use up any remaining dough. If you own ceramic baking tiles for your oven, you can prepare the pizzas directly on a wooden pizza board with a little cornmeal on it and slide the pizzas directly onto the hot tiles. The baking times will be reduced slightly.

FOCACCIA

MAKES 2 LOAVES

This is a most versatile bread product in that it is great just as it comes from the oven, but it also makes terrific sandwiches. It goes back several hundred years in Rome and it certainly has something to do with the contemporary pizza.

2 packages fast-rising
    dry yeast
2 cups tepid water
    (about 110°)
2 tablespoons sugar
4 tablespoons olive
    oil
½ cup salad oil
1 teaspoon table salt
5½ cups unbleached
    white bread
    flour

3 cloves garlic,
    crushed
¼ cup olive oil for
    topping
1 tablespoon whole
    rosemary
1 tablespoon kosher
    salt for topping

Dissolve the yeast in the tepid water. Use a yeast/cheese thermometer (page 45) to check on the temperature. Add the sugar, olive oil, salad oil, and regular salt. Mix in 3 cups of the flour and whip until the dough begins to leave the sides of the mixing bowl, about 10 minutes. I use my KitchenAid mixer for this whole process.

Mix in the remaining flour by hand or with a dough hook and knead the dough until it is smooth. Allow the dough to rise twice, right in the bowl, and punch down after each rising.

Oil 2 baking sheets, each 11 × 17 inches, and divide the dough between the 2 pans. Using your fingers, press the dough out to the edges of each pan. Cover and allow to rise for about 30 minutes and brush with the crushed garlic mixed with the oil for topping. Sprinkle the rosemary and kosher salt on top.

Bake at 375° for about 30 minutes.

TUNA AND EGG FOCACCIA

This one is easy and delicious. Your kids will love it. Simply prepare a batch of Focaccia (page 267) and allow it to cool. In the meantime, hard-boil 6 eggs and peel them. Slice them and place them shingle style on top of one of the focaccias. Top with a can or two of good tuna packed in water. Just flake the tuna and spread it on the top of the eggs. Drizzle with good extra virgin olive oil and cut into serving squares.

This is a great sandwich or snack, and certainly great for parties.

ASPARAGUS PIZZA

MAKES 2 PIZZAS

Can you imagine serving an asparagus pizza to a little kid just a few years ago? Everyone would have thought you were crazy. In the Italy of our time, just about anything goes when it comes to a pizza topping, and I think this one is just great for that growing number of asparagus lovers ... those people who don't like overcooked asparagus. In Italy we found that most vegetables are overcooked, so this asparagus is just barely blanched prior to being placed on the pizza. A real delight!

1 recipe Pizza Dough
  (page 266)

1 pound thin
  asparagus
3 tablespoons olive oil
6 cloves garlic,
  crushed
⅔ cup Fresh Tomato
  Sauce Sicilian
  (page 139)

4 cups (1 pound)
  grated aged
  mozzarella (page
  469)
2 tablespoons freshly
  grated Parmesan
  cheese
Black pepper to
  taste

Break off the tough ends of the asparagus and discard. Cut the asparagus into 3-inch pieces. Bring a kettle of water to a boil and add 1 tablespoon of the oil. Blanch the asparagus 2 to 3 minutes and drain. Rinse with cold water to stop the cooking and drain well.

Roll out 2 portions of dough 14 inches in diameter on a lightly floured surface and place on two Wilton Pizza Pans (page 39). Combine the remaining two tablespoons of oil and the garlic together and rub on both rolled-out doughs. Spread ⅓ cup of sauce on each and top with the mozzarella and blanched asparagus. Sprinkle with Parmesan cheese and top with black pepper.

Bake in the upper third of a preheated 450° oven for 10 to 12 minutes or until bubbly and lightly browned.

PANCETTA AND ONION PIZZA

MAKES 1 PIZZA

This is the ham and onion pizza to end all ham and onion pizzas. Pancetta does not have that strong smoky flavor that is typical of American bacon, so I think you will really enjoy this one. Yes, it is a tad rich but a great pizza.

1 recipe Pizza Dough
(page 266)

2 teaspoons olive
oil

2 cloves garlic,
crushed

⅓ cup Fresh Tomato
Sauce Sicilian
(page 139)

1 cup grated
mozzarella cheese

½ cup thinly sliced
yellow onion

¼ pound pancetta
(page 23), very
thinly sliced
(purchase lean
good-quality
pancetta from an
Italian deli-
catessen and have
them slice it for
you)

½ teaspoon coarsely
chopped fresh
rosemary needles

1 tablespoon freshly
grated Parmesan
cheese

Roll out 1 portion of the dough as instructed in the recipe for Pizza Dough. Place the dough on a Wilton Pizza Pan (page 39). Smear the rolled-out dough with the oil and garlic. Spread the tomato sauce on the dough, making sure that the sauce doesn't run over the edge of the dough. Sprinkle with the mozzarella cheese and sliced onion. Lay the sliced pancetta on top in an attractive manner and sprinkle with rosemary and Parmesan cheese. Bake the pizza in the upper third of a preheated 450° oven for 10 to 12 minutes. The pizza should be lightly browned near the center with crispy brown edges.

FOUR-CHEESE PIZZA WITH ONION AND RED PEPPER FLAKES

MAKES 1 PIZZA

If you are going to make a pizza, make a pizza! The cheeses that flavor this one provide something that a pizza parlor or a freezer can never give you. I think we tasted this one in Naples, where pizza actually holds court!

1 recipe Pizza Dough
   (page 266)

2 teaspoons olive oil
2 cloves garlic,
   crushed
⅓ cup Fresh Tomato
   Sauce Sicilian
   (page 139)
½ cup grated
   mozzarella cheese
¼ pound Italian
   Fontina cheese
   (page 468), cut
   into strips

¼ cup goat cheese
   (page 470)
⅔ cup thinly sliced
   yellow onion
Pinch of red pepper
   flakes
1 tablespoon freshly
   grated Parmesan
   cheese

Roll 1 portion of the dough out as instructed and place on a Wilton Pizza Pan (page 39). Smear the dough with the oil and garlic. Spread on the tomato sauce and top with the mozzarella. Arrange the Fontina on top of the mozzarella and place the goat cheese in little blobs on top as well. Top with the onion, red pepper, and Parmesan cheese. Bake in the upper third of a preheated 450° oven 10 to 15 minutes or until lightly browned with crisp edges.

RADICCHIO, PORCINI, AND ONION PIZZA

MAKES 2 PIZZAS

Aren't we getting fancy? No, this is not unusual for the pizza joints in the North, although it may be a bit out there for the traditional lovers of pizza in the South. This one has a wonderful blend of flavors as the radicchio gives it a bitter taste that plays off the tomato sauce, mushrooms, and onions in a beautiful way.

1 recipe Pizza Dough (page 266)

½ ounce dried porcini (page 415)

¾ cup hot tap water

⅔ cup Fresh Tomato Sauce Sicilian (page 139)

4 cups (1 pound) grated mozzarella cheese

1 cup peeled and thinly sliced yellow onion

2 cups coarsely chopped radicchio (page 24)

2 tablespoons freshly grated Parmesan cheese

4 teaspoons olive oil

Place the porcini in a small glass and add the hot water. Allow to soak 45 minutes and drain, discarding the liquid. Rinse the porcini to be sure there is no dirt or sand. Squeeze out the excessive water and chop coarsely.

Roll out 2 portions of dough on a lightly floured surface and place on Wilton Pizza Pans (page 39). Spread ⅓ cup of sauce on each and top the two with mozzarella. Add the reserved porcini, onion, and radicchio and sprinkle each with 1 tablespoon of Parmesan. Drizzle each with 2 teaspoons of olive oil. Bake in the upper third of a preheated 450° oven for 10 to 12 minutes or until lightly browned and the edges are crispy.

EGG PIZZA

MAKES 1 PIZZA

This is a beauty. Who says you can't put anything you want on a pizza? This sort of thing is not uncommon from Rome to the North, and it is especially appreciated in Milan. We have cooked ample eggs for this dish so that you need not use the small end of the boiled eggs for the final presentation. The shingled egg slices should be as much as possible the same size, and you will want to arrange them carefully so that they really do look like a lovely tiled roof . . . on a pizza. This is good!

1 recipe Pizza Dough
  (page 266)

½ cup Fresh Tomato
  Sauce Sicilian
  (page 139)

2 tablespoons freshly
  grated Parmesan
  cheese

6 hard-boiled eggs,
  sliced

1 tablespoon chopped
  parsley

1 tablespoon extra
  virgin olive oil

Roll out 1 portion of the dough on a lightly floured counter and place on a Wilton Pizza Pan (page 39). Spread on the sauce along with the cheese and bake in the upper third of a preheated 450° oven for 10 to 15 minutes until the sauce dries out a bit in the center. Remove from the oven and cool for 2 minutes. Shingle the cooked egg slices on top and sprinkle with parsley. Drizzle with the oil. Serve at room temperature.

COVERED FILLED FOCACCIA

MAKES 2 FILLED PIES

This is a New York Italian dish and we saw nothing like it in Italy. The gang at the Italian Food Center in Little Italy, Manhattan, is always coming up with good things. This is as close as we could come to their "Stuffed Focaccia." The recipe looks very complicated, but just read it through once and you will find that the dish is quite simple, and simply delicious.

THE DOUGH

2 packages fast-rising dry yeast
2 cups tepid water (about 110°)
2 tablespoons sugar
2 tablespoons olive oil
½ cup salad oil
1 teaspoon salt
5½ cups unbleached bread flour

THE FILLING

2½ tablespoons olive oil
¾ pound mild Italian sausage links
4 cloves garlic, sliced
1 medium yellow onion, thinly sliced
¾ pound mushrooms, sliced
1 teaspoon dried oregano
Pinch of red pepper flakes
¾ cup Fresh Tomato Sauce Sicilian (page 139)
1 cup grated mozzarella cheese (page 469)
¼ cup freshly grated Parmesan cheese
Salt and pepper to taste

THE EGG WASH
1 egg beaten with 1
   tablespoon water

THE TOPPING
3 cloves garlic,
   crushed

2 tablespoons olive oil
2 teaspoons chopped
   fresh rosemary
   needles
Kosher salt to taste

In the bowl of your electric mixer dissolve the yeast in the tepid water. Add the sugar, olive oil, salad oil, and the 1 teaspoon salt. Stir to dissolve and mix in 3 cups of the flour. Beat until the dough begins to leave the sides of the mixing bowl, about 10 minutes. I use my KitchenAid mixer for this whole process.

Mix in the remaining flour by hand or with a dough hook and knead the dough until it is smooth. Allow the dough to rise twice, right in the bowl, and punch down after each rising. Prepare the filling below as the dough is rising.

Heat a medium-size frying pan and add ½ tablespoon of the oil for the filling. Fry the sausage in the oil until browned and cooked through. Remove the sausage and slice crosswise into ⅛-inch-thick pieces. Discard any fat in the pan and heat it again with the remaining 2 tablespoons of oil. Sauté the garlic and onion until tender. Add the mushrooms and sauté until tender; remove to a bowl and cool. Stir in the oregano, red pepper flakes, tomato sauce, mozzarella, and Parmesan cheese. Add salt and pepper to taste.

Divide the dough into 4 equal parts. Lightly oil 2 10-inch-round cake pans and place a portion of the dough in the bottom of both pans. Press the dough out with your fingers so that it lines the bottom and sides of the pans evenly. Divide the filling between the 2 pans and even it out across the bottom of the dough. Roll out the 2 remaining portions of dough so that they are barely larger than the cake pans. Brush the inner sides of the dough in the pans with the egg wash and lay the rolled dough on top. Tuck the top layer down to adhere to the egg wash on the dough in the pan. Pinch the 2 layers together to seal.

Brush the tops of the pies with garlic and oil. Sprinkle with rosemary and kosher salt. Bake in a preheated 400° oven for 40 minutes.

SPINACH FOCACCIA

SERVES 8 AS A BREAD COURSE

We tasted this in Milan. Those people love breads of all kinds, and they have got to be the sandwich geniuses of Italy. This stuff is great as a bread course but it makes an outstanding sandwich.

1 package fast-rising
   dry yeast
1 cup tepid water
   (about 110°)
1 teaspoon sugar
½ teaspoon salt
2 tablespoons good
   olive oil
¼ cup salad oil
2¾ cup bread flour
   (not all-purpose)
½ 10-ounce package
   frozen chopped
   spinach, thawed
   and squeezed
   dry

THE TOPPING

2 cloves garlic,
   crushed
2 tablespoons olive
   oil
2 teaspoons kosher
   salt

Dissolve the yeast in the tepid water along with the sugar. Add salt, both oils, and 1½ cups of the flour. Beat together to form a sticky batter, about 10 minutes. Stir in the spinach. Knead in the remaining 1¼ cups flour until a smooth dough is achieved. Allow the dough to rise right in the bowl, covered, until doubled in bulk, about 1 hour. Punch the dough down and allow to rise the same way a second time.

Lightly oil an 11 × 17-inch nonstick sheet pan and press the dough out with your fingers evenly to the edges of the pan. Allow to rise 30 minutes more. Combine the crushed garlic with the 2 tablespoons olive oil for the topping. Brush onto the risen dough and sprinkle with the kosher salt. Bake at 375° for 30 to 35 minutes until lightly browned. Remove the focaccia from the pan to a cooling rack. Cut into serving pieces.

SAUSAGE AND BROCCOLI RABE PIZZA

MAKES 2 PIZZAS

This is one of the best that we found in Naples, home of the tomato-topped pizza. The secret, of course, is the broccoli rabe, a thin and tiny bit deliciously bitter member of the broccoli family. You will probably find this only during the spring and summer, and even then only in Italian communities. But someday you are going to see some and you will know what to do with it.

In the meantime, if you wish to make this great dish, I suggest that you substitute Chinese broccoli. You can find it in any Chinatown and it is long and thin just like its Italian cousin. It also has that wonderfully sharp and mustardy flavor that marks the Italian version. The Chinese broccoli should be available year-round if you live in New York, Chicago, Seattle, San Francisco, or Los Angeles. You might even try Chinese mustard greens. Same family.

1 recipe Pizza Dough
   (page 266)
1 pound broccoli rabe
   (trim off any
   tough ends near
   the roots)
⅔ cup Fresh Tomato
   Sauce Sicilian
   (page 139)
2 cups (8 ounces)
   grated mozzarella
   cheese
1 pound mild Italian
   sausage, removed
   from casings
2 tablespoons freshly
   grated Parmesan
   cheese

Blanch the broccoli rabe in lightly salted water for 2 minutes. Drain and rinse in cold water; drain well. Chop the vegetable coarsely and set aside.

Roll out 2 portions of dough to 14 inches in diameter on a lightly floured surface. Place the rolled dough on on Wilton Pizza Pans (page 39). Spread ⅓ cup of sauce on each portion of dough and top with mozzarella cheese. Arrange the sausage in little pieces on the pizzas and top with the blanched broccoli rabe. Top with grated Parmesan cheese and bake in the upper third of a preheated 450° oven for 12 to 15 minutes.

SANDWICHES

Most of us in this country think of an Italian sandwich as meatballs and tomato sauce on a hard roll ("grinder") or perhaps an Italian "submarine." However, in the Northern cities in Italy, the cities of the "beautiful people," sandwich making has risen to an art form.

Milan has sandwich bars that are among the most elegant and sophisticated places that you can imagine. And they are full bars. Alcohol in every form is served, along with wonderful coffee and cold drinks, and all of this is celebrated in broad daylight. Hardly what you think of when you hear the word *bar* in this country.

The sandwich counter at the Blitz Bar in Milan, for instance, offers some thirty varieties of sandwiches and they are all prepared and stacked in front of you. Just trying to decide among these creations is frustrating. You might also try the Samarini Bar in the same neighborhood.

I have simply described these sandwiches and you may choose from many possibilities.

I have also included recipes from great Italian sandwiches that we found in New York City and Philadelphia. They are more like the old-style sandwich, while the Northern Italian ones are much more artistic.

Milano Toasted Sandwiches

These are made with crustless white bread and then placed in a sandwich press and toasted on order. The bread is like our Pullman or square sandwich loaf, but the slices are a bit larger. I know that you are surprised that I enjoyed white bread sandwiches but they really are fresh and delicious.

Fresh Mozzarella and Cotto Ham, toasted
Mushrooms and Fresh Mozzarella, toasted
Parma Ham and Fontina, grilled, not crushed
Fresh Spinach and Mozzarella, toasted
Cotto Ham, Provolone, Baby Artichokes in Oil, toasted

Milano Fancy Sandwiches

Use crusty Italian sandwich rolls for these or bake your own Bread for New York Sandwiches (page 262). White bread is fine as well, as is pocket bread or focaccia. If you can find soft flat bread, such as Armenian bread, you can make wonderful rolled sandwiches.

Ham, Fresh Mozzarella, and Tomato

Prosciutto, Mozzarella, and Anchovy

Tuna, Egg Slices, Provolone, and Tomato

Mortadella, Provolone, Mayonnaise, Lettuce, and Tomato

Salami, Provolone, and Roasted Peppers

Prosciutto, Grilled Eggplant, and Cheese

Grilled Zucchini, Prosciutto, and Fresh Mozzarella

Pancetta, fried, Tomato, Mortadella, and Fresh Mozzarella (A real P.T.M., not a B.L.T.)

Fresh Basil, Tomato, Cheese, and Prosciutto

Frittata (page 457) Sandwich with Lettuce and Mayonnaise

Veal Cutlet, breaded and fried, with Tomato, Fresh Basil, and Mayonnaise

Shrimp Salad on White

Artichoke Salad on White

Cotto Ham and Hard-Boiled Egg on White

Asparagus and Sliced Egg on White

Tuna and Sliced Egg on White

Mushrooms and Ham with Cheese on White

Variations

Spinach Focaccia Sandwich. Try slicing Spinach Focaccia (page 276) up into sandwich-size pieces and use a
filling of spinach and cream cheese. Just delicious.

Crepes. Make sandwiches and roll up. Cut on an angle.

Tortilla, 12-inch. Make sandwiches and roll up. Cut on
an angle.

Roasted Peppers can be served on almost any sandwich.

Arugula or Radicchio instead of lettuce will work on
almost anything.

Hot Italian Sandwiches

The sandwiches that follow all come from the Italian communities in this country, with the single exception of the
Boiled Beef from Florence. Further, you will note that most
of them have been around a long time, and most show the
influence of Sicily.

NEW YORK SPECIAL SANDWICH

In Little Italy, New York City, there is a shop called the Italian Food Center that claims to have invented this jewel in 1971. The bread must be fresh and hot so they bake their own sandwich rolls throughout lunchtime.

FOR ONE SANDWICH
1 hot loaf of Bread for New York Sandwiches (page 262)
Genoa salami
Prosciutto

Mortadella
Provolone
Marinated mushrooms
Red sweet bell peppers, sautéed (page 387)

The roll is hot, the meats are very thinly sliced, as is the cheese. Delicious.

TRIPE SANDWICH, PHILLY STYLE

Please don't back away from tripe. It is an ancient food product enjoyed by the Romans and everyone since.

I had never had a tripe sandwich until I visited Willie's Sandwich Shop on Christian Street in Philadelphia. The place is a little dark and dingy but the sandwiches are great.

Use Tripe Florentine (page 365) and place some on a good hard roll or our Bread for New York Sandwiches (page 262). I love this sort of thing.

ROAST PORK SANDWICH, PHILLY STYLE

This recipe is going to make enough for a lot of sandwiches ... so warn the relatives and neighbors. Or simply cook the roast and slice it as needed as you go through the week. The wonderful thing about such sandwiches is that the meat can be heated up in a little of the broth. So you can make one or a dozen.

Have ready hard rolls or Bread for New York Sandwiches (page 262).

Prepare 1 Porchetta roast (page 334) and allow to cool a bit. Slice very thin for sandwiches or chill and slice later.

Deglaze the roasting pan with ¼ cup water. Add to a small saucepan along with 2 cups Chicken Stock (page 116). Simmer for about 10 minutes and skim the fat.

Salt the broth to taste, and use au jus for the Philly Pork Sandwiches.

VEAL SANDWICH, PHILLY STYLE

In Philadelphia there is a tiny sandwich shop on Christian Street in the Italian Street Market. The place is called Willie's Sandwich Shop and it turns out sandwiches dripping with juice and loaded with flavor. This is as close as Craig and I can come to the veal sandwich. Unusually good.

6 sandwich loaves,
either poor boy
or our
homemade
Bread for New
York
Sandwiches
(page 262)

1 tablespoon olive oil
3 cloves garlic,
crushed
¼ pound pork fat,
coarsely ground

1 cup finely chopped
yellow onion
2½ pounds lean veal,
very coarsely
ground
1 cup Chicken Stock
(page 116)
Salt and pepper to
taste
1 tablespoon finely
chopped parsley

Heat sauteuse and add the oil, garlic, pork fat, and onion. Sauté until clear and add the veal and brown lightly, about 5 minutes. Add the Chicken Stock, parsley, and salt and pepper to taste and bring to a simmer. Cover and simmer gently 25 minutes until the veal is very tender.

Fill each of the six sandwich loaves and drizzle the remaining juices over the meat. Serve the sandwiches all hot and drippy.

SAUSAGE SANDWICH

I think the secret to this sandwich is the toasting of the hard roll or poor boy roll on the griddle until the edges of the roll are crunchy. Use a bit of olive oil on the grill, of course.

Split and pan-fry the Italian sausages (page 351) of your choice and then simmer them for a few minutes in a bit of Fresh Tomato Sauce Sicilian (page 139), or if you want a dish that is very rich, simmer them in Italian Gravy (page 141). Place the sausages on the toasted roll along with enough sauce to make a mess. Enjoy!

CHICAGO ITALIAN BEEF SANDWICH

MAKES 4–6 SANDWICHES,
DEPENDING ON HOW HIGH YOU WANT TO STACK THE
MEAT

I had an argument with Craig. I always lose when I have an argument with Craig. For years I drove around Chicago reading those signs that advertised "Italian Beef Sandwich" and I thought that the sandwich obviously had tomato sauce on it. Craig claimed I was naive. This is his recipe for the Chicago classic, and he is a Chicago man. I just told him that he had too much beef for this preparation, and he reminded me that I was still naive. Get ready for a treasure, but you will not need potatoes, pasta . . . you will be lucky to take on a salad.

1 **4-pound sirloin tip roast**	2 **medium yellow onions, sliced**
Salt and pepper to taste	2 **cups Beef Stock (page 115)**
1½ **teaspoons dried oregano**	1½ **cups Chicken Stock (page 116)**
1 **teaspoon dried thyme**	½ **cup dry white wine**
3 **tablespoons olive oil**	2 **tablespoons chopped fresh parsley**
6 **cloves garlic, sliced**	**Salt and pepper to taste**
2 **large red bell peppers, cored and cut into 1-inch strips**	4–6 **individual Italian poor boy rolls (sliced lengthwise but not cut all the way through)**
2 **large green bell peppers, cored and cut into 1-inch strips**	

Season the meat with salt and pepper, oregano, and thyme. Place on a rack in a roasting pan and roast in a preheated

375° oven for about 2 hours or until the meat reaches 130° in the center. Remove and allow to cool. Deglaze the roasting pan with a little water and place the juices in a 6-quart pot.

Heat a large nonstick frying pan and add the oil, garlic, red and green bell peppers, and onions. Sauté for 5 minutes and add to the pot. You may have to do this in batches.

Slice the cooled meat very thinly across the grain. (You will need an electric meat slicer to do this properly.) Place the sliced meat in the 6-quart pot along with any meat juices that may have accumulated during cooling. Add the Beef Stock, Chicken Stock, wine, and parsley. Cover and simmer gently for 1 hour and 15 minutes. Stir the pot a couple of times while cooking. Add salt and pepper to taste.

Turn off the heat and allow the pot to rest, covered, for 15 minutes. Dip each roll in the broth in the pot so that it is saturated and heavy. Fill the roll with plenty of simmered beef and vegetables.

PHILLY STEAK SANDWICH

MAKES 1 SANDWICH

The steak or beef sandwich varies a great deal as you move about the country, but every large Italian community claims theirs is the best. In Philadelphia the competition is murder, but our driver, "Big Dennis," always takes us to Geno's. His is a fine sandwich because he uses good beef. The rest of the community must agree with me because Geno sells fifteen hundred of these each weekday, and twice that on weekends.

Thinly slice boneless beef ribeye (6 slices).

Butter a split-open poor boy sandwich roll and grill lightly.

Oil the griddle and quickly fry the beef slices (only a minute total).

Layer the meat together on griddle. Top with sautéed onion and slices of provolone. Assemble with a bit of salt and pepper to taste. Cover with a pot lid and let the cheese melt into the meat. Arrange the meat, cheese, and onions on the roll. Serve with garnishes: Tabasco, pepper relish, jalapeño peppers, cherry peppers, whatever else you like.

Note: You can also ask Geno to put that yellow gooey American Processed Cheese Product sauce on your Philly steak. I think it is a terrible thing to do, but they tell me that if you were raised in the City of Brotherly Love, then you still like the yellow goo.

FRIED EGGPLANT SANDWICH

This one has got to be a favorite for all eggplant lovers, and for those who think that they don't like eggplant. Give it a chance.

Prepare some fried eggplant as in Pasta with Eggplant Sicilian (page 173), but do not cut it into strips. Leave the slices whole and place on a warm sandwich roll. Top with a bit of warmed Fresh Tomato Sauce Sicilian (page 139). This is a mess to eat, but within two days you will want another.

BOILED BEEF SANDWICH FLORENTINA

MAKES ENOUGH MEAT FOR AT LEAST 10 GOOD SANDWICHES

There is a shop in the central market in Florence that serves a terrific boiled beef sandwich. The place is called Nerbone Sandwich Bar, in the covered market. They sell one item, the sandwich, but the meat is cooked that day and terribly moist. Of course you need a glass of wine . . . but in the Florence market that comes from another merchant. Turn around; he is right behind your table. Such a good lunch, and easy to make for a group of friends.

THE BEEF
1 4-pound beef brisket
Salt and pepper to
   taste

THE BROTH
2 tablespoons olive oil

8 (Yes!) cloves garlic,
   chopped
2 carrots, chopped
2 ribs celery, coarsely
   chopped

Place the brisket on a rack in a roasting pan and salt and pepper to taste. Roast at 375° for 1½ hours. Allow the roast to cool a bit and deglaze the pan with a cup of water. Reserve the deglazings for the broth.

Place the oil, garlic, carrots, and celery in a 6-quart stove-top casserole and gently sauté until all is lightly browned. Place the roast on top of the vegetables. Add the liquid from the deglazing of the pan along with enough water to come about halfway up the side of the roast. Bring to a boil, cover, and turn down the heat to a simmer. Simmer very gently for 2 hours. Turn off the heat and allow to rest covered for 30 minutes.

When ready to serve, slice the meat as thinly as possible and stack it on a warm sandwich roll. We suggest the homemade Bread for New York Sandwiches (page 262). Otherwise, use poor boy rolls or loaves.

Be sure that you drizzle enough of the broth on the sandwich to make it really moist and wonderful.

Note: The remaining part of the unused roast can be stored in the broth and refrigerated. When you want a sandwich, simply slice some meat and heat it in a bit of the broth. What a good thing to have in your refrigerator!

POULTRY AND GAME

In this country we eat much more red meat per capita then white meat. I think it is the reverse in Italy. The poultry markets in major cities are just beautiful, while in this country such a thing is hard to find. We find a chicken cut up and wrapped in plastic and placed in the cooler of the supermarket. In Italy you can buy birds like that, but you can also buy them whole, freshly slain and complete, feathers and all. Further, the bird is aged a bit as the Italians feel that this improves the flavor. Whether or not you want to get into that sort of thing is probably another issue. In any case you can buy a whole chicken, rabbit, pheasant, or quail anytime you want.

There are some really excellent recipes in this section, even if I have to say that myself. The Chicken Twice Cooked, from Parma, will surprise you as it is so simple to prepare and so delicious at the table. The Game Hens Stuffed with Sausage, Fennel, and Mushrooms, one of Craig's ideas, is delightful. The Rolled Chicken Breast with Sausage is a great idea as is the Tied Chicken Bundles with Rosemary. We saw such prepared poultry all over Italy, tied bundles that needed nothing more than to be carried home and broiled. I have no idea why American markets have not caught onto this. I am not talking about cooked barbecue chickens, I am talking about chicken breasts seasoned and stuffed and tied, ready to go for the person who works outside the home. Why not?

The dietitians of our time are urging us to eat less red meat and more white meat. I think the real problem with our red meat love affair is our affection for beef fat, an affection that we must lose and yet still enjoy good lean beef, lean pork, and lean lamb. We can do it!

In any case, you will like these poultry recipes, I am sure.

In addition to the recipes in this chapter you may also wish to see:

Pappardelle with Duck Ragù (page 202)

QUAIL GRILLED WITH ROSEMARY

I need only describe this dish. It is a common way of grilling quail or squab, though squab, or pigeons, are not as common a food in Italy as you might think. The pigeons are all over the piazzas and city center and city squares. They are everywhere and they are filthy. So much for the question as to why the Italians don't get into eating the squab or pigeons.

Try this one. Butterfly the quail by simply cutting them down the back with a pair of good poultry shears. Place in a bowl and marinate with a bit of good olive oil, crushed fresh garlic, salt and pepper, and fresh rosemary. Let them marinate for an hour or so and then place them on the charcoal barbecue. Grill about 12 minutes. Be careful not to overcook these little birds. They are wonderful cooked this Italian way.

GAME HENS STUFFED WITH SAUSAGE, FENNEL, AND MUSHROOMS

SERVES 4–6

I really like game hens. If not overcooked they make an elegant presentation, and the flavors in this recipe will certainly increase your enjoyment of this small bird. Fresh fennel in poultry stuffing may become a habit for you.

THE STUFFING
- ½ pound mild Italian sausage
- 2 tablespoons olive oil
- 2 cloves garlic, crushed
- 1 cup peeled and chopped yellow onion
- 2½ cups julienned fresh fennel bulb

- ¼ pound mushrooms, sliced
- 2 tablespoons chopped parsley
- ¾ cup bread crumbs
- ½ cup Chicken Stock (page 116)
- 2 eggs, beaten
- Salt and pepper to taste

- 4 1¾-pound birds

Brown the sausage until crumbly. Drain and discard the fat. Combine the sausage with the rest of the stuffing ingredients.

Rub the hens with crushed garlic, oil, salt and pepper, and paprika, and stuff. Roast at 350° in the center of the oven for 1 hour 15 minutes max!!! Allow to stand 5 minutes. Split in half and serve.

GAME HENS DIAVOLO

Try doing the same thing with game hens as in the Chicken Diavolo recipe on page 310. Butterfly them in the same way, but remember that they will not take as long to cook since they are a much smaller bird. Pan-fry them about 10 minutes on each side, or until done to your taste. Remember that the juices should run clear when you cut into the bird.

Since this little bird has a much lighter flavor than chicken, you may wish to be a little light-handed on the seasonings. The result should be very moist.

CHICKEN WITH OLIVES AND PICKLED VEGETABLES

SERVES 4

This chicken dish is a bit spicy and vinegary due to the pickles and olives. It seems to be quite popular in the Southern regions where pickles are so common. This is an old rustic-style dish.

1 3½-pound chicken, cut into eighths
3 cloves garlic, chopped
1½ tablespoons fresh rosemary
Freshly ground black pepper to taste
¾ teaspoon salt
3 tablespoons olive oil
1 cup drained pitted green olives
½ cup peeled and sliced yellow onion
1½ teaspoons grated lemon peel
½ cup dry white wine
½ cup Chicken Stock (page 116)
1 cup rinsed and drained bottled Gardiniera (find in grocery stores)
1 tablespoon chopped parsley
Salt and pepper to taste (if needed)

Combine the chicken, garlic, rosemary, pepper, salt, 2 tablespoons of the olive oil, the drained olives, onion, and lemon peel in a mixing bowl. Toss together, cover, and refrigerate 3 hours. Rub the marinade off the chicken pieces and reserve.

Heat a large nonstick frying pan and add the remaining 1 tablespoon of oil. Brown the chicken on both sides and drain off the excess oil. Place the chicken pieces in a heavy 6-quart pot. Add the wine, Chicken Stock, and reserved marinade and bring to a simmer. Cover and simmer gently for 25 minutes.

Coarsely chop the rinsed and drained Gardiniera and add to the pot along with the parsley. Simmer gently, covered, for 10 minutes more. Remove the chicken pieces to a warm plate. Heat the sauce in the pot to a boil and simmer 2 to 3 minutes to reduce a bit. Add salt and pepper to taste if necessary. Ladle the sauce with the vegetables over the chicken and serve.

CHICKEN BREASTS WITH LEMON SAGE BUTTER

SERVES 6 AS A MEAT COURSE

Sage is terribly popular with the Northern Italians. So is chicken. Thus this recipe. I do not cook chicken breasts very often as they tend to be dry, but this method of putting the sage butter under the skin solves the problem in a delicious way.

4 tablespoons butter, at room temperature

2 tablespoons finely chopped fresh sage leaves

2 tablespoons lemon juice

Salt and pepper to taste

6 individual chicken breasts (buy large ones with the bone in and the skin attatched)

½ cup dry white wine

Place the butter, sage, and lemon juice in a small bowl and blend together with a fork until smooth. Add the salt and pepper to taste and set 2 tablespoons of the mixture aside. Rub the remaining butter mixture on the meat underneath the skin on each breast. Barely lift the skin up and rub the butter on the meat without removing the skin. Replace the skin in its original position. If the skin falls off you may have to tie it back onto the breast with some kitchen string. Rub the outside of the chicken with the reserved 2 tablespoons of the butter mixture.

Place the chicken skin side up on a rack in a roasting pan. Bake the chicken in a preheated 350° oven for 35 to 40 minutes or until the juices run clear when the meat is pierced with a knife. Place the chicken on warm plates and deglaze the roasting pan with the wine. Simmer the pan juices a bit to reduce and serve over the chicken.

CHICKEN PARMIGIANO WITH TOMATO CREAM SAUCE

SERVES 6 AS A MEAT COURSE

This dish is very tasty and quite rich, due to the cream, but the flavors are very clean. Please remember that you must not overcook chicken breasts or they will be dry and tasteless.

6 **individual chicken breasts (boneless and skinless)**
Salt and pepper to taste
1 **tablespoon olive oil**

THE SAUCE
1½ **cups Fresh Tomato Sauce Sicilian (page 139)**

⅓ **cup whipping cream or half-and-half**
⅓ **pound mozzarella cheese, grated**
¼ **cup freshly grated Parmesan cheese**
½ **teaspoon dried marjoram**

Season the chicken with salt and pepper to taste. Heat a large nonstick frying pan and add the oil. Brown the chicken lightly on both sides and remove to a plate.

Combine the fresh tomato sauce with the cream and place ½ cup of the mixture in the bottom of a 9 × 13-inch glass baking dish. Arrange the chicken in the dish and top with the remaining sauce. Add the mozzarella, Parmesan, and marjoram. Bake in a preheated 350° oven for 20 to 25 minutes until nicely browned.

CHICKEN WITH BALSAMIC VINEGAR

SERVES 4

Chicken in vinegar may sound odd to you at first but remember that balsamic is not a normal vinegar. It is a wonderful condiment that goes with just about everything. You do not need to use a very expensive balsamic in this dish. A medium-priced condiment will do just fine.

8 large chicken thighs, about 3 pounds, skin on

3 cloves garlic, crushed

2 tablespoons chopped fresh basil

¼ cup balsamic vinegar (page 495)

2 tablespoons olive oil

Combine all the ingredients in a large bowl and toss together. Allow to marinate 2 hours. Toss together a few times while marinating. Reserve the marinade for basting in the oven. Charcoal-grill the chicken over medium heat for 10 minutes on each side to brown and flavor the thighs (be careful not to burn the chicken). Remove to a preheated 350° oven and bake for 15 to 20 minutes or until the juices run clear when the bottom of the chicken thigh is pierced in the center. Baste the chicken with the reserved marinade while baking in the oven.

CHICKEN WITH CAPERS AND OLIVES

SERVES 1–4

Spicy stuff, this one. Spicy not in terms of heat as with a pepper sauce but spicy in terms of the wonderful flavors of the olives and capers. This type of dish is very common in the South, and you might want to try this recipe with pork chops, spareribs, maybe even game hens.

6 chicken thighs, skin on
Salt and pepper to taste
1 tablespoon olive oil
¼ cup dry white wine
½ cup chopped ripe tomato
Pinch red pepper flakes
⅓ cup oil-cured Italian olives (page 485), pitted

1 tablespoon drained capers
1 bay leaf
¼ cup Chicken Stock (page 116)
½ cup whipping cream or half-and-half

GARNISH
Chopped parsley

Season the chicken with salt and pepper to taste. Heat a large nonstick frying pan and add the oil. Brown both sides and remove the chicken to a 4- to 6-quart stove-top casserole. Add the remaining ingredients except the cream and bring to a simmer. Cover and cook gently for 40 minutes. Remove the chicken to a warm platter and add the cream to the casserole. Simmer the sauce 2 to 3 minutes to reduce and thicken. Adjust salt and pepper to taste and pour the sauce over the chicken. Garnish with the parsley.

ITALIAN CHICKEN ROLLS

SERVES 4

It is a delight to go into a market in Milan or Torino and find things so carefully prepared and ready for your frying pan. I admit you have to pay a fortune for such food in Italy but you can do this recipe from scratch and not have to sell any of the children. I usually dislike chicken breasts pan-fried because they are too dry, but the cheese and prosciutto, and the fact that they are rolled, keep these breasts in moist and flavorful shape.

4 6- to 8-ounce
 boneless, skinless
 chicken breasts
Salt and pepper to
 taste
¼ pound provolone
 cheese, thinly
 sliced
4 thin slices prosciutto
1 egg
1 tablespoon water
½ cup flour
½ cup fine bread
 crumbs
¼ cup olive oil

THE SAUCE
1 tablespoon butter
¼ cup finely chopped
 shallots
¼ pound mushrooms,
 thinly sliced
2 tablespoons flour
1 cup Chicken Stock
 (page 116)
¼ cup dry Marsala
 wine
¼ cup dry white wine
Salt and pepper to
 taste

GARNISH
Chopped parsley

Pound each chicken breast evenly between two sheets of plastic wrap to ¼-inch thickness. Use a flat meat pounder (page 36) for this. Or you can use a heavy glass. Season the inside of each breast with salt and pepper to taste. Add a slice of provolone and then a slice of prosciutto. Roll the chicken up tightly and secure with toothpicks. Season the outside with salt and pepper to taste.

Beat the egg in a small bowl with the water. Place the flour and the bread crumbs in separate bowls. Roll each chicken roll in flour and pat off the excess. Roll in the egg and then into the bread crumbs.

Heat a frying pan and add the oil. Brown the breaded chicken rolls lightly on all sides and remove the toothpicks. Place the rolls seam side up in an 8 × 8-inch glass baking dish. Bake at 350° for 20 to 25 minutes or until a meat thermometer registers 155° when inserted in the center of the rolls.

While the chicken is baking, prepare the sauce: Discard the oil in the frying pan and heat the pan again. Add the butter, shallots, and mushrooms and sauté until the the shallots are clear. Add the flour and cook together a few minutes to form a roux. Add the Chicken Stock and whisk together until smooth over low heat. Add the Marsala and white wine and simmer 5 minutes until smooth and lump free. Add salt and pepper to taste. Serve the sauce over the chicken and garnish with the parsley.

BRAISED RABBIT IN WINE SAUCE

SERVES 2–4 AS A MEAT COURSE

It is a shame that Americans cannot get used to eating rabbit. It has been common food in Europe for as long as anyone can remember, but in this country we seem to get hung up on Bugs and Peter and the Easter Bunny. I love this dish, and if you don't make a big thing about the contents, your kids will love it as well.

1 2¾-pound rabbit, cut into serving pieces	1 cup sliced yellow onion
Salt and pepper to taste	1 cup sliced mushrooms
1 cup flour	⅓ cup dry red wine
2 tablespoons butter	2 tablespoons chopped parsley
1¼ cups Chicken Stock (page 116)	1 teaspoon dried marjoram
¼ pound chopped pancetta	1 tablespoon tomato paste
1 tablespoon olive oil	
2 cloves garlic, crushed	

Season the rabbit with salt and pepper to taste. Place the flour in a bowl and dredge the pieces of rabbit in the flour. Pat off the excess flour, leaving a thin coating of flour on the meat. Heat a large frying pan and melt the butter. Lightly brown the rabbit on both sides and remove the meat to a 6-quart casserole. Deglaze the pan with ¼ cup of the Chicken Stock and add to the casserole.

Heat the frying pan again and brown the pancetta until clear. Add the pancetta to the casserole. Heat the pan again and add the oil, garlic, and onion. Sauté until the onion is tender. Add the mushrooms, sauté 2 minutes, and add the remaining ingredients, including the remaining Chicken Stock. Stir together until the tomato paste dissolves. Pour over everything in the casserole.

Bring to a simmer and cover. Simmer gently 35 minutes, turning the meat a couple of times. Turn off the heat and leave covered for 10 minutes to allow the meat to relax. Add salt and pepper to taste if needed.

Option: Debone any leftover meat and sauce and use as a sauce for pasta.

ROLLED CHICKEN BREAST
WITH SAUSAGE

SERVES 6

These wonderful little chicken and sausage bundles are sold ready to go in the public market in Torino. The sausage solves the problem that I have with chicken breasts. They are always too dry! The small amount of work involved in this preparation is really worth the moist and tender reward.

3 ¼-pound mild
    Italian sausage
    links
3 1-pound double
    chicken breasts,
    boneless with
    skin on (each
    piece has 2
    breasts intact)
Salt and pepper to
    taste (easy on
    the salt)
1½ tablespoons
    chopped parsley
1½ tablespoon
    chopped fresh
    sage

¼ cup dry white wine

THE MARINADE
3 tablespoons olive
    oil
2 tablespoons lemon
    juice
3 cloves garlic,
    crushed
Salt and pepper to
    taste

GARNISH
Chopped parsley

Bring a 4-quart pot of water to a boil and poach the sausage links for 5 minutes. Drain and allow to cool completely.

Using a meat pounder (page 36) pound out the 3 double breasts skin side down to about ⅜ inch thick. Season the inside with salt and pepper to taste. Rub the inside of the breasts with the parsley and sage. Place a cooled sausage in the center of the breasts. Tie into little roasts with string. Tie the breasts crosswise and lengthwise.

Combine the ingredients for the marinade in a large bowl. Add the tied chicken breasts and marinate for 30 minutes. Place on a rack in a roasting pan and roast at 375° for 55 minutes. Reserve the marinade.

Place the roasted chicken on a plate, covered, in a warm oven. Deglaze the roasting pan with the wine and the reserved marinade. Remove the string from the chicken breasts and slice each crosswise into 6 pieces. Add any extra juice from the warming plate to the deglazed pan juices. Serve the sliced chicken with pan juices over the top. Garnish with parsley.

CHICKEN TWICE COOKED

SERVES 3–4

The title of this dish is a bit odd but then so is the process. We tasted this at a very fine restaurant in Parma, where the chef, in her seventies, cooks the chicken the second time while patting it down with a heavy spatula. Craig is convinced that a second heavy frying pan used as a weight does a fine job. I agree. You may not agree with the size of the servings in this dish as the pieces will disappear before you get around to serving yourself. So increase, increase!

6 chicken thighs	⅓ cup dry white wine
Salt and pepper to taste	
2 tablespoons butter	
1½ tablespoons fresh rosemary stripped from the stem	

Season the chicken thighs with salt and pepper to taste. Heat a large frying pan and melt the butter. Brown the chicken lightly on both sides along with the rosemary. Remove all to a roasting pan, uncovered. Place in a preheated 350° oven. Bake skin side up for 10 minutes. Turn the chicken and roast 10 minutes more. Remove the chicken to a plate and reserve the fat in the pan.

Heat a lightly oiled flattop griddle or a heavy cast-iron frying pan. Place the chicken skin side down in the pan. Place another heavy cast-iron pan directly on top of the chicken and press it down. Brown the chicken very well on both sides, using the weight of the second frying pan, about 2 minutes on each side. Remove the chicken again to the plate.

Heat the roasting pan juices, adding any juice, from the plate, and deglaze with the wine. Reduce a bit. Pour the sauce over the chicken.

Note: If the thighs are quite large, the initial roasting time may be increased, but do not dry the chicken out.

Note: A good exhaust fan that draws smoke out of the house is necessary!

Note: You will get the best results if you do not refrigerate the cooked pieces in between the two cooking processes. Do the whole recipe as a single event.

CHICKEN DIAVOLO

SERVES 2–4

We have tasted a dish by this name before, a dish that was heavy with pepper sauce and thus called "Hot as the Devil" (Diavolo). This particular version we saw in Bologna, where heavy spices are rarely used. The method of weighting down the chicken while cooking results in a most wonderful texture and flavor. Still, I add lots of black pepper. Bologna will forgive me, I am sure.

1 3½-pound chicken	2 tablespoons olive
6 cloves garlic,	oil for frying
crushed	
1 tablespoon olive oil	GARNISH
Salt and pepper to	Lemon wedges
taste (use plenty	
of pepper)	

Cut the chicken down the back only and open the chicken up. Place on the counter skin side up and press to flatten out. Place in a large bowl and add the garlic, 1 tablespoon oil, and salt and pepper to taste. Rub the bird all over and allow to marinate for 1 hour. Preheat a 325° oven.

Heat a 14-inch nonstick frying pan and add the 2 tablespoons of oil. Place the chicken skin side up in the hot pan and place a 12-inch heavy cast-iron pan on top of the bird. Fry over medium-low heat about 12 minutes per side with the pan weighting the chicken down. (You will need an exhaust fan that draws smoke out of the house to do this.) Remove to a roasting pan and place skin side up in the preheated oven.

Bake an additional 10 to 15 minutes or until the juices run clear when the underside of the thigh is pierced with a knife. Serve with lemon wedges.

COLD CHICKEN WITH GREEN SAUCE BALSAMIC

SERVES 4 AS AN APPETIZER

This dish is from Bologna. Modena, the home of balsamic vinegar, and Bologna, come up with the most wonderful uses for the balsamic condiment. This recipe is very close to one that we tasted at Leonida, in Bologna. It is a fine first course, main course, or, with a bit of lettuce, a terrific salad.

4 individual chicken breasts (bone in, skin on)

THE SAUCE
½ teaspoon dried marjoram
½ cup extra virgin olive oil

¼ cup finely chopped parsley
2 tablespoons minced shallots
1½ tablespoons balsamic vinegar (page 495)
Salt and pepper to taste

Fill a 6-quart pot two-thirds full with cold water. Bring to a boil and add the chicken. Cover and gently poach the chicken for 10 to 15 minutes or until the juices run clear when the meat is pierced with a knife. Do not overcook! Drain and allow the chicken to cool enough to handle. Remove the meat from the bones in whole pieces and discard the bones and skin.

Slice the meat ¼ inch thick across the grain and arrange neatly on a serving platter. Combine the ingredients for the sauce in a small bowl. Mix together and pour over the sliced chicken. Cover and chill for 1 hour.

TIED CHICKEN BUNDLES WITH ROSEMARY

SERVES 4 AS A MEAT COURSE

The only way to keep chicken breasts moist, as far as I am concerned, is to cook them rolled and tied, as a roast. You can purchase these already tied and seasoned in the markets of Milan and Torino. However, they are easy to prepare at home.

Please note that you must tell your butcher that you want the whole two breasts of the chicken in one piece. In that way you will have a large piece of breast meat that can be rolled. This dish is well worth the effort.

2 whole chicken breasts, boneless with skin on (that means 2 pieces of chicken, each piece with 2 breasts attached and the skin intact)

2 chicken thighs, boneless and skinless

Salt and pepper to taste

2 cloves garlic, crushed

2 teaspoons olive oil

2 teaspoons coarsely chopped fresh rosemary needles

½ cup dry white wine

Pull the skin off the breast and reserve. Place the 2 whole breasts skin side down on the countertop and lay a sheet of plastic wrap on top. Gently pound out the chicken breast to a ⅜-inch thickness. Place a chicken thigh on top of each and flatten out a bit. Season with salt and pepper, garlic, oil, and rosemary. Roll the chicken up into a bundle while folding and tucking the edges in. Wrap the reserved chicken skin around the bundles, and tie with kitchen string to secure.

Season the outside with salt and pepper to taste and place on a rack in a roasting pan. Roast in a preheated 375° oven for about 40 to 50 minutes or until a meat thermometer inserted in the center registers 160°. Remove the chicken to a plate and allow to rest for 2 minutes.

Discard the fat, then deglaze the roasting pan with the wine and simmer to reduce a bit. Remove the string and slice the chicken bundles crosswise into ½-inch-thick medallions. Place the sliced chicken on warm plates and spoon the pan juices over the top.

CHICKEN THIGHS WITH
PARMESAN AND BROWN BUTTER
WITH SAGE SAUCE

A very quick and delicious dish, using Chef Estanzo's hot sage butter sauce.

Bake eight chicken thighs for about 30 to 40 minutes or until done to taste. The juices should run clear. Place on a heated platter and top with Parmesan cheese and the Brown Butter with Sage Sauce (page 149). The hot butter should sizzle up on the cheese and the chicken. This is one of the most interesting chicken dishes that I have ever found.

CHICKEN, FARMER STYLE
(Pollo Contadino)

SERVES 4

This is not a complicated recipe, but it is a good one. Carmine, who runs one of the best Italian kitchens on the West

Coast, gave us this one. He did a show with us and charmed even the TV crew, and that is a tough audience!

His fine restaurant in Seattle is called Il Terrazzo, near Pioneer Square. Such class!

4 large chicken breasts, boneless and skinless (I also like to use chicken thighs with the skin on. Use two thighs per person and be sure to cook them a bit longer so that the juices run clear when the underside of the thigh is pierced with a knife.)

Salt and pepper to taste

½ cup flour

½ cup olive oil

2 medium carrots, peeled and diced

1 large red bell pepper, cored and julienned

1 large green bell pepper, cored and julienned

1 large yellow onion, peeled and julienned

6 large mushrooms, sliced

12 medium Italian or Greek black olives, not pitted

1 teaspoon capers

6 ripe plum tomatoes, chopped (Carmine peels his tomatoes)

1 tablespoon fresh rosemary

¼ cup dry white wine

Season the chicken lightly with salt and pepper. Place the chicken in a large bowl and add the flour. Toss together and pat off the excess flour from each piece of chicken. Heat a large frying pan and add half of the olive oil. Brown the chicken on both sides and remove to a roasting pan, leaving the oil in the frying pan.

Heat the pan again and add the carrots. Sauté for 3 minutes and add the red and green peppers and the onion. Sauté until the onion is translucent. Place the vegetables on top of the chicken in the roasting pan.

Heat the frying pan again and add the remaining oil. Add the mushrooms, olives, capers, and tomatoes. Bring to a simmer and cook gently for 5 minutes. Add salt and pepper to taste and pour over the chicken. Sprinkle with rosemary and drizzle the wine over all.

Cover the roasting pan with aluminum foil and bake in a preheated 400° oven for 20 minutes. Uncover the pan and bake for 15 minutes more. Turn the chicken a couple of times in the vegetable sauce while cooking. Serve the chicken with the vegetables and sauce over the top.

CHICKEN SALAD VENETIAN

SERVES 4 AS A HEARTY SALAD COURSE

This rather different chicken salad was offered us at Harry's Dolce, a part of the famous Harry's Bar but farther on down the canal in Venice. One can sit on the sides of the canal during a lovely evening and feel quite elegant.

This dressing is not from the restaurant but from Craig, our kitchen genius. It works very well and is not the least bit heavy.

4 chicken breasts, bone in, lightly poached, cut into strips

4 cups iceberg lettuce, shredded taco style

THE DRESSING

½ cup mayonnaise

2 tablespoons fresh lemon juice

3 tablespoons balsamic vinegar (page 495)

1 teaspoon Worcestershire sauce

2 tablespoons olive oil

Salt and pepper to taste

GARNISH

Chopped parsley

Please be careful not to overcook the chicken. A light poaching of 20 minutes should be ample for nice moist meat. Do not put salt in the water while poaching since the salt will draw moisture out of the bird.

Cool and debone the meat, discarding the skin. Cut into strips.

Make a mound of cold shredded lettuce on each of 4 plates. Top with chicken. Prepare the dressing and pour over all. Sprinkle with parsley. Each person can toss his or her own salad at the table.

GRILLED CHICKEN AND PANCETTA SPIEDINI WITH THREE SAUCES

SERVES 4 AS A MAIN COURSE OR MANY MORE AS AN APPETIZER

I adore Sue Wilkens. She is crazy enough, and wise enough, to run a fine restaurant in San Francisco, on Washington Square, called Little Italy Antipasto Bar. You can walk in and order a fine dinner or several antipasto treats, such as the one that is offered here.

Bamboo skewers
(Find in most
supermarkets.
Soak them in
water overnight
to prevent
splintering; this
will also prevent
the ends of the
skewers from
burning so
quickly when you
cook over an open
flame.)

2 pounds chicken
breasts or thighs,
boneless and
skinless
½ to ¾ pound
pancetta (page 23)
very thinly sliced
(Have the
delicatessen do
this for you if you
don't own an
electric meat
slicer. You can
also substitute a
good-quality
thinly sliced
bacon from the
supermarket.)

Red onion, peeled
and cut in 1-inch
pieces
Portobello
mushrooms cut in
1-inch pieces
Sweet bell peppers,
cored and cut into
1-inch pieces (use
a combination of
red, green, and
yellow bell
peppers)

THE MARINADE
1 cup olive oil
2 tablespoons chopped
garlic
2 tablespoons chopped
rosemary
⅓ cup good-quality
red wine vinegar
2 teaspoons kosher
salt
½ teaspoon freshly
ground black
pepper

Cut the chicken into 1-inch cubes and wrap each piece with a small piece of the pancetta. Skewer the wrapped chicken pieces alternately with the onion, mushroom, and pepper pieces. Combine the ingredients for the marinade and allow the skewers to marinate for several hours or overnight in the refrigerator.

Grill the spiedini over a charcoal fire or on a Le Creuset stove-top grill (page 35) to taste. Serve the spiedini over a nice rice dish with any or all of the sauces that follow. These versatile sauce recipes will yield more than you will need, so use any leftovers to accompany fresh grilled tuna or swordfish, or as a dressing for crostini or vegetables.

MIXED HERB PESTO
- 1 cup olive oil
- 2 teaspoons chopped garlic
- 1 teaspoon kosher salt
- 3 cups Italian parsley leaves
- 2 tablespoons fresh thyme leaves
- 1 tablespoon chopped rosemary
- ½ cup toasted nuts (walnuts or pine nuts)
- ½ cup grated Asiago cheese (page 468) or Parmesan cheese

Chop all the ingredients in a food processor, but don't puree until completely smooth. Use the pulse button on your processor to achieve a coarsely chopped sauce. This sauce should be made close to serving time as the thyme will begin to turn black after a while.

BLACK OLIVE VINAIGRETTE

1 anchovy fillet
½ cup pitted Kalamata olives (find in most supermarkets)
1 tablespoon capers
½ teaspoon chopped garlic
½ cup extra virgin olive oil
4 to 5 teaspoons balsamic vinegar (page 495)
½ cup roasted red bell peppers, minced (buy roasted peppers packed in glass, not in a can)
2 tablespoons minced green onion
2 tablespoons chopped parsley

Chop the anchovy, pitted olives, capers, and garlic coarsely in a food processor. Remove to a small bowl and stir in the remaining ingredients by hand.

TOMATO ARUGULA SALSA

1 pound plum tomatoes, chopped (remove the seeds)
1 cup chopped arugula (you can substitute basil, Italian parsley, or watercress)
1 tablespoon minced red onion
½ cup extra virgin olive oil
1 teaspoon Dijon mustard
2 tablespoons white wine vinegar
2 tablespoons lemon juice
Salt and pepper to taste

Chop the tomatoes, arugula, and red onion by hand and stir together with the remaining ingredients.

RED MEATS

This is getting to sound a bit repetitive, but as with all food habits in Italy, the consumption of red meat varies from region to region. Throughout the South, seafood and fresh vegetables are favored, while in the North, red meats of all kinds are appreciated, along with the fish and vegetables.

In Torino we saw beautiful shops selling fresh pork, beef, veal, horse, lamb, and goat. These were some of the most attractive shops I have ever seen. In Milan anything can be purchased, though the red-meat shops are much smaller than those of Torino, where real meat eaters hold forth. The meat shops of Bologna are wonderful, though nothing like the kind of supermarket displays of beef that we have in this country. In Bologna everything is quality and classy. I cannot say enough good things about Bologna in terms of eating habits. How I would love to have a kitchen there!

The Florentines are famous red-meat eaters and the meat and sausage shops you find there are outstanding. Steak Florentine is a well-known dish.

Even Venice offers some interesting red-meat dishes but the Venetians' diet centers around their great fresh fish. The public market in Venice offers many red-meat shops but I do not think the quality of beef is equal to our own. Neither does any Italian who travels in this country. Venetian fish . . . now that is another matter. The best!

You will enjoy some classic dishes in this section. The Osso Bucco is great as are the beef Short Ribs with Wine and Porcini Sauce. Beef in Rosemary Butter will tickle you and the Meatball and Cabbage Couscous is fun to prepare and to eat. However, I think the best recipe in this section is the simple peasant pork dish called Porchetta, from Umbria, where pork is king of the red meats.

In addition to the recipes in this chapter you may also wish to see:

Steak Grilled with Olive Oil (page 490)

SHORT RIBS WITH WINE AND PORCINI SAUCE

SERVES 6

I love short ribs. Rich and tender in this wine and porcini sauce, they go great with Cannellini Beans (page 408). It is a perfect match that we first tasted at a fine restaurant in San Francisco called Ecco.

¾ ounce dried porcini mushrooms (find in Italian markets, or you might use the South American variety, which are good and much cheaper than the Italian variety)

½ cup hot tap water

3½ pounds beef short ribs (6 large meaty pieces, crosscut 1 inch thick)

Salt and pepper to taste

2 tablespoons olive oil

2 cloves garlic, crushed

1 rib celery, diced

1 medium carrot, peeled and diced

½ cup peeled and diced yellow onion

½ cup good Beef Stock (page 115) or use canned

½ cup dry red wine

THE SAUCE
1 tablespoon olive oil
Reserved soaked
    porcini, chopped
Reserved pan juices
¼ cup dry red wine

½ cup good Beef Stock
    (page 115) or use
    canned
2 tablespoons chopped
    parsley
Salt and pepper to
    taste

Place the porcini in a small glass along with the hot water. Allow to soak for 45 minutes. Drain, reserving the liquid. Chop the porcini and set aside.

Trim any excess fat from the short ribs and season with salt and pepper. Heat a heavy frying pan and add 1 tablespoon of the oil. Brown the ribs well on all sides. Place the browned meat in a shallow baking dish.

Discard the excess grease in the frying pan and heat the pan again. Add the remaining 1 tablespoon olive oil and sauté the garlic and vegetables until lightly browned. Add to the baking dish of meat. Deglaze the frying pan with the Beef Stock and add to the meat along with the wine and the reserved porcini liquid. Cover with foil and bake at 325° for 2½ hours or until the short ribs are very tender. Remove the meat and strain the vegetables and pan juices. Discard the vegetables. Skim the fat from the juices and discard. Return the short ribs to the baking dish and cover.

Heat the frying pan again and add the olive oil and reserved chopped porcini. Sauté for 2 minutes and add the remaining ingredients for the sauce. Simmer for 5 minutes and pour over the ribs. Cover the baking dish and return to the 325° oven. Bake 40 minutes more. Serve the short ribs on a bed of Cannellini Beans and ladle some porcini sauce over the top.

OSSO BUCCO WITH GREMOLADA

SERVES 4–6

This is a classic creation in terms of Italian cuisine. I have had it most properly prepared in this country at Felidia's Restaurant in New York City, but I have had this dish wonderfully prepared in many restaurants in Italy. I think you can do better on your own, providing you can find a butcher who can provide quality meat. Call around, and then prepare this dish for a grand dinner party. You may have to keep a few shanks in the freezer until your butcher can gather enough for you. All of this is worth the effort, I promise.

3 2¼-pound veal shanks, cut into 2-inch pieces (have your butcher do this)
Salt and pepper to taste
4 tablespoons olive oil
½ cup water
3 cloves garlic, chopped
2 medium carrots, sliced into ¾-inch pieces
2 ribs celery, sliced into ¾-inch pieces

1 medium yellow onion, chopped
½ cup dry white wine
¼ cup chopped parsley
1¾ cups Mock Veal Stock (page 116)

GREMOLADA TOPPING

1 lemon rind, coarsely grated and finely chopped
1 clove garlic, minced
¼ cup finely chopped parsley

Season the shanks with salt and pepper to taste. Heat a large frying pan and brown the shanks in 2 batches, using 1 tablespoon of the oil each time. Remove the shanks to a large roasting pan. When all of the meat is browned, return the pan to the heat and deglaze with the water. Add the juices to the roasting pan.

Heat the frying pan again and add the remaining 2 tablespoons of oil. Add the garlic, carrots, celery, and onion. Sauté for 5 minutes until browned and add to the roasting pan. Return the pan to the burner and deglaze with the wine. Add the juices to the roasting pan along with the parsley and the Mock Veal Stock.

Cover the roasting pan with doubled-up aluminum foil. Bake in a preheated 325° oven for 3 hours. Add water ½ cup at a time if the pan begins to dry out. The shanks should be very tender but not falling off the bone.

Remove the shanks to a platter, cover with aluminum foil, and place in a warm oven. Strain the vegetables, reserving the pan juices. Discard the vegetables. Skim any fat from the juice and discard. Stir together the ingredients for the Gremolada in a small bowl. Serve the Osso Bucco with Gremolada sprinkled over the top. Ladle on the pan juices.

SHORT RIBS ITALIAN

SERVES 6–8

In the Bible fatness is a sign of joy. Only a people who spent most of their time hungry could come up with such a wonderful image. This is my version of biblical fatness, and certainly joy at the table. If I can't have beef short ribs once a month I am going to cash in my cookbooks!

5 pounds beef short ribs, trimmed of most of the fat (not all, or you will have a dry dish)

Salt and pepper to taste

3 tablespoons olive oil

3 cloves garlic, crushed

¼ cup chopped carrot

¼ cup sliced celery

2 yellow onions, peeled and sliced

2 bay leaves

1 tablespoon dried oregano

1 cup dry red wine

2 cups Beef Stock (page 115) or canned

2 tablespoons tomato paste

1 cup chopped fresh parsley

1 teaspoon dried basil

½ cup dry vermouth

4 tablespoons butter

6 tablespoons flour

GARNISH
Chopped parsley

Season the ribs with salt and pepper to taste. Heat a large heavy frying pan and brown the ribs in 2 batches, using 1 tablespoon of the oil each time. Brown the ribs well on all sides and remove to an 8- to 10-quart stove-top casserole, discarding the fat in the pan.

Heat the frying pan again and add the remaining 1 tablespoon oil. Add the garlic, carrot, celery, and onions. Sauté until the onion is tender and add to the ribs. Deglaze the pan with ½ cup water and add the juices to the casserole. Add the bay leaves, oregano, red wine, Beef Stock, tomato paste, parsley, and basil. Add enough cold water to just barely cover the contents in the pot, about 2 cups. Bring the pot to a boil, cover, and simmer gently for 2 hours or until the ribs are very tender.

Remove the meat to a platter and keep warm. Strain the sauce, discarding any solids. Return the sauce to the pot, add the vermouth, and bring to a gentle simmer.

Melt the butter in a small frying pan. Add the flour and cook together a few minutes to form a roux. Do not burn. Whisk some of the roux into the simmering pot until

smooth and thickened. Add more roux to thicken to taste.
Add salt and pepper to taste. Pour the sauce over the ribs,
garnish with the parsley, and serve.

BRACIOLE

SERVES 6

*Boston is the home of this one, though I know that a thou-
sand Italian grandmas will tell me of their similar fillings
for this wonderful dish. I guess anything goes, and the results will always be good providing you don't overcook this
tied steak roast. It is a classic in Italy.*

1 1¾-pound flank
   steak
   Salt and pepper to
   taste
2 tablespoons pine
   nuts, toasted
⅓ cup chopped fresh
   mint
⅓ cup chopped fresh
   parsley
4 cloves garlic,
   crushed

¼ cup freshly grated
   Parmesan cheese
   Juice of 1 lemon
2 tablespoons olive
   oil
1½ cups Fresh Tomato
   Sauce Sicilian
   (page 139)
½ cup red wine

Place the meat on the counter and pound it out a bit to
tenderize and flatten. Add salt and pepper to taste.

Place the pine nuts in a small frying pan and toast them
over low heat until golden brown. Allow to cool and place
in a small bowl with the mint, parsley, garlic, cheese, lemon
juice, and 1 tablespoon of the oil. Stir together and rub on
the meat. Roll the steak up tightly across the grain of the
meat like a jelly roll. Tie the roll together with string to
secure. Season the outside with salt and pepper to taste.

Heat a large nonstick frying pan and add the remaining
1 tablespoon of oil. Brown the meat roll on all sides over

medium heat. Place the roll in an oval-shaped stove-top casserole. Add the tomato sauce and the wine. Bring to a boil and simmer very gently, covered, for 1 hour. Turn the Braciole a few times while cooking.

Turn off the heat and allow to rest in the casserole with the lid on for 15 minutes. Remove the string and slice across the grain into ½-inch-thick pieces. Serve the sliced meat roll with the sauce that has formed in the casserole.

MEATBALLS, CRINITI STYLE

SERVES 8–10

Criniti's, of Philadelphia, is no big operation. It is a small Sicilian restaurant in which the owner/chef does all the cooking. The meatballs that he makes are unusual in that he grinds the meat so fine that the texture of the final product is closer to a quenelle than a meatball, but certainly not as light. This is a Sicilian meatball, not a quenelle. I am very taken by this method.

6 cups dried bread cubes (cut up leftover bread and dry it on the counter overnight)
1 pound boneless veal stew meat, ground
1 pound boneless pork butt, ground
½ pound boneless beef chuck, ground
⅓ pound pork fat, ground
⅓ cup finely chopped yellow onion
4 tablespoons freshly grated Parmesan cheese

2 cloves garlic, crushed
½ teaspoon dried marjoram
2 tablespoons chopped parsley
2 teaspoons salt
1 teaspoon freshly ground black pepper
2 eggs, beaten
2 tablespoons olive oil
½ recipe Fresh Tomato Sauce Sicilian (page 139)
½ pound sliced mozzarella

Place the dried bread cubes in a large bowl and cover with plenty of cold water. Allow to soak for 1 hour and drain. Squeeze the water out with your hands. Place the bread in a large bowl and add the remaining ingredients, except the olive oil, tomato sauce, and mozzarella. Mix everything together with your hands very well.

Grind the mixture very fine in a food processor with the 2 tablespoons of oil. (If you have a good-size food processor, you can do this in 2 batches, using 1 tablespoon of the oil each time.) Grind the mixture very fine until almost emulsified. This will take a few minutes and you will need to scrape the bowl of the food processor down a few times as you go.

Return all to the bowl and mix together with your hands again. Form into meatballs a little smaller than a golf ball. Moisten your hands with cold water whenever your hands begin to stick to the mixture. Place the meatballs on a lightly oiled sheet pan and bake at 375° for 25 minutes.

Cut the meatballs in half and place in individual baking dishes. Top with some fresh tomato sauce and mozzarella. Bake in a 375° oven until bubbly and lightly browned on top.

FARSUMAGRU

SERVES 8

This dish is from Sicily. It is flank steak rolled and tied around a rather involved meatloaf. Craig suggested the ad-

dition of asparagus in the middle of the roll, so this is even more complex then the normal Sicilian version. It is unusually good and well worth the effort that this will take to produce. Have a kitchen helper at your side and you will have no trouble with this dish.

2 ¾-pound flank steaks
Salt and pepper to taste
½ cup sliced and chopped pancetta (page 23)
2 tablespoons olive oil
3 cloves garlic, chopped
1 medium onion
1 raw egg, beaten
⅓ cup bread crumbs
2 tablespoons chopped parsley
1 teaspoon dried oregano
¼ cup freshly grated Parmesan cheese

½ pound thin asparagus
⅓ pound salami, sliced and julienned
½ pound mozzarella cheese, in julienned strips
4 hard-boiled eggs, peeled
1 pound ground pork

THE SAUCE
1½ cups Chicken Stock (page 116)
½ cup dry red wine
¼ cup tomato paste

Pound out the 2 flank steaks to about ¼-inch thickness. Lay the steaks out on the counter with the grain running crosswise. Overlap one of the steaks by 2 inches onto the other. Salt and pepper the meat to taste.

Heat a medium-size frying pan and add the pancetta. Sauté until browned. Reserve the pancetta and discard the fat. Heat the frying pan again and add 1 tablespoon of the oil. Add the garlic and onion and sauté until clear. Remove to a bowl and add the raw egg, bread crumbs, parsley, oregano, Parmesan cheese, and the reserved pancetta. Stir together so that the bread crumbs absorb the egg. Break off the tough ends and blanch the asparagus in boiling water for 2 minutes. Drain well and cool.

Spread the bread-crumb mixture onto the meat in an even layer. Lay the blanched asparagus in a line down the center of the meat. Lay the salami and mozzarella in a line on top of the asparagus. Arrange the hard-boiled eggs in a line as well. Spread the ground pork over all to hold everything in place. Season with salt and pepper to taste. Roll up like a jelly roll and tie with kitchen string. (You will probably need help to do this.) Tie the roll up well so that it doesn't fall apart. Season the roll with salt and pepper to taste.

Heat a large nonstick frying pan and add the remaining 1 tablespoon of oil. Brown the meat roll on all sides and place in a small roasting pan. Combine the ingredients for the sauce in a small bowl and stir together until smooth. Pour over the meat roll in the pan and cover with parchment paper. Cover the pan tightly with aluminum foil. Bake, covered, in a preheated 325° oven for 1 hour.

Remove the meat roll from the pan and allow to rest on a plate for 5 minutes. Simmer the pan juices a few minutes to reduce and thicken slightly. Remove the string and slice the roll crosswise into ½-inch slices. Serve with the reduced sauce spooned over the top.

MEATBALLS BAKED IN TOMATO SAUCE WITH FONDUTA

SERVES 10–12

Rich, rich, rich! The Fonduta sauce adds a new depth to a meatball dish. Please understand that this tastes even better when it is warmed up a second time, so don't worry about leftovers.

1 recipe Meatballs,
    Criniti Style (page
    330)
2 cups Fresh Tomato
    Sauce Sicilian
    (page 139)

1 recipe Fonduta (page
    80)

Prepare the meatballs as instructed in the recipe, but don't bake them in individual casseroles as it states. Instead, place the baked meatballs in a large ovenproof casserole and top with the tomato sauce. Pour the Fonduta over all and bake at 375° until bubbly and nicely browned on top.

PORCHETTA

SERVES 8–10

This pork dish is much appreciated in Umbria where it originated, though you can find it all over the North. I first saw it on a street stand where you could simply buy a slice or two and take it home for dinner. This recipe is from the Giovannucci family of Philadelphia, friends for years. They operate the best kitchen-supply shop outside of New York. It is called Fante's and it is found in the Italian Market. When we are in the city of Brotherly Love they will prepare a whole roast pig, from Esposito's Meats, in this style. What a party! What a family! What a piggy!

This is just great for a dinner party.

1 7- to 8-pound whole
    fresh pork
    shoulder (you will
    have to order this
    from your butcher
    and it must have
    the pork skin
    attached)

Salt and pepper to
    taste
3 cloves garlic, crushed
1 tablespoon fresh
    rosemary or 2
    teaspoons dried

Lay the meat skin side up on the counter and prick the skin all over with a sharp object such as an ice pick. Turn skin side down and season the meat with the salt and pepper, garlic, and rosemary. Roll up the roast with the skin on the outside and tie with kitchen string. Place on a rack in a roasting pan.

Roast in a preheated 375° oven for about 2½ hours or until a meat thermometer registers 165°. Let stand 15 minutes and slice across the grain.

LITTLE TIED PORCHETTA ROASTS

SERVES 6

This is the same dish as the previous Porchetta but these are a bit smaller and each will serve two to three people. I suggest that you cook two of these so that your refrigerator will be ready for you when you decide that you need a late-night cold-pork sandwich. This will really do the job . . . or you can cut up a bit of cold Porchetta and toss it with hot pasta. So good.

You can find little roasts like this in any good meat shop in Northern Italy. Why do our butchers not catch on to these little tricks?

1 3-pound boneless
   pork roast, tied
   Salt and pepper to
   taste
2 cloves garlic, crushed

1 tablespoon chopped
   fresh rosemary
   needles
1 tablespoon olive oil

Untie the roast and cut it into 2 1½-pound pieces. Place in a large bowl and season the pork with salt and pepper, garlic, rosemary, and olive oil. Rub the meat all over. Retie the 2 pieces into smaller roasts with the grain of the meat the same as the original piece. Place on a rack in a roasting pan and roast at 350° about 1½ hours or until a meat thermometer regiters 165°. Remove and allow to rest 5 minutes before slicing.

DEEP-FRIED VEAL MEATBALLS

MAKES ABOUT 2½ DOZEN

In Milan you find traces of several culinary traditions. These meatballs obviously had something to do with Austria or Switzerland. The flavors are Italian but the method of cooking had to come in from farther north. Regardless of their pedigree they are delicious.

THE MEATBALLS
½ cup milk
½ cup fine bread crumbs
1½ pounds veal, coarsely ground
½ pound pork fat, ground
1 clove garlic, crushed
1 egg, beaten
1 tablespoon chopped parsley

Salt and pepper to taste

THE BREADING
1 cup flour
2 eggs, beaten
2 cups fine bread crumbs

FOR FRYING
3 cups olive oil
3 cups peanut oil

Stir the milk and ½ cup bread crumbs together in a medium-size bowl. Allow to soak for 5 minutes and add the remaining ingredients for the meatballs. Mix together very well with your hands and form into balls containing 2 tablespoons of the meat mixture. Moisten your hands with cold water if the meat mixture begins to stick to your hands.

Place the flour, eggs, and remaining bread crumbs in separate bowls. Roll the meatballs in flour and pat off the excess flour. Coat with beaten egg and roll in bread crumbs.

Heat the olive oil and peanut oil for frying. Fry the meatballs at 375° until brown and the center is cooked through,

but don't overcook. Drain on paper towels. These can be
eaten plain or served with Fresh Tomato Sauce Sicilian
(page 139).

VEAL AND PARMA HAM ROLLS

SERVES 6 AS A MEAT COURSE

*These little bundles are to be found in the lovely butcher
shops of Turin, Parma, Milan, and Florence. The meats
are all tied and ready to go home with you.*

*Italians eat less meat than we do, in terms of sheer bulk,
and they therefore will spend more money on those tasty
little meat dishes that they do enjoy. While this one is not
cheap to make, you will be pleased by the richness of flavors. You don't need a whole plate of these in order to be
happy and content. This is a fine dish!*

6 4-ounce veal cutlets	Salt and pepper to
Freshly ground	taste
black pepper to	1 cup flour
taste	2 tablespoons butter
2 teaspoons chopped	1 tablespoon olive oil
parsley	½ cup dry white wine
6 thin slices prosciutto	½ cup Chicken Stock
(page 355) (buy at	(page 116)
a good Italian	
delicatessen and	**GARNISH**
have them slice it	Chopped parsley
for you)	

Pound the veal out thinly with a meat pounder (page 36),
making sure not to tear the meat. Season the meat with a
little black pepper to taste (no salt because the prosciutto
is salty). Sprinkle the pounded meat with chopped parsley.
Lay a slice of prosciutto on each cutlet and roll up tightly
like a jelly roll. Secure the rolls with toothpicks and season
the outside with salt and pepper to taste.

Preheat a 375° oven. Dredge the rolls in the flour and pat off the excess flour. Heat a large ovenproof frying pan (a frying pan with a metal handle). Add the butter and oil, and brown the veal rolls on all sides over medium-low heat. Place the whole pan in the oven and roast at 375° for 10 minutes. Remove the rolls to individual warm plates and remove the toothpicks.

Heat the pan on the stove top and add the wine and Chicken Stock. (Remember that the handle is hot.) Simmer a couple of minutes to form a thin sauce. Add salt and pepper to taste and spoon the sauce over the veal rolls. Garnish with chopped parsley.

BEEF IN ROSEMARY BUTTER

SERVES 4–6 AS A MEAT COURSE

Ermina, the chef for thirty-eight years at the highly respected Trattoria Vecchio Molinetto in Parma, uses water from the pasta pot as she is cooking. I had to think about this for some time. Now I understand it. She probably learned this trick from her mother, a woman who could not go to the hot water faucet all the time (she didn't have one) nor did she want to ask the children to keep running to the well. She was Italian and therefore wasted nothing. Nothing! The result of this frugality is that water from the pasta pot gives a bit of additional starch to any dish, and further, the boiling water from the pot does not reduce the temperature of the other dish that is cooking. Such a clever thought, all out of peasant practices. Also consider the fact that a tiny addition of hot pasta water now and then prevents the butter from burning and the dish from cooking too quickly. All of this from a pot of hot pasta water sitting on the corner of the stove!

1 2½-pound boneless New York steak (You will have to ask your butcher for this and specify the "center cut." The steak should be about 4 inches thick.)

Salt and pepper to taste
1½ tablespoons fresh rosemary needles
1 tablespoon olive oil
6 tablespoons butter, melted

Trim off the heavy gristle at the large end of the steak. Trim off any excess fat on the outside, leaving ⅛ inch of fat. Place the trimmed meat in a bowl and rub the meat with salt and pepper and rosemary. Add the olive oil and rub again. Allow the meat to marinate in the refrigerator for 2 hours. Turn the meat a few times while marinating. Pick the rosemary off the meat and reserve.

Heat a large nonstick frying pan and brown the meat lightly on all sides. Remove to a baking pan without a rack. Deglaze the frying pan with ¼ cup water. (*Our friend Ermina would use pasta water.*) Pour the pan juices over the meat. Add the reserved rosemary and pour the melted butter over all.

Roast in a preheated 350° oven for about 25 minutes or until a meat thermometer registers 125° (for medium-rare). Turn the meat a few times while cooking, and add a little water to the pan (about 2 tablespoons at a time). This will prevent the butter from burning and help form a sauce. Allow the meat to rest for a few minutes and slice ¼ inch thick. Slop each piece in the butter sauce in the pan and serve. ("Slop" is Craig's term, not mine!)

MEATBALL AND
CABBAGE COUSCOUS

SERVES 8–10

*This is a bit of Craig's imagination. He read that there is
a meatball and cabbage dish served with couscous in Italy.
Obviously the couscous came along when people from
North Africa moved into Sicily. The Sicilians still enjoy
couscous but the dish there is usually served with seafood.
When the people from North Africa moved farther up the
coast of Italy this version was developed. We have not been
able to locate a recipe for it so Craig decided that he would
develop one for us. The results of his study are most im-
pressive.*

THE MEATBALL MIXTURE

- 1 tablespoon olive oil
- 2 cloves garlic, crushed
- 1 cup minced yellow onion
- ¾ cup fine bread crumbs
- ¾ cup milk
- 1 egg, beaten
- ½ pound ground beef
- 1 pound pork butt, finely ground
- ¼ pound pork fat, finely ground
- 2 teaspoons ground fennel seed
- 2 tablespoons chopped parsley
- 1½ teaspoons salt
  Freshly ground black pepper to taste

THE SAUCE

- 2 tablespoons olive oil
- 2 cloves garlic, crushed
- 1 medium yellow onion, chopped
- 1½ pounds green cabbage, coarsely chopped
- ¾ cup dry white wine
- 2 cups Fresh Tomato Sauce Sicilian (page 139)
- ½ cup Chicken Stock (page 116)
  Salt and pepper to taste

THE COUSCOUS

- 1 pound (3 cups) couscous (page 22)
- 1 teaspoon salt
- 2½ cups boiling water
- 2 tablespoons olive oil

Heat a medium-size frying pan and add the oil, garlic, and onion for the meatball mixture. Sauté until the onion is clear; allow to cool. Place the bread crumbs in a small bowl and stir in the milk. Allow to stand for 5 minutes so that the crumbs absorb the milk. Place the cooled onion and soaked bread crumbs in a large bowl. Add the remaining ingredients for the meatballs and mix together very well until all is incorporated.

Form into 1-inch balls and place on an oiled sheet pan.

Moisten your hands with a bit of cold water if the mixture sticks to your hands. Bake the meatballs in a preheated 350° oven for 10 minutes. Remove and let the meatballs cool on the pan. The meatballs should be firm yet barely cooked because they will be cooked again in the sauce.

Heat a large frying pan and add the oil, garlic, and onion for the sauce. Sauté until the onion is clear and add the cabbage. Sauté, covered, for 5 minutes and remove to a 6-quart pot. Add the wine, tomato sauce, and Chicken Stock. Simmer, covered, for 10 minutes or until the cabbage is just tender. Add the baked meatballs to the pot and simmer gently for 20 minutes. Stir gently a few times while cooking. Add salt and pepper to taste.

TO PREPARE THE COUSCOUS

Place the couscous and salt in a large bowl and add the boiling water. Allow to stand for 5 minutes or until the couscous absorbs the water and expands. Heat a large frying pan and add the oil and the expanded couscous. Cook, covered, over medium heat about 5 minutes, stirring occasionally. Do not burn the couscous. Turn off the heat and salt to taste. Allow to stand, covered, about 3 minutes.

Serve the meatball stew over the couscous.

BEEF WITH BALSAMIC VINEGAR SAUCE

SERVES 4

This dish is common in Northern Italy, though usually it is too heavy for my taste. In this recipe we have lightened it up a bit with the chicken broth and I really think it plays much better. American beef is much more tender than the meat you see in Italy, so you do not need so much additional flavor. This is going to be popular at your house.

4 6-ounce fillets of
   beef
Salt and pepper to
   taste
1½ tablespoons olive
   oil
⅔ cup Chicken Stock
   (page 116)

¼ cup dry white wine
2 tablespoons
   balsamic vinegar
1½ tablespoons
   chopped parsley

Season the steaks with salt and pepper to taste. Heat a medium-size frying pan and add the oil. Add the meat and sauté over medium-high heat to your liking (about 3 minutes per side for medium-rare). Remove to a warm plate and add the Chicken Stock, wine, and vinegar to the frying pan. Bring to a boil and simmer for about 3 minutes to reduce the sauce. Add the parsley and salt and pepper to taste if needed. Add any juices from the meat that have formed on the plate. Serve the sauce over the steaks.

COLD PORK SALAD

SERVES 8

This colorful dish for pork lovers can go in the antipasto section, or the salad section, or the red meat section, since it is perfect for a summer evening's whole meal.

I love meat salads, and this one, typical of Milan and Florence, is a delight.

1½ pounds boneless pork loin roast	**THE DRESSING**
½ cup cored and julienned red bell pepper	½ cup extra virgin olive oil
½ cup julienned celery	1 tablespoon fresh lemon juice
½ cup peeled and julienned white onion	1 tablespoon white wine vinegar
1 tablespoon chopped parsley	Salt and pepper to taste

Prepare the roasted pork loin as in the recipe for Marinated Roast Pork Slices (page 67).

Slice the cooled meat about ³⁄₁₆ inch thick. Julienne the slices and place in a large bowl. Add the pepper, celery, onion, and parsley.

Mix the ingredients for the dressing, add to the bowl, and toss everything together. Cover and allow to marinate 1 to 2 hours in the refrigerator. Toss the salad a couple of times while chilling.

PORK ROAST STUFFED WITH MORTADELLA

SERVES 6–8

In the city of Bologna, mortadella reigns supreme. We had a dish like this in that fine eating center in the Emilia-

Romagna region and we found it very easy to duplicate in Seattle. The flavor of the mortadella blends a bit with the pork roast and the resulting slices of meat are pinwheels of very moist and delicious roast. This is to be enjoyed with some serious eaters. Don't forget a tortellini course so you can be truly Bolognese.

4 pounds boneless pork butt roast, tied	**Salt and pepper to taste**
2 cloves garlic, crushed	**½ pound mortadella (page 23), thinly sliced**
2 tablespoons chopped parsley	

Untie the roast and using a meat pounder (page 36) pound the roast out evenly to about 1 inch thick. Rub the meat with the garlic, parsley, and salt and pepper to taste. Lay the sliced mortadella all over the seasoned meat. Roll the roast up tightly and retie with kitchen string. (You will probably need help with this.)

Season outside with salt and pepper to taste. Roast at 350° for 1 hour. Reduce the temperature to 325° and roast 1½ hours more or until a meat thermometer registers 165°. Allow the roast to stand 10 minutes before slicing.

ROAST PORK WITH BLACK OLIVE PASTE

SERVES 6–8 AS A MEAT COURSE

When we tried this great olive paste recipe on a pork roast we were amazed. There is a certain sealing that goes on with this paste and the results are nothing but moist and flavorful. Craig, my chef, took the remains of this dish home to his brother Jeff, who is no light eater. Jeffrey announced that it was the best pork roast he had ever eaten. I agree. Don't pass this one up!

1 4-pound pork butt roast, tied Salt and pepper to taste (easy on the salt)	½ cup Black Olive Paste (page 490)

Salt and pepper the roast to taste. Rub with the black olive paste. Allow to marinate ½ hour. Place on a roasting rack and roast at 350° for about 2 hours and 15 minutes or until it is 160° in the center when tested with a meat thermometer. Remove and allow to stand for 15 minutes before slicing.

ROAST LAMB WITH BLACK OLIVE PASTE

SERVES 8–10

The lamb and the olive belong together, and have since ancient times. I love lamb and this is a very interesting and delicious variation.

1 5½-pound leg of lamb Salt and pepper to taste (easy on the salt)	½ cup Black Olive Paste (page 490)

Season the lamb with the salt and pepper to taste and rub with the olive paste. Allow to marinate at room temperature for ½ hour. Place on a roasting rack and roast at 325° for about 1 hour and 45 minutes or until a meat thermometer registers 130° (for medium-rare to medium; insert the thermometer into the thickest part of the leg without touching the bone). Remove the roast and allow to stand in a warm place for 15 minutes before slicing.

SAUSAGES AND PROSCIUTTO

Sausages are everywhere in Italy. Every meat shop prepares its own and they are all very proud of them. In the Campo De Fiori, the great open market square in Rome, there is a sausage shop that will bring tears to your eyes, if you feel as I do about sausage.

The number of ingredients that can be put into a sausage is simply startling. Further, the flavors vary from region to region, of course. I once received a fine recipe for sausage from a bunch of Sicilian butchers from Brooklyn. I published the recipe in one of my earlier books and a woman wrote to tell me that I was a jerk! "Italians never use fennel in sausage." Well, madam, perhaps not in the regions of your childhood but certainly in other regions of Italy.

The sausage is probably very Roman, and I think there is good evidence to prove that it goes back to ancient times. When the Romans had their great feasts and parties the guests were all to eat reclining on couches. You ate leaning on one elbow and therefore a knife and fork were out of the question. You would slip and break your neck if you tried to cut something while in such a position. So casings were filled with meats and they could be eaten with the fingers of one hand. How clever!

Please do not think that making your own sausages is too much work. It is not, and the rewards are worth the minor effort. Your kids will get a kick out of helping and if you have a sausage machine, you will be having sausage parties every so often.

All of these recipes work well and are delicious, but if I were to pick a favorite I suppose it would be the Italian Dried Sausage. Cook these in Fresh Tomato Sauce Sicilian and you are in Southern Italian Heaven!

In addition to the recipes in this chapter you may also wish to see:

Sausage and Spinach Polenta (page 234)

On Making Sausage

1. The casings: Your butcher can tell you of a source for the casings. You will need the size for Italian sausage or garlic sausage for all of these recipes except the small-style Italian, which requires breakfast-sausage–size casings.

   The casings will probably be packed in salt. They must be rinsed well and the inside rinsed of the salt before use.

2. Test out the mixture for proper seasoning by cooking a tiny amount first. Simply pan-fry a little patty. Then correct the seasonings to your taste and proceed to stuff the casings.

3. Stuff the filling into the casings using a sausage-stuffing funnel (page 44) or a sausage-stuffing tube on your meat grinder. Do not pack the meat in too tightly as the sausages will expand a bit when cooking.

4. Tie into individual sausages using kitchen string. Or you might just twist them into shape—but be careful as they will pop.

5. Prick the casings in several places before cooking. This will prevent them from exploding. I use a little corn-on-the-cob holder for this job.

6. Cook the sausages slowly. High heat will make them pop.

7. A pound of filling will fill about one yard of casing.

8. Cure the sausages in the refrigerator 1 day before cooking and serving them. Do not attempt to keep these sausages longer than 3 to 4 days as they contain no chemicals, with the exception of the dried Italian. It will keep a bit longer.

   If a sausage feels slippery or slimey, it has gone to sausage heaven. Discard the body!

9. Each person will eat about ½ pound of sausage at dinner.

ITALIAN DRIED SAUSAGE

MAKES 2 POUNDS

This is great fun to make. Please remember that salt and saltpeter are common perservatives in meat, and I think the salt and nitrate scare in our time is much overrated. Italians do not like sausage that is all wet and filled with water. So, in order to dry them out, and to improve the flavor, I offer the following.

Prepare a batch of Italian Sausage, Sicilian Style (page 352) and add ½ teaspoon saltpeter (any drugstore) to the mixture. Stuff into casings and hang in a cool place. Hang them in such a way that they are not touching one another. Each one must have free air circulating around it.

I hang a batch in the pantry and then aim an electric oscillating fan at them. Use this drying method for 2 or 3 days, depending on how hard you want the sausages to be. When they are dry you can put them into plastic sacks in the refrigerator. They will keep for at least an additional week, but they are best cooked upon drying.

To cook, prick each sausage and simmer in Fresh Tomato Sauce Sicilian (page 139). Be prepared for a very rich dish as the drying concentrates all flavors.

Serve over pasta or polenta.

ITALIAN SAUSAGE WITH LEMON

MAKES A LITTLE OVER 2 POUNDS

Lemon is just great with pork, and this sausage with lemon is delightful. It is not heavy but rather very refreshing.

2 pounds pork butt, coarsely ground	3 cloves garlic, crushed
¼ pound pork fat, coarsely ground	1 teaspoon salt
1 tablespoon freshly ground fennel seed	4 tablespoons dry white wine
1 tablespoon dried parsley	2 tablespoons freshly grated lemon peel

Mix all the ingredients together. Let stand for 1 hour and mix again. Stuff into casings.

ITALIAN SAUSAGE, SICILIAN STYLE

MAKES 2 POUNDS

This will be better than any sausage you can find in a market, except perhaps Fretta Brothers in New Jersey and Esposito's in Philadelphia. Well, there are some fine com-

panies in Seattle also. Fresh-made sausage, homemade, is a forgotten thing in our culture and I think that is a shame.

2 pounds lean pork butt, coarsely ground	3 cloves garlic, crushed
¼ pound pork fat, coarsely ground	⅛ teaspoon dried hot red pepper flakes
1 tablespoon coarsely ground fennel seed	1 teaspoon salt
	¼ teaspoon freshly ground black pepper
2 bay leaves, crushed	4 tablespoons dry white wine
1 tablespoon dried parsley	

Mix all the ingredients and let stand for 1 hour. Mix again and then stuff into casings.

ITALIAN SAUSAGE WITH PARSLEY AND CHEESE

MAKES A LITTLE OVER 2 POUNDS

This is a bit lighter than the sausages with red pepper flakes and I think this is a perfect sausage for a nice dinner with friends.

2 pounds pork butt, coarsely ground	1 teaspoon salt
¼ pound pork fat, coarsely ground	¼ teaspoon freshly ground black pepper
3 tablespoons chopped fresh parsley	4 tablespoons dry white wine
3 cloves garlic, crushed	½ cup freshly grated Parmesan cheese

Put all the ingredients together, and mix them well. Let sit for an hour and mix again. Stuff into casings.

ITALIAN SAUSAGE WITH CHEESE AND WINE

This one is great for pasta dishes. It is not strong in flavor but it is bright in flavor. The wine always has a cleansing effect on meat.

Make the recipe for Sausage with Parsley and Cheese (page 353), but omit the parsley and the white wine. Substitute ½ cup of dry red wine and proceed with the recipe. Terrific!

ITALIAN SAUSAGE WITH PARSLEY, SMALL STYLE

MAKES ABOUT 2¼ POUNDS

These little sausages are a bit more delicate than those above, and they are also much smaller. These are great for breakfast or for a summer luncheon party. The parsley really does quiet the flavors.

<table>
<tr><td>2 pounds pork butt, ground medium</td><td>½ teaspoon freshly ground black pepper</td></tr>
<tr><td>¼ pound pork fat, ground medium</td><td></td></tr>
<tr><td>½ cup chopped fresh parsley</td><td>4 tablespoons white wine</td></tr>
<tr><td>1 teaspoon salt</td><td>2 cloves garlic, crushed</td></tr>
</table>

Mix all the ingredients together well, and then let stand for one hour. Mix again and stuff into breakfast-sausage–size casings.

SAUSAGE CACCIATORE
OVER POLENTA

The dried sausages (page 351) have a very concentrated flavor, due to the drying, of course. Try simmering them in a bit of our Fresh Tomato Sauce Sicilian (page 139) along with a splash of dry red wine for about ½ hour. Don't forget to prick them first. Serve over polenta, either soft (page 224) or hard (page 225). Grill the hard polenta and top with the sausages and tomato sauce. I would like some freshly grated Parmesan cheese on mine.

Prosciutto di Parma

In the past we were not been allowed to enjoy the great dried ham of Parma, the prosciutto. Our government was concerned about hoof-and-mouth disease, but now we may import this great delicacy and we are doing so to the tune of 900,000 hams per year. Wonderful!

We make a similar ham in this country and some fine imitations are made in Canada, but once you taste the real thing you will be frustrated with our American efforts. I know of two exceptions to this statement, one being the fine prosciutto that Lorenzo makes himself at the North Beach Restaurant in San Francisco and the other being that made by Dante at Felidia's Restaurant in New York City.

Let's talk frugal, no waste. One of the reasons that the hams of Parma are so delicious is that the pigs are fed the whey from the dairies that produce that wonderful Parmigiano-Reggiano cheese. Every dairy has its own herd of pigs. Such a rich meal . . . twice around.

Only the rear legs of the pig are used for this great ham. The leg is salted and hung in a cold room, where the temperature is carefully controlled, for about 3 months. It is then moved to an aging room, where the wind of the Italian hills can draw out the moisture. After 7 months the meat becomes hard on the outside, so it is rubbed with kidney fat or lard so that the outer coating will soften and the drying process can continue. At the end of the year, or perhaps a few months more, the ham is tested for flavor and purity by a member of the Consortium Prosciutto di Parma. If he passes the ham, it is branded with the official seal and put out for sale.

That is it. No preservatives, no nitrates, no pepper; nothing but salt and piggy.

This whole process is very carefully controlled by the consortium so quality is assured. Some 210 factories participate in the Consortium and they produce some 7.5 millon hams a year. By the time the hams reach this country they are terribly expensive by American standards but they cost just about as much in Italy. The Italians seem to have no problem with the price of this unquestionable delicacy.

INNARDS

In our country we have trouble finding fresh innards. In Italy there are special shops that sell nothing but innards. One can purchase pork and lamb liver, sweetbreads, heart, lungs, brains, kidneys, tripe, tongue, oxtails, and pigs' feet, all in one shop. In America we are reluctant to eat most of these things for some strange reason but we will buy commercial wieners. Hmmmm. I am not quite sure what to make of our understanding of the production of our food.

The appreciation of these specialty meats goes back to pre-Roman times. While it is true that many innards were used by the lower classes since the meats were cheap, it is also true that the upper classes would serve many fine dishes made from innards at formal banquets. Apicius, in a collection of recipes from the first century, delights in tripe, lung, and kidneys. And we must not forget the meals celebrated by the Emperor Heliogabalus who used to enjoy eating a hundred or so ostrich brains at dinner. That is even too much for me!

To this day innards are still enjoyed throughout Italy. It is a shame that we refuse to try so many things in this country, but those who have lived in hard times in Italy came to love things that we would call peasant food. And they continue to eat those things today not because they have to but because they love them. These are wonderful dishes cooked by a thousand wonderful Italian grandmas.

We are proud of the tripe dishes in this section. Please, be patient enough to try one or two. Then I will have you hooked. The mild Veal Kidneys with Gorgonzola Sauce is an ingenious dish, as is the Risotto with Sweetbreads and Mushrooms. Incidentally, sweetbreads are from the thymus gland. They are *not* "Rocky Mountain oysters."

Florence seems to be a major center for the appreciation of innards, and a visit to the City of the Renaissance must include a dish of Tripe Florentine. That is where I first tasted tripe some thirty-three years ago. I have never recovered from that lovely surprise.

TRIPE WITH TOMATO AND FENNEL

SERVES 6 AS A MAIN COURSE

This dish goes back a long way in terms of Italian history. In the old days fennel and spices were added to inexpensive meats to cover up any sharp flavors from meat that was not fresh. Today we can enjoy fresh meats, certainly innards, that have been carefully cleaned, processed, and refrigerated or frozen. Still, the flavor of the fennel bulb is supportive and delicious.

3 pounds tripe, pre-
blanched (discuss
this with your
butcher)

3 tablespoons olive
oil

3 cloves garlic,
peeled and
chopped

½ pound boneless
pork, medium
diced

1 medium onion,
peeled and
chopped

1 medium carrot,
coarsely grated

½ cup chopped
parsley

1 cup red wine

1¼ cups Fresh Tomato
Sauce Sicilian
(page 139)

Peel from ¼ lemon

½ cup Beef Stock
(page 115)

½ teaspoon dried
basil

Salt and black
pepper to taste

1 1½-pound fennel
bulb, sliced (trim
the top and
discard)

Trim off any fat on the tripe. Cut the tripe into 2 × ½-inch strips. Place the cut tripe in a 4- to 6-quart pot. Heat a large frying pan and add the oil, garlic, and pork. Brown a few minutes and add the onion and carrot. Sauté 5 minutes and add to the pot of tripe. Add the parsley, wine, fresh tomato sauce, lemon peel, Beef Stock, basil, and salt and black pepper to taste. Bring to a boil, cover, and simmer gently for 4 hours. Stir occasionally. Add the sliced fennel bulb and simmer until the fennel is tender, about 30 minutes.

Taste for the correct amount of salt and pepper.

Serve on any pasta or on the side of any vegetable.

TRIPE ON POLENTA CROSTINI WITH CHEESE

Try this for a very attractive way to serve tripe. Slice some Hard Polenta (page 225) thinly and brush it with olive oil and garlic. Broil so as to make crostini, or literally "crunchy" polenta. Place the polenta slices on the plate and top with Tripe Florentine (page 365). I would add some additional Parmesan cheese on the top.

TRIPE AND POLENTA

In Boston I found a strange and very good rendition of what I call Poached Polenta Cubes (page 233). The cook at Piccola Venezia poaches the polenta a second time, as you would with gnocchi, and then serves Tripe Florentine (page 365) over the poached polenta pieces. The result is a very soft and enjoyable dish. Add more cheese!

VEAL KIDNEYS WITH
GORGONZOLA SAUCE
SERVES 6

There are those of you out there who now think that I have gone over the edge. Relax. I know that people either like kidneys or do not like kidneys. There is no "sort of" about it.

Northern Italy has been influenced by the rest of Western Europe much more than the South. This dish is obviously one of those influenced by the French or perhaps even the Austrians. In Milan we found a version similar to this one, and if you enjoy veal kidneys you must try it. The flavors are much lighter than you would imagine. Rich, yes.

THE KIDNEYS	THE SAUCE
2 1-pound veal kidneys	¼ cup dry white wine
3 quarts boiling water	½ cup Chicken Stock (page 116)
¼ cup white vinegar	¼ cup cream
1 tablespoon salt	½ cup Gorgonzola Sauce (page 148)
1 tablespoon olive oil	

Blanch the kidneys for 1 minute in the boiling water, along with the vinegar and salt. Remove and cool. Trim any excessive fat and discard. Slice the kidneys ¼ inch thick. Sauté quickly in a large frying pan along with the 1 tablespoon olive oil for 30 seconds per side and remove to a warm plate. You may have to do this in two batches.

Add the sauce ingredients to the frying pan and simmer until all is hot. Return the kidneys to the pan and heat for a moment.

This is great served over toast or polenta. You might even try rice.

TRIPE WITH CRANBERRY BEANS

SERVES 6–8 AS A MAIN COURSE

I know that many of you are not as fond of tripe as am I. Further, I know that most of you have never tried it, and I think that is a shame.

We had this version in Bologna and I am pleased to tell you that I shared it with our driver, Giorgio. He is a true Italian and therefore a great lover of tripe. Thank goodness I found him.

¾ cup cranberry
  beans (find in
  Italian markets)
3 cups cold water
3 pounds tripe, pre-
  blanched (ask
  the butcher)
3 tablespoons oil
2 cloves garlic,
  crushed
½ pound pork, diced
1 medium onion,
  chopped
1 medium carrot,
  coarsely grated
½ cup chopped
  parsley

1 cup red wine
1¼ cups Fresh Tomato
  Sauce Sicilian
  (page 139)
Peel from ¼ lemon
½ teaspoon dried
  basil
2½ cups Chicken
  Stock (page 116)
Salt and pepper to
  taste

GARNISHES
Chopped parsley
Grated Parmesan
  cheese

Place the beans in a bowl and add the water. Allow to sit on the countertop overnight. Drain the beans and set aside. Trim any fat off the tripe and rinse and drain it. Cut the tripe into ½ × 1½-inch strips. Place the tripe in a 6-quart pot.

Heat a large frying pan and add the oil, garlic, and pork. Brown a few minutes and add the onion and carrot. Sauté 5 minutes and add to the pot of tripe. Add the parsley, wine, tomato sauce, lemon peel, basil, and Chicken Stock. Bring to a boil, cover, and simmer gently for 3 hours. Drain the soaked beans and add to the pot. Bring to a simmer and cook gently for 1 hour more. Stir the pot occasionally. Add salt and pepper to taste. Serve with the garnishes.

RISOTTO WITH SWEETBREADS
AND MUSHROOMS

Serves 6–8

I think this is a very elegant dish. Sweetbreads are a part of the thymus gland of the young calf. The flavor is close

*to a very mild liver, but sweetbreads are superior to liver,
I promise.*

1 veal sweetbread (a
   small one, about
   ½ pound)
4 quarts cold water
   for poaching
1 medium yellow
   onion, peeled and
   quartered
2 bay leaves
10 whole black
   peppercorns

3 tablespoons distilled
   white vinegar
4 sprigs parsley
1 recipe Risotto with
   Mushrooms (page
   245)

GARNISH
Chopped parsley

Rinse the sweetbread and drain. Bring the 4 quarts water
to a boil with the onion, bay leaves, peppercorns, vinegar,
and parsley. Simmer covered for 10 minutes. Place the
sweetbread in the pot and gently poach for 20 minutes.
Remove and plunge into cold water and allow to cool completely. Discard the poaching liquid. Pull off the clear
membrane that surrounds the sweetbread. Pull the gland
apart and separate into nuggets. Remove or trim any other
skin, fat, or gristle attached. Prepare the risotto and stir the
prepared sweetbreads into the rice in the last few minutes
of cooking. Heat through and serve with parsley garnish.

TRIPE FLORENTINE

SERVES 8

*In Florence this dish is served in all of the fine restaurants.
Americans seem to think that it is cheap food, what with
all of our talk about something being just "tripe." Come
now. This is a fine dish and I urge you to try it. As a matter
of fact, tripe has become so much more popular in this
country during the last few years that the price has increased dramatically. Still, I love it and I will continue to
plead with you to try it.*

2 pounds tripe, pre-
  blanched (talk to
  your butcher)
4 tablespoons olive oil
2 carrots, grated
½ cup chopped celery
1 yellow onion, peeled
  and chopped
½ cup chopped parsley
3 cloves garlic,
  crushed
1 cup Fresh Tomato
  Sauce Sicilian
  (page 139)
½ cup Beef Stock
  (page 115) or use
  canned

½ cup dry red wine
1 teaspoon oregano
1 bay leaf, crushed
½ teaspoon basil
  Salt and pepper to
  taste
2 1-inch-long pieces
  lemon peel
1 cup half-and-half
½ cup freshly grated
  Parmesan or
  Romano cheese

GARNISH
Additional
Parmesan or
Romano cheese

Trim and remove the fat from the tripe. Slice the tripe into ½-inch-wide pieces. Sauté very quickly in half the oil in a large frying pan. Place the tripe in a 4- to 6-quart heavy stove-top casserole.

In the frying pan sauté in half the oil the carrots, celery, yellow onion, parsley, and garlic until the onion is clear. Add the tomato sauce, Beef Stock, and red wine along with the oregano, bay leaf, basil, salt and pepper, and lemon peel. Simmer the sauce for a few minutes, and then add to the pot with the tripe.

Cook on top of the stove, covered, for 3 hours, or until tender. Or bake in a moderate oven. (Watch the water content during the cooking; you may need to add a bit of water as the liquids cook away.)

When the tripe is tender, add the half-and-half and the cheese. Simmer again until all is hot. When it is ready to serve, add a little Parmesan or Romano cheese as a garnish.

Serve with pasta.

SWEETBREADS WITH FRESH FENNEL

SERVES 4–6

One of you dear readers is going to make some comment about sweetbreads. You are going to say something about Rocky Mountain oysters or something worse. Sweetbreads are only found in young animals and they are the thymus gland, as explained earlier. The flavor of this great delicacy is very close to a young liver flavor, but much more delicate. The use of fennel with innards is a very old Italian custom, and I think this dish is "to die for," as they say in Brooklyn.

Note that we have used a very light sauce on this dish so that you can taste the very delicate flavor of the wonderful sweetbreads.

2 ¾-pound veal
    sweetbreads
2 tablespoons olive oil
2 cloves garlic, peeled
    and thinly sliced
2 cups julienned fresh
    fennel bulb (trim
    the top and
    discard or use in
    soup stock)

Salt and pepper to
    taste
1 cup flour
1 tablespoon butter
½ cup Chicken Stock
    (page 116)
⅓ cup dry white wine

GARNISH
Chopped parsley

Poach the sweetbreads as instructed in the recipe for Risotto with Sweetbreads and Mushrooms (page 364), but leave the sweetbreads whole. Remove the clear membrane that surrounds the gland and slice the sweetbreads lengthwise into ¼-inch-thick pieces; set aside.

Heat a medium-size frying pan and add 1 tablespoon of the olive oil, the garlic, and the julienned fennel. Sauté, covered, until the fennel is just tender, about 10 minutes. Set aside.

Season the sliced sweetbreads with a little salt and pepper to taste. Dredge them in the flour and pat off the excess so that there is a very thin coating of flour. Heat a large frying pan and add the remaining 1 tablespoon olive oil and the butter. Sauté the sweetbreads 1 minute per side and remove to warm plates.

Deglaze the pan with the Chicken Stock and add the wine. Add the sautéed fennel and simmer the sauce for 2 to 3 minutes to reduce and thicken slightly. Add salt and pepper to taste. Serve over the sweetbreads and garnish with parsley.

VEGETABLES

The Italians love vegetables. We have seen whole buffets of cold vegetables set out as a first course, enough vegetables to comprise an entire meal. Not a bad idea!

The dietitians of today are telling us that we must eat more vegetables, grains, and starches, and cut down on animal fat. That is how the Italians have been eating for hundreds of years. We would be wise to catch up with them.

In this section you will find some unusual dishes, all of them very delicious in my opinion. Vegetarians, take note. You stop me on the street often and demand a vegetarian cookbook. This section is as close as I can come as I am not a vegetarian. However, I have included all-vegetable recipes in every cookbook that I have ever written, so take heart, calm down, and read through this batch of fine dishes.

I must warn you that when you eat in Italy you will find yourself complaining that the vegetables, each and every one, are generally overcooked. This is especially true for such tender treasures as fresh asparagus and broccoli. Cook these following dishes a bit more American style and you will be pleased.

I especially enjoy the Braised Endive, Cipolline Braised with Marsala, and the Peppers Piedmont. The Cold Spinach Balls will please any spinach lover.

In addition to the recipes in this chapter you may also wish to see:

Asparagus Tonnato (page 77)

PAN-ROASTED POTATOES WITH RADICCHIO

SERVES 4–6

While the potato was a gift to Italy from the New World, we have to admit that the Italian kitchen has come up with supportive flavors for the old spud that we have not even thought about. This is easy and creative and delicious. Even your junior high kids will give you a high sign on this one. And it is not even deep-fried!

2 tablespoons olive
   oil
2 pounds russet
   potatoes, peeled
   and cut into ¾-
   inch chunks
   (Keep the cut
   potatoes in
   lightly salted
   water to prevent
   browning. Drain
   very well and
   pat dry on paper
   towels before
   cooking.)

2 cloves garlic
1½ cups coarsely
   chopped
   radicchio, about
   6 ounces
1½ tablespoons
   chopped parsley
   Salt and pepper to
   taste

Preheat the oven to 375°. Heat a large ovenproof frying pan and add the oil and potatoes. Brown the potatoes over medium-high heat for 5 minutes, tossing regularly. Toss in the garlic, stir a moment, and place the whole pan in the hot oven for 15 minutes or until the potatoes are just tender. Toss the potatoes a couple of times while in the oven.

Remove from the oven (remember the handle is hot!) and place on a hot burner. Add the radicchio, parsley, and salt and pepper to taste. Sauté and toss together 1 minute until the radicchio becomes tender and collapses onto the potatoes.

GRILLED EGGPLANT

SERVES 6

I am on a personal campaign to get Americans to eat more eggplant. The Italians know how to cook it properly and thus their affection for the vegetable. In this country we seem to be stymied by memories of gushy eggplant from the lunch lady at Brooklyn Grade School Number 306. Enough! This is a fine dish and it will not be bitter at all. The oil will offer a very rich support.

1 1-pound eggplant
1½ tablespoons salt
⅓ cup olive oil for
   grilling

1 tablespoon lemon
   juice
Salt and pepper to
   taste

THE DRESSING
¼ cup extra virgin
   olive oil

GARNISH
Chopped parsley

Slice the eggplant crosswise ¼ inch thick. Sprinkle both sides of the slices with some of the salt and place them in a colander. Allow the eggplant to drain 45 minutes. Rinse the slices in cold water and pat dry on paper towels. Brush one side of the slices with some of the olive oil and place the oiled side down on a medium-hot barbecue or Le Creuset stove-top grill (page 35). Grill until very brown on the oiled side. Brush the top side with more oil and turn the eggplant slices. Grill until very brown on the second side and the eggplant is tender. Remove to a sheet pan to cool.

Arrange the slices in a shingle pattern on a serving platter. Mix the ingredients for the dressing together and drizzle it over the eggplant. Garnish with chopped parsley.

CIPOLLINE BRAISED WITH MARSALA

SERVES 4 AS A SIDE DISH OR VEGETABLE

Cipolline are very small onions. You can buy them in an Italian market, but they are not cheap since they are imported. You can substitute small white boiling onions from your local supermarket but be sure they are fresh and firm.

In the old days they used to import a very small dark-skinned cipollina that the old-timers loved to eat peeled and pan-fried with eggs or sausage. They are somewhat bitter and the younger people do not seem to get into them.

In our time I am quite sure that you will be very happy with this version.

3 tablespoons olive oil
4 cups cleaned cipolline (peeled but left whole), about 1½ pounds, or substitute small white boiling onions (see above)
½ cup dry white wine
Salt and pepper to taste
¼ cup sweet Marsala
2 tablespoons chopped parsley

Heat a medium-size frying pan and add the oil and onions. Sauté over medium heat until lightly browned, about 2 minutes. Add the wine, cover, and reduce the heat to low. Cook the onions for 15 to 20 minutes or until just tender. Toss the onions a couple of times while cooking. When the onions are just tender, add the salt and pepper to taste, Marsala, and parsley. Toss all together over the heat until the liquid is evaporated and a glaze forms. Serve at once.

BRAISED ENDIVE

SERVES 2–4 AS A SIDE DISH

I hope you know endive. The Italian kitchen cannot be without it. It is sort of a slightly bitter lettuce and can be found in any Italian produce market. In a big city you can find it year-round. You can boil it, fry it, use it in salads, and it is just great in soups. In this dish we braise it and then use the juice to make a light gravy.

3 tablespoons olive oil
2 cloves garlic, chopped
½ cup finely chopped yellow onion
1½ pounds endive, washed and drained
¼ cup chopped prosciutto
¾ cup Chicken Stock (page 116)
½ cup dry white wine
1 tablespoon butter
1 tablespoon flour
Salt and pepper to taste

Heat a large deep frying pan and add the oil, garlic, and onion. Sauté until just tender. Core the endive and add the whole leaves to the pan. Add the prosciutto, Chicken Stock, and wine. Cover and simmer gently 5 minutes until tender. Turn the endive a few times while cooking. Strain the endive, reserving the broth. Return the broth to the pan.

Melt the butter in a small pan and stir in the flour to form a roux. Heat the broth in the pan and stir in the roux to thicken. Return the endive to the pan and fold together with the sauce. Salt and pepper to taste.

ASPARAGUS PARMIGIANO

SERVES 4–6

Asparagus in Italy goes back to the first century in Rome. All Italians seem to love the stuff and this recipe, which involves the blending of the flavor of my favorite vegetable with my favorite cheese, is almost too much. Easy to prepare—you will love this classic!

1 pound thin asparagus	3 tablespoons melted butter
Pinch of salt	Freshly ground
2 teaspoons olive oil	black pepper to
¼ cup freshly grated Parmesan cheese	taste
1½ tablespoons lemon juice	

Break the tough woody ends off the asparagus and discard. Fill a 12-quart pot two-thirds full with cold water. Bring to a boil and add the salt and the oil. Blanch the asparagus for 2 minutes and drain. Immediately rinse in cold water to stop the cooking. Drain very well.

Place the asparagus in an 8 × 8-inch glass baking dish and sprinkle with the Parmesan cheese. Drizzle with the lemon juice and melted butter and top with freshly ground black pepper to taste. Bake in a preheated 350° oven for 5 to 7 minutes or until the cheese is melted.

ASPARAGUS MILANESE

SERVES 4–6

This very dish actually goes back to ancient Rome, where Apicius, a famous cooking authority of the first century, held forth. He was the one to suggest that scrambled eggs are just great over asparagus. This old recipe is actually very much up to date.

1 pound thin asparagus
1 teaspoon salt
1 tablespoon olive oil
3 tablespoons melted butter
3 tablespoons freshly grated Parmesan cheese

Salt and freshly ground black pepper to taste
2 eggs, beaten

Break off the tough woody ends of the asparagus and discard. Fill a 12-quart pot two-thirds full with cold water and bring to a boil. Add 1 teaspoon of salt and the oil. Blanch the asparagus 2 minutes and drain. Immediately rinse in cold water to stop the cooking. Drain very well.

Place in a bowl and toss with 2 tablespoons of the melted butter, the cheese, and salt and pepper to taste. Arrange in an 8 × 8-inch glass baking dish. Bake in a preheated 350° oven for 5 to 7 minutes until the cheese is melted.

Heat a frying pan and add the remaining 1 tablespoon of melted butter. Scramble the eggs but do not overcook. The eggs should be hot but not cooked hard. Top the asparagus with the soft-cooked eggs. Sprinkle with a little bit of salt and top with plenty of freshly ground pepper.

BRAISED RADICCHIO WITH
LEMON MAYONNAISE

SERVES 4

Radicchio is a delicate leafy vegetable with a nice bite. It has become very popular in this country during the last few years and has usually been used in salads. In this dish we braise or sauté the vegetable and then dress it with lemon juice and good mayonnaise. The result is a dish that is fine as a vegetable or as a salad or as an antipasto or as . . . well, it goes well with just about anything.

2 8-ounce heads radicchio (page 24) (buy large heads that are dense and not wilted)	**THE DRESSING**
	1½ tablespoons lemon juice
	½ cup mayonnaise
	Tiny pinch of salt to taste
2 tablespoons olive oil	
2 cloves garlic, crushed	**GARNISHES**
⅓ **cup dry white wine**	Freshly ground black pepper
	Chopped parsley

Cut the radicchio in half lengthwise. Do not remove the core. Heat a large nonstick frying pan and add the oil, garlic, and radicchio, cut side down in the pan. Cook the cut side over medium-low heat a few minutes until brown and caramelized. Add the wine and cook, covered, over low heat for 5 to 7 minutes until the radicchio is just tender. Do not turn the radicchio while cooking. Remove to a platter with the browned side up and allow to cool.

Stir the ingredients for the dressing together until smooth. Drizzle the dressing over the radicchio and garnish with a bit of ground black pepper and chopped parsley. Serve at room temperature.

CARROTS, SICILIAN STYLE

SERVES 4-6

When I was a little kid we had carrots often. They were one of the few vegetables available during World War II. My mother would always overcook them—no, she does not do that now—and the vegetable turned soggy and tired. I said earlier that I think most Italian restaurants overcook all their vegetables, but if you will use this recipe and not overcook it, you will be very pleased. I am back to eating my carrots!

1¾ pounds carrots, peeled (trim ends)
Salted water to taste
1 tablespoon butter
2 tablespoons olive oil
2 cloves garlic, chopped

2 teaspoons stripped and chopped fresh oregano
2 teaspoons chopped parsley
⅓ cup dry Marsala
2 tablespoons Parmesan cheese
Salt and pepper to taste

Slice the carrots diagonally ¼ inch thick. Blanch 3 to 4 minutes in lightly salted water until almost tender. Drain and cool with water. Drain well.

Heat a large frying pan and add the butter, oil, garlic, and carrots. Sauté over medium heat, tossing until the carrots become tender, about 5 to 7 minutes. Do not burn the garlic, but a little bit of brown is good! Add the oregano and parsley and toss together one minute. Add the Marsala and cook over high heat until evaporated to a glaze. Sprinkle with Parmesan and salt and pepper. Serve at once.

FRIED MIXED VEGETABLES WITH GARLIC AND LEMON OLIVE OIL

SERVES 8

I dislike overcooked vegetables. No, I don't dislike them, I hate them! Here is a variation on the regular fried mixed-vegetable dish that is common with good Italian chefs in this country. In Italy it would be overcooked for sure.

We have added our Lemon Olive Oil, which gives a fine accent to the vegetables.

1½ cups cauliflower florets
1 medium green zucchini, sliced into ¼-inch pieces
1 medium yellow zucchini, sliced into ¼-inch pieces
2 tablespoons olive oil
4 cloves garlic, peeled and sliced
1 cup peeled and sliced yellow onion

1 cup julienned fresh fennel bulb
1 small cored and julienned red sweet bell pepper
Salt and pepper to taste
1 cup coarsely chopped radicchio (page 24)
2 tablespoons Lemon Olive Oil (page 489)

Parboil the cauliflower in lightly salted water until almost tender, about 4 minutes. Remove with a strainer, reserving the boiling water. Rinse the cauliflower in cold water to stop the cooking. Drain well. Blanch both types of zucchini for 1 minute in the same water; drain. Rinse and drain like the cauliflower. Set the parboiled vegetables aside.

Heat a large frying pan and add the 2 tablespoons of plain olive oil, the garlic, onion, julienned fennel, and red bell pepper. Sauté until almost tender, about 5 minutes. Add the reserved vegetables and sauté everything together until tender. Add salt and pepper to taste, the radicchio, and Lemon Olive Oil. Sauté for 30 seconds to make the radicchio collapse.

STUFFED EGGPLANT HALVES

SERVES 4–8, DEPENDING ON HOW YOU WISH TO SERVE. ONE SHOE, CUT IN HALF, WILL EASILY SERVE TWO PEOPLE AS A VEGETABLE COURSE.

The Anatolians probably taught this dish to the Greeks, who in turn taught it to the Romans when Rome invaded Greece and took fine cooks back home as slaves. In any case, I love this sort of thing and it remains popular throughout Italy.

The natural sugar of the eggplant becomes highlighted in this preparation. It is unusually good. Even those who claim they don't like eggplant will enjoy this one. The vegetarians will also be pleased because this dish is very rich and contains no meat whatsoever.

3 ¾-pound eggplants
1 tablespoon salt
3 cloves garlic, crushed
3 tablespoons olive oil
¼ cup thinly sliced celery
½ cup diced yellow onion
3 tablespoons tomato paste
½ cup Chicken Stock (page 116)
1 tablespoon white wine vinegar
1 teaspoon sugar
2 tablespoons chopped parsley
½ cup dry white wine
2 teaspoons pine nuts (toasted in a frying pan until lightly browned)
Salt and pepper to taste

GARNISHES
Chopped parsley
Drizzle of extra virgin olive oil

Trim off the tops of the eggplants and discard. Dice only 1 of the eggplants and place in a bowl. Cut the other 2 eggplants in half lengthwise and dig out the flesh in the center, leaving about a ¼-inch layer of eggplant attached to the skin. Chop the flesh and add to the bowl of diced eggplant. Add the 1 tablespoon of salt to the bowl and toss together well. Place in a colander and allow to drain for 45 minutes.

Heat a large frying pan and brown the 4 eggplant halves and the garlic in 2 tablespoons of the oil (you may have to do this in batches). Remove from the pan and add the remaining 1 tablespoon of oil. Add the celery and onion and sauté until the vegetables are very tender. Rinse the salted eggplant with cold water and drain well. Add to the frying pan and sauté for 5 minutes. Add the remaining ingredients except the salt and pepper to taste. Cover and simmer 20 to 30 minutes until the eggplant is very tender and a thick sauce has formed, stirring often.

Fill the eggplant halves with the mixture and place in an oiled baking dish. Bake in a preheated 375° oven for 25 minutes, or until the eggplant shells collapse and are very tender. Serve warm or cold with the garnish.

DANDELION GREENS

Dandelion greens are similar in flavor to bitter lettuces like escarole or endive. Dandelions are not readily available, but if you are lucky enough to find them in your grocery store or from a farmer, try them. These greens are not the same as those annoying weeds you will find in your backyard. They can be eaten raw in salads or cooked in olive oil and garlic like Braised Endive (page 375).

BRAISED LEEKS

SERVES 4–6

This is a very old vegetable, this leek. It is mentioned several times in the Bible and it was common in ancient Rome. The Italians of every region have been enjoying it ever since.

I delight in braised leeks. Please don't overcook them. Just barely tender is enough. Then, enjoy.

6 leeks (large ones that are at least 1 inch in diameter)	**2 cloves garlic, crushed**
1½ tablespoons olive oil	**½ cup dry white wine Salt and pepper to taste**

Slice the leeks in half lengthwise. Trim off the tops where the white portion begins to turn green. Discard the tops. Trim off the root end, leaving enough of the core so that the leek will still hold together. Rinse well in cold water to remove any sand or dirt in the layers. Drain well.

Heat a large frying pan and add the oil, garlic, and the leeks with the cut side down. Sauté for a few minutes to brown slightly. Do not turn the leeks in the pan. Add the wine and simmer gently, covered, for 7 to 10 minutes or until the leeks are just tender. Add salt and pepper to taste and serve.

CIPOLLINE IN TOMATO AND OIL

SERVES 6-8

I love this dish because it is so rich and sweet just from the natural sugar in the little onions. And yes, if you cannot find the imported cipolline, small white boiling onions will be just fine for this dish. Just be sure that when you buy them they are firm and fresh. Don't overcook them.

1 tablespoon olive oil	¼ cup dry white wine
2½ pounds (about 6 cups) cleaned cipolline (page 374) (peeled but left whole) or small white boiling onions	1 cup Fresh Tomato Sauce Sicilian (page 139)
	⅓ cup extra virgin olive oil

Heat a large frying pan and add the oil and cleaned onions. Sauté for 5 minutes but don't brown too much. Add the wine and fresh tomato sauce and simmer, covered, 20 minutes until the onions are tender. Allow to cool and add the ⅓ cup of extra virgin olive oil. Stir together and marinate at room temperature for at least 1 hour. Serve at room temperature.

BROCCOLI DI RAPA

SERVES 4

Our bartender in Milan was fascinated that we were writing a cookbook. Marino is his name. He had to get in on the act and offered us this recipe. It is typical of the cooking of Naples, his home.

If you cannot find broccoli rabe (broccoli di rapa in Italian) in your Italian produce section go to Chinatown and buy Chinese broccoli. You will get very similar results, and very good results indeed.

1 **pound broccoli rabe**	1 **tablespoon small**
3 **tablespoons olive oil**	**capers, drained**
2 **cloves garlic**	**Pinch of red pepper**
¼ **cup sliced pitted**	**flakes**
black olives,	**Salt to taste**
California style	
¼ **cup sliced pitted**	
green olives	

Trim off the tough ends of the vegetable near the roots and discard. Bring a large pot of water to a boil. Lightly salt the water and add 1 tablespoon of the oil. Blanch the vegetable for 2 minutes and drain well.

Heat a large frying pan and add the remaining 2 tablespoons of oil, the garlic, and the broccoli rabe. Sauté over high heat for 1 minute and add the remaining ingredients. Cook 2 to 3 minutes more until the stems are just tender (do not overcook).

SWEET AND SOUR CIPOLLINE

SERVES 4–6 AS A SIDE DISH

You may have trouble finding imported cipolline from Italy. Large Italian communities bring them in each fall, but this dish is so good that you may want to serve it more often. I suggest you find small boiling-onions and use them as a substitute. The Italian variety is a little more bitter and thus a tad more flavorful, but in a pinch our American variety will do. This is a great dish, if you like onions.

4 cups cipolline (about 1½ pounds) (page 374), cleaned (peel the small onions but leave them whole)
1 tablespoon olive oil
⅓ cup dry white wine
¼ cup Fresh Tomato Sauce Sicilian (page 139)

1 tablespoon sugar
2 tablespoons white wine vinegar
1 tablespoon chopped parsley
Salt and pepper to taste

Sauté the cipolline in oil for 2 minutes. (Do not brown too much!) Add the wine and simmer gently, covered, for 10 minutes. Add the remaining ingredients, cover, and simmer 5 to 10 minutes or until the onions are just tender.

PAN-ROASTED POTATOES WITH SAGE AND ROSEMARY

SERVES 4–6

Since I love potatoes so much it was great to find this recipe in Bologna. We do not do enough with the potato in this country, so I suggest this delicious recipe.

2 pounds russet
   potatoes, peeled
   and cut into ¾-
   inch-thick cubes
   (Keep the potatoes
   in lightly salted
   water to prevent
   browning. Drain
   very well before
   cooking. Pat dry
   with paper towels.)

2 tablespoons olive oil
2 cloves garlic, peeled
   and thinly sliced
2 tablespoons chopped
   fresh sage
1 tablespoon fresh
   rosemary needles
Salt and pepper to
   taste

Preheat the oven to 375°. Heat a large ovenproof frying pan and add the potatoes and oil. Brown the potatoes over medium heat for 5 minutes, tossing regularly. Add the garlic and fresh herbs. Toss together and place the whole pan in the oven, uncovered. Roast for about 15 minutes or until the potatoes are tender. Toss a few times while in the oven. (Remember the handle is hot!) Add salt and pepper to taste.

BELL PEPPERS CARAMELIZED

SERVES 4 AS AN ANTIPASTO WITH BREAD

This appears so simple that you cannot believe it will really make a change in your Italian kitchen. Trust us. The caramelizing of the peppers really toasts the sugar in them, and the result is delicious, just delicious.

1 large red bell
   pepper
1 large green bell
   pepper
1 large yellow pepper

3 tablespoons olive oil
1 teaspoon sugar
¼ cup dry white wine
Salt and pepper to
   taste

Core and cut the peppers into 1-inch-wide strips. Heat a large frying pan and add the olive oil and the peppers. Sauté over medium-low heat, covered, for 20 minutes. Toss the peppers often while cooking. Sprinkle the peppers with the sugar and add the wine. Continue to sauté, covered, 5 minutes more until the peppers are very tender and caramelized. The peppers should look very brown but not burned. Add salt and pepper to taste.

ARTICHOKES IN OIL

SERVES 6

This method of cooking artichokes is common all over Northern Italy. I cannot improve on it, except to say that generally an artichoke is overcooked in Italy, at least by American standards. So watch this glorious thistle while cooking and do not overdo it. The olive oil and the artichoke seem to know each other well, and besides, you are avoiding all of that butter that we usually put on the vegetable.

6 medium artichokes Lemons to prevent cleaned artichokes from discoloring	½ cup extra virgin olive oil Salt and pepper to taste

Clean the artichokes using the method in the recipe Artichokes, Jewish Style (page 390) and rub with lemon juice. Place the cleaned artichokes in a steamer and steam 35 to 45 minutes until the artichokes are very tender when pierced with a knife. Remove to a medium-size bowl and add the oil and salt and pepper to taste. Gently toss together and allow the artichokes to cool in the oil. Arrange the artichokes on a platter and pour the oil over the top.

SWEET BELL PEPPER HALVES

SERVES 6–8

Sweet bell peppers make a wonderful vegetable course, although in America we usually use them only in cooking, chopped up in some other dish. Italy loves the sweet pepper and it is not uncommon to see an entire course of sweet peppers served at a formal dinner. I like this version. Craig is to be credited for this one. It is typical of Italy but Craig always has his own special touch.

3 small red bell peppers
3 small yellow bell peppers
2 tablespoons butter, melted
2 tablespoons olive oil
2 cloves garlic, crushed
½ cup bread crumbs
½ teaspoon sugar
1 tablespoon chopped parsley
¼ pound provolone cheese (page 469), grated
¼ cup freshly grated Parmesan cheese (page 465)
Salt and pepper to taste

Toast the peppers over an open flame on an asador grill (page 35) until charred all over. You can also toast them under a broiler in the oven just until they begin to blister. Place in a baking pan and bake in a preheated 350° oven for 20 minutes. Remove the pan from the oven and place a clean heavy kitchen towel over the peppers in the pan. Allow the peppers to cool under the towel. Cut the peppers in half lengthwise and remove the core and seeds. Scrape the charred skin off the peppers with a table knife and discard. Place the pepper halves in a greased baking dish with the cut side up.

Mix the remaining ingredients in a bowl and divide the mixture among the pepper halves in the dish. Bake in a preheated 350° oven for about 20 minutes or until lightly browned and hot throughout.

BITTER GREENS

Leafy vegetables like kale, collards, and Swiss chard can seen in markets all over Italy. They are readily available in our country and should be eaten more often. Coarsely chopped bitter greens are delicious in soups or simply sautéed in olive oil and garlic. A drizzle of balsamic vinegar (page 495) on cooked greens is terrific. If you don't overcook this type of vegetable you will enjoy the bright flavors and texture.

You might even hit the Chinese markets to find Chinese broccoli. It would work well in this recipe.

ARTICHOKES, JEWISH STYLE
SERVES 6

This recipe actually goes back to the Jewish Ghetto in Rome. There are several restaurants in the old ghetto that still serve these, though the recipe varies from place to place. This is a fine version of a classic and ancient dish.

6 medium artichokes,   5 tablespoons olive oil
    cleaned (see below)   Salt to taste
Lemons to prevent   Lemon juice to taste
    cleaned artichokes
    from discoloring

CLEANING AN ARTICHOKE

Break off the first two or three rows of the lower outer leaves. Using a paring knife, cut off the top half of the remaining leaves. Do this by holding the artichoke on its side, cutting down on an angle away from the stem. Turn the choke as you cut until the purple thistle center is exposed. Using a grapefruit spoon, remove the purple center, exposing the meaty artichoke bottom. Cut off the stem, leaving about an inch. Trim off the tough exterior skin of the stem. Rub the whole choke with fresh lemon juice to prevent it from discoloring. The artichokes are now ready to cook in a number of ways.

Trim the stems off the cleaned artichokes so that they will sit flat. Heat a large frying pan and add 2 tablespoons of the oil. Brown the artichokes on both sides with the lid on. Add ½ cup of water and cover and cook gently over low heat for 25 minutes. Turn the artichokes halfway through the cooking time. The artichokes should be tender when a knife is inserted in the center. If the pan begins to dry out, add a little more water to the pan during cooking. Remove the artichokes and drain any liquid left in the pan.

Heat the pan again and add the remaining 3 tablespoons of oil. Return the artichokes to the pan and fry until browned and a little crispy on both sides. Serve with salt to taste and a squeeze of lemon juice.

SPINACH FRITTERS

MAKES 1½ DOZEN DEPENDING ON SIZE

We enjoyed this one evening as guests of the Bologna family at their fine winery in Asti. I cannot tell you how wonderful it is to come under their care and concern . . . but better you should come to their table.

STEP 1
1 pound spinach,
    washed and
    chopped (about 6
    cups lightly
    packed chopped
    leaves)
1 tablespoon olive oil
¼ cup sliced yellow
    onion

2 green onions, finely
    chopped
6 tablespoons flour
2 eggs, beaten
1 teaspoon baking
    powder
    Salt and pepper to
    taste

STEP 2
1 tablespoon finely
    chopped parsley

Prepare the spinach. Heat a medium-size frying pan and add the oil and onion. Sauté until clear but not browned. Add the spinach and sauté 5 minutes until very limp and no more liquid remains. Cool completely.

Blend all the ingredients for Step 2 and stir into the spinach mixture. Use 2 tablespoons to form a patty. Push it out of the spoon and flatten it a bit in the hot oil. Pan-fry 1 to 2 minutes on each side until golden brown. Do not get the oil too hot or it will burn.

Drain on paper towels and serve.

PEPPERS PIEDMONT

SERVE 2–4 AS A SIDE DISH

We discovered this great recipe while in the household and care of the Bologna family in Asti. No, they have nothing to do with the region called Bologna as they are Piedmontese. The winery that they run is just wonderful and the food that they serve their guests is beautiful.

We tasted a dish very close to this version while enjoying their hospitality one night in Asti. You must try this!

1 large sweet red bell pepper
1 large sweet yellow bell pepper
⅓ cup olive oil
4 anchovy fillets (packed in oil), minced
2 cloves garlic, crushed
¼ cup fine bread crumbs
¼ cup water (you may need a bit more)
Salt and pepper to taste

GARNISHES
Chopped parsley
Extra virgin olive oil

Toast the peppers over an open flame on an asador grill (page 35) until charred all over. Place in a baking pan and bake in a preheated 350° oven for 20 minutes. Remove the pan from the oven and place a heavy kitchen towel on top of the peppers in the pan. Allow the peppers to cool under the towel. Cut the peppers into quarters lengthwise and remove the core and seeds. Scrape the charred skin off the peppers using the back of a table knife. Lay the pepper strips out on a nonstick sheet pan with the outside down.

Heat a small frying pan and add the oil, anchovies, and garlic. Sauté for 15 seconds and add the bread crumbs. Sauté 1 minute more and remove to a bowl to cool. Gradually stir in the water and add salt and pepper to taste. You should have a thin loose bread-crumb mixture. Spread onto the pepper quarters and heat in a 350° oven for 10 to 15 minutes. Serve warm with a sprinkle of parsley and a drizzle of olive oil.

COLD SPINACH BALLS

In the fanciest food shops in Italy or just at a little produce stall you can purchase fresh spinach that has already been cooked. The cooked spinach has been drained of excess water and shaped into the size of a tennis ball or smaller. You simply buy whatever you need and use it in any dish you like. In the Northern regions it is common to season the cold or room-temperature balls with extra virgin olive oil, vinegar, or lemon juice, and salt and pepper to taste. You might consider serving a nice platter of cooked spinach balls on your next buffet and allow your guests to season their own at the table. Simple and delicious.

Purchase fresh spinach, clean it, trim off the stems, and sauté it lightly in a bit of olive oil. When cool, form into small balls and gently squeeze out the excess water. Cover the balls with plastic wrap and chill until dinner.

FRIED MARINATED POTATOES

SERVES 4–6

I rarely eat fried potatoes, though I do enjoy them. I just don't allow myself that much fat.

Having read that, you are now going to glance at the following recipe and you are going to scream at me! We are going to fry these potato chunks in a blend of freshly rendered pork fat and olive oil. The flavor is out of this world . . . and so is the cholesterol count. But you must try these once in a while. They are some of the best fried potatoes that I have ever eaten.

You might substitute peanut oil for the freshly rendered lard, but the flavor will not be as bright.

The recipe comes from a joint in Modena, a joint where old men gather to play bocce ball. The dining room is late peasant and the kitchen is about the same. The food is basic but very good and not at all expensive. The place is called Caffè Roberta and it is best to go with a friend who speaks fluent Italian. I do not recall seeing a printed menu in the place.

2 pounds russet
potatoes
¼ cup balsamic
vinegar (page
495)
3 cloves garlic,
crushed
1½ tablespoons fresh
rosemary needles
Salt and pepper to
taste
¼ cup olive oil

THE FRYING OIL
2 cups olive oil

1½ cups fresh
rendered pork
fat (Buy a couple
of pounds of
fresh pork fat
from your
butcher and
cook it to melt it
down. Simply
cut the fat into
strips and gently
pan-fry in a
large black
frying pan over
low heat until
the fat is
rendered and the
remains are
golden and
crisp.)

Peel the potatoes and quarter them lengthwise. Cut into 1-inch chunks and place in a bowl. Add the vinegar, garlic, rosemary, salt and pepper, and the ¼ cup oil. Toss together and marinate 2 hours. Drain the potatoes very well and discard the marinade.

Heat the oil and rendered pork fat to 375°. Fry the potatoes in batches until golden brown. Drain on paper towels and place on a fine wire cooling rack inside a baking pan. Bake in a preheated oven, uncovered, at 375° for 7 to 10 minutes or until the potatoes are tender. Add salt to taste.

ARTICHOKES AND FRIED RADICCHIO

SERVES 4–6

This is a fine blend of vegetables that Craig came up with when he fell in love with fried radicchio in Italy. While we did not see this very dish in any of the Italian regions that we visited, it does seem to me that this is something that a lot of grandmas know about. At least I hope that they have tried it.

5 medium artichokes
(about 2¾
pounds)
Lemons to prevent
cleaned artichokes
from discoloring
3 tablespoons olive oil
2 cloves garlic,
chopped
1 cup peeled and
sliced yellow
onion
½ cup dry white wine

½ cup Chicken Stock
(page 116)
2 cups coarsely
chopped radicchio
(page 24)
2 tablespoons chopped
parsley

THE DRESSING
⅓ cup extra virgin
olive oil
Salt and pepper to
taste

Clean the artichokes as in the recipe for Artichokes and Caponata (page 65) and rub with lemon juice.

Slice the cleaned artichokes lengthwise ¼ inch thick. Toss with a little more lemon juice to prevent browning. Heat a large frying pan and add the oil, garlic, onion, and sliced artichokes. Sauté for 5 minutes and add the wine and Chicken Stock. Cover and simmer gently 15 to 20 minutes, tossing occasionally, until just tender. Add the radicchio and parsley and toss together over high heat less than 1 minute until the radicchio collapses. Remove to a bowl to cool.

Mix the olive oil and salt and pepper to taste for the dressing and toss with the artichoke mixture.

BEANS

Beans are wonderful things. Some beans belong to the Americas and are now shared with other cultures around the world, the most common being the navy bean, kidney bean, lima bean, and string bean.

It is hard to imagine our early colonial culture getting along without the baked-bean pot, or the Latin Americans without their pinto beans, or the Cubans without their black beans. And Italians without their beans in pasta.

In the region of Tuscany you will find wonderful bean dishes. As a matter of fact, the Tuscans are called "The Bean Eaters," and this regional affection seems to have been going on for a long time. However, you will find the popularity of the bean is common throughout the North. South of Rome pasta is the preferred starch, while in the North pasta must compete with beans and rice.

We enjoyed so many legume dishes in the North, and most were made with Italian brown beans, called *borlotti*. We found them both dried and fresh, and the public markets were absolutely filled with fresh beans during the fall. When they are purchased whole in the pod, there is a bit of work in preparing these, but they are terribly popular in soups and stews, cooked with pasta and even with tripe.

When I returned to this country I thought I would have no trouble finding this bean. I began to inquire and got nowhere with my description of "the regular Italian popular brown bean." I found Italian stores that did not know what I was talking about. Finally, I talked to Patty, my wife. She is a serious Italian food lover. "Borlotti beans? In this country they are called cranberry beans." After some further research I realized that she was right. It all sounded too simple to me, but cranberry beans they are. While they are generally beige striped with red lines when raw, the colors even out in cooking and the final dish is brown.

I like all of these following dishes but I am partial to Pasta e Fagioli, White Beans and Tuna, and Beans in a Flask.

In addition to the recipes in this chapter you may also wish to see:

Cannellini Bean Salad (page 98)
Tripe with Cranberry Beans (page 363)

PASTA E FAGIOLI

SERVES 6–8

A dish of pasta and beans is hearty, to say the least. It is very simple food but also comforting and sustaining. There are as many variations on this dish as there are grandmas in Italy.

2 cups cranberry beans (page 401)
6 cups cold water
½ cup dry white wine
2 cups Beef Stock (page 115)
4½ cups Chicken Stock (page 116)
3 cloves garlic, crushed
1 tablespoon tomato paste
2 tablespoons chopped parsley

1 cup tubetti pasta (page 152), not cooked!
⅓ cup grated Parmesan cheese

GARNISHES
Chopped parsley
Extra virgin olive oil
Grated Parmesan cheese

Place the beans and the cold water in a 6-quart pot and bring to a boil. Cover the pot and turn off the heat (leave the pot covered on the very burner you used). Allow to stand 1 hour. Drain the beans and return to the pot. Add the wine and the Beef and Chicken Stock, and bring to a boil, cover, and simmer gently for 30 minutes. Strain out half the beans and puree. Return the pureed beans to the pot. Add the garlic, tomato paste, parsley, and the raw tubetti pasta and simmer gently, uncovered, for 25 to 30 minutes or until the pasta is very tender and the soup is thick. Stir the soup regularly to prevent the pasta from sticking to the bottom of the pot. Stir in the ⅓ cup of Parmesan cheese. Garnish with chopped parsley, a drizzle of extra virgin olive oil, and grated Parmesan cheese.

PASTA E FAGIOLI FRIED

MAKES 8 PATTIES

This is a very clever way to use up leftovers. We had this dish in a very tiny restaurant in Modena, and even though it was indeed made of leftovers, we paid plenty for our lunch! I very much enjoy this kind of peasant cooking.

2 cups Pasta e Fagioli (page 403) (use leftovers that are cold from the refrigerator)	**4 tablespoons flour Additional flour for dredging Olive oil for pan-frying**

Mix the Pasta e Fagioli and 4 tablespoons flour together in a small bowl. Form into patties 2½ inches in diameter by ¼ inch thick. Roll the patties in flour and pan-fry in a nonstick frying pan with a little olive oil until nicely browned on both sides. Remove and drain on paper towels.

VARIATION: Serve the fried patties with Fresh Tomato Sauce Sicilian (page 139) ladled over the top.

BEANS IN A FLASK

SERVES 4 AS A SIDE DISH

Some old peasant dishes are so colorful that you feel you need to try the process right away and worry about the flavor later. Well, this one is quaint and Old World, and the flavor is bright and heavy at the same time.

In the old days a wine flask—what we would call a Chianti bottle—was filled with beans and herbs and stock and oil . . . and then placed in the dying embers of the fire before you went to bed. In the morning, beans for breakfast, lunch, or dinner.

The wine bottles in the old days must have been much tougher than ours as I am not convinced that you should place such a bottle in the embers of a romantic fire. Besides, I doubt that you have a dying fire in your apartment just before going to bed. Better you should use a water bath on the top of the stove.

Carlo Middione, author of The Foods of Southern Italy *and chef/owner of San Francisco's terrific restaurant Vivande, serves this dish at catering parties. It is great fun to dump cooked beans from a wine bottle onto the plates of your guests. Some dishes are just plain fun. This is such a dish. Craig suggested an old-fashioned milk bottle for this dish rather than the Chianti bottle. The neck of the old milk bottle is much wider than the wine bottle's and you will find serving to be much easier. Find these real milk bottles in junky antique stores anywhere in the country. Worth the search and worth the dish!*

1 1-quart old-fashioned glass milk bottle or heavy glass wine carafe (buy a heavy one from Italy and avoid the lighter versions from the Orient found in import houses) or a 750 ml. Chianti bottle with the decorative basket removed	2 cloves garlic, crushed
	1 teaspoon chopped fresh parsley
	1 teaspoon chopped fresh sage
	½ teaspoon chopped fresh rosemary needles
	½ teaspoon salt
	½ teaspoon freshly ground black pepper
	2 tablespoons extra virgin olive oil
1 cup northern white beans	

Place the beans in a bowl and cover with 4 cups cold water. Allow the beans to soak overnight. Drain the soaked beans and add to the bottle in layers with the garlic, the herbs, and the salt and pepper. Tap the bottle on the counter a few times to make the beans settle evenly in the bottle. Add the olive oil and enough cold water so that it is just even with the level of the beans. Place a heavy heat diffuser (page 45) in the bottom of a tall kettle. Or you might make a nest of aluminum foil to hold the bottle. Wad it up a bit and set the bottle firmly in the middle. Anything to keep it off the bottom of the kettle.

Place the bottle on the diffuser or aluminum nest inside the kettle. Fill the kettle with enough water so that it is 1 inch higher than the level of the beans in the bottle. Bring to a boil, reduce the heat, and simmer 1 to 2 hours, or until all is tender. Leave both the bottle and the kettle uncovered. Add hot water to the kettle as the water level lowers but maintain a gentle simmer. Remove the bottle from the kettle. (Careful! This is hot!) Serve the beans at the table by shaking or pouring them out of the bottle into individual servings. Drain off some of the cooking liquid, if you want, to use in soups. Have your guests add salt and pepper to their taste if needed.

Freshly grated Parmesan cheese might be a welcome garnish.

WHITE BEANS AND TUNA

SERVES 6 AS A STARCH COURSE

Fine-quality canned tuna is common in the Italian diet and I am particularly fond of this match.

Prepare a batch of Cannellini Beans for Short Ribs (page 408). You will not need the short ribs, of course. Place the beans on a serving platter while they are still hot and sprinkle with bits of good-quality canned tuna, broken into chunks. This will take a small can or two, depending on how heavy the dish is to be.

If you use tuna canned in water, you might wish to drizzle the dish with some extra virgin olive oil just before serving.

CANNELLINI BEANS FOR
SHORT RIBS

SERVES 6

This is a fine side dish and a good base for almost any kind of red meat dish. I can enjoy these beans as they are, but with a rich, brown gravy I am really content.

1½ cups dry cannellini beans or northern white beans
1 teaspoon salt
2 tablespoons olive oil
4 cloves garlic, crushed
1 medium yellow onion, chopped
1 medium-size ripe tomato, diced

½ cup dry white wine
½ cup Chicken Stock (page 116) or use canned
2 teaspoons fresh rosemary
1 tablespoon tomato paste
Salt and pepper to taste

Place the beans and 4 cups cold water in a 4-quart pot and bring to a boil. Cover, turn off the heat, and allow to stand 1 hour. Do not lift the lid. Drain and return the beans to the pot along with 2½ cups fresh cold water and 1 teaspoon salt. Bring to a boil, cover, and simmer 25 minutes. Drain the beans and return to the pot.

Heat a frying pan and add the oil, garlic, and onion. Sauté until the onion is tender. Add the diced tomato and sauté 3 minutes more. Add to the pot of beans along with the wine, Chicken Stock, rosemary, and tomato paste. Partially cover and simmer gently for 35 minutes until the beans are tender and a sauce has formed. If the beans are tender but the sauce is thin, uncover and boil to reduce the sauce. Salt and pepper to taste. Allow the beans to stand uncovered for 5 minutes.

Serve as a bed for short ribs and other red meat stews.

BEAN SOUP WITH FRIED ESCAROLE
OVER BRUSCHETTA

SERVES 8

This is almost too much of a good thing! When Craig tasted this soup he wanted to go one step further. He always does. So, his addition of the fried escarole and the Bruschetta turns this soup into a meal, I promise.

2½ cups cannellini
    beans or navy
    beans
  6 cups cold water
¼ pound pancetta,
    thinly sliced and
    chopped
  1 medium yellow
    onion, chopped
  2 tablespoon chopped
    parsley
  2 teaspoons chopped
    fresh rosemary
  6 cups Chicken Stock
    (page 116)

Salt and freshly
    ground black
    pepper to taste
2 tablespoons olive oil
4 cloves garlic,
    chopped
½ pound escarole,
    washed and the
    leaves removed
    from the core
8 slices Bruschetta
    (page 261)

Place the beans in a 6-quart pot and add the water. Bring to a boil, cover, and turn off the heat. Allow the beans to stand on the stove for 1 hour. Drain the beans and return them to the pot.

Heat a large frying pan and add the pancetta. Brown until it begins to turn crisp; add the onion, parsley, and rosemary. Sauté until the onion is clear, about 10 minutes. Add to the pot of beans along with the Chicken Stock. Bring to a boil, cover, and simmer gently for 30 minutes or until the beans are just tender. Strain the pot, reserving the stock. Puree half the strained beans in a food processor until smooth with a little of the stock. Return the pureed beans to the pot along with the remaining beans and stock. Heat the pot to a gentle simmer and cook, covered, 15 minutes more, stirring often. Season the soup with salt and pepper to taste.

Heat the frying pan again and add the oil and the garlic, and the escarole leaves. Sauté 3 to 4 minutes or until very tender and limp. To serve, place a slice of Bruschetta in the bottom of a soup bowl and ladle on the soup. Top each serving with some of the fried escarole.

PISAREI

SERVES 6–8

When you experience the hospitality of Rafaella Bologna, of the Braida winery in Asti, get ready for a surprise. This young woman, who is running the fine winery founded by her late father, knows her wine and the history of her Piedmont community to a degree that you would expect from a much older person. I loved being with her, but I could never work as hard as does she.

One night she threw a dinner party for all of us on the television crew, and the young woman who cooked the dinner offered this unusually good dish. Easy to make!

THE THICK SOUP OR SAUCE

- ¾ cup cranberry beans (find in Italian markets)
- 2 cups cold water
- ⅓ cup chopped pancetta (page 23)
- 2 tablespoons olive oil
- 3 cloves garlic, crushed
- ¾ cup diced carrots
- ½ cup chopped celery
- ¾ cup peeled and chopped yellow onion
- ½ cup chopped tomato
- 1½ cups peeled, quartered, and thinly sliced potato
- 2 cups Chicken Stock (page 116)
- 2 tablespoons chopped parsley
- 1 bay leaf
  Salt and pepper to taste

THE DUMPLINGS

- 1 cup fine bread crumbs
- ¾ cup flour
- 1 teaspoon salt
- 1 teaspoon baking powder
- 1 egg, beaten
- ½ cup cold water
  Additional flour for dusting

GARNISHES

Butter to taste
Grated Parmesan cheese

Place the beans in a small saucepan and add 2 cups cold water. Bring to a boil, cover, and turn off the burner. Allow the beans to sit for 1 hour and drain.

Heat a 4- to 6-quart pot and add the pancetta and olive oil. Brown the pancetta and add the garlic, carrots, celery, and onion. Sauté until the onion is clear. Add the remaining ingredients for the sauce, except the salt and pepper, along with the drained beans and bring to a simmer. Cover and simmer gently for 50 minutes. Add salt and pepper to taste.

Combine the dry ingredients for the dumplings in a bowl. Stir in the beaten egg and cold water and knead together to form a smooth dough. Cover the dough and allow to rest 5 minutes.

Cut the dough into 8 equal pieces. Roll each piece of dough out into a snake about ¼ inch thick. Cut the rolls of dough crosswise into pieces about ³/₁₆ inch thick. Place the dumplings on a sheet pan and dust them with flour. Bring a large pot of water to a boil and add salt to taste. Boil the dumplings 3 minutes and drain well.

Add the drained dumplings to the pot of sauce and simmer gently for 20 minutes. Stir gently a couple of times while cooking. Serve in shallow bowls with a pat of butter and grated Parmesan cheese.

MUSHROOMS

People all over Italy are just crazy about mushrooms. On our last visit we were in Turin, Alba, Venice, and Milan . . . all during the height of the mushroom season. Heaven from rotting leaves in the forest!

The varieties celebrated there are numerous. The big Portobello, the Crimini, the tiny long-stemmed brown mushrooms—all are seen in abundance. But the most popular, the most expensive, and certainly the most delicious mushroom is the great porcini.

You can buy dried porcini in America, and Italian restaurants are now using a frozen porcini from Italy. I was suspicious when I first saw the product but it does hold up very well, as long as you cook the porcini before they entirely defrost and become soggy.

The dried porcini, which have a rich and deep flavor, are very expensive. Expect to pay between seventy and one hundred dollars a pound for them in this country. We bought extra-fine quality in Italy for about fifty-five dollars a pound. I know this sounds crazy, but they are worth the price if you are a mushroom lover.

However, a very decent substitute can be found in any Italian market. These are dried mushrooms from South America, and they cost much less than the Italian version, at least a third the price. Those from South America will be labeled as boletus . . . same mushroom variety but with a bit more smoky flavor. They may have a bit more sand in them than the expensive Italian variety, but you can simply rinse them after soaking them. Don't worry about flavor loss since they tend to be stronger in flavor than the more expensive ones. Many of my friends who are Italian chefs and teachers in this country use these fungi from South America, generally Chile.

You must have some dried mushrooms in your Italian kitchen. They work very well in sauces, stews, soups, and so forth.

In addition to the recipes in this chapter you may wish to see:

Spaghetti with Black Truffle Paste (page 198)
Truffle Oil over Pasta (page 170)
Fried Cheese Polenta with Truffle Oil (page 228)

POTATO AND MUSHROOM TIMBALE

MAKES 8 TIMBALES

You will never see mashed potatoes in Italy unless you go to one of those boring American eating houses. The Italians are much more creative with the potato as shown in this delicious recipe. I cannot even remember where we tasted this but we enjoyed it very much. The dried mushrooms certainly tell the potato where he stands!

¼ ounce dried porcini
  (page 415)
¾ cup hot water
1 pound russet
  potatoes
2 tablespoons olive oil
¾ pound fresh
  mushrooms, sliced
  and chopped
1 cup whipping cream
1 egg, beaten
¼ cup freshly grated
  Parmesan cheese
Salt and black
  pepper to taste
2 tablespoons butter,
  melted

Place the dried porcini in a water glass and add the hot
water. Allow to soak for 45 minutes and drain, discarding
the soaking water. Rinse the porcini to be sure it contains
no sand and chop coarsely. Peel the potatoes and slice very
thin, using a mandoline (page 41). Keep the sliced potatoes
in cold water to prevent browning.

Heat a large frying pan and add the oil and the chopped
porcini. Sauté for 2 minutes and add the fresh mushrooms.
Sauté a few minutes until the mushrooms are tender and
there is no liquid in the pan. Drain the sliced potatoes well
and add to the frying pan along with the cream. Cover the
pan and cook over medium-low heat for about 10 minutes,
carefully folding the potatoes in the pan occasionally so that
they cook evenly. When the potatoes are just tender, remove to a bowl and allow to cool completely. Add the
beaten egg, Parmesan cheese, and the salt and pepper to
taste. Fold together until evenly incorporated.

Grease 8 4-ounce timbale molds with the melted butter.
Lightly pack the cooled potato mixture into the buttered
molds and even out the tops. Place the molds in a baking pan
and add enough hot water to the pan to come one quarter of the
way up the sides of the molds. Bake in a preheated 375° oven
for 1 hour.

Remove the molds from the baking pan and allow to cool
enough so that you can handle them. Run the back of a
table knife around the inside edge of each mold and invert
onto serving plates. You may have to tap the molds a bit
to get the timbale to release from the mold.

CREPES WITH PORCINI
AND MUSHROOMS

SERVES 8 AS A VERY RICH AND WONDERFUL PASTA
COURSE OR 4
AS A MAIN DISH

They are crazy for mushrooms in Northern Italy. We tasted this dish, or one close to our version, at a great place that you will find in an alley in Bologna. It is called Leonida, and in this place I think we tasted some of the best food that we had in Italy.

This dish is superbly rich and flavorful, well worth the mild work in preparation.

1 recipe Basic
  Cannelloni Crepes
  (page 207)
¼ ounce dried porcini
  mushrooms (The
  real Italian
  version is very
  expensive. Look
  for a cheaper
  South American
  version in any
  Italian market.)
¾ cup hot water
4 tablespoons butter
¼ cup flour
2 cups hot milk
  Salt to taste
2 teaspoons olive oil
1 clove garlic, crushed
¾ cup sliced and
  chopped *fresh*
  button
  mushrooms

½ pound fresh frozen
  porcini (page
  415), thinly sliced
  (allow to thaw
  just enough so
  that the porcini
  can be sliced)

OR SUBSTITUTE

½ pound large fresh
  brown
  mushrooms
  (Crimini would be
  fine)
1 tablespoon chopped
  parsley
  Salt and pepper to
  taste
¼ cup freshly grated
  Parmesan cheese

Prepare the cannelloni crepes and set aside, covered. Place the dried porcini in a water glass and add the hot water. Allow to soak 45 minutes.

Melt the butter in a small frying pan and stir in the flour. Cook together a few minutes to form a roux; do not brown! Stir the roux into the hot milk and whisk until smooth and lump free. Add salt to taste. Simmer gently, uncovered, for 5 minutes until thickened and smooth. Set aside.

Drain the liquid from the dried porcini and discard. Rinse the soaked porcini and chop coarsely. Heat a medium-size frying pan and add the oil, garlic, and chopped soaked porcini. Sauté for 1 minute but don't burn. Add the button mushrooms, sliced fresh porcini or brown mushrooms, and parsley and sauté 2 minutes. Add salt and pepper to taste.

Stir in ¾ cup of the prepared cream sauce to the mushroom mixture and allow to cool. Stir the Parmesan cheese into the remaining cream sauce.

Lightly oil the inside of 4 single-serving oblong baking dishes (approximately 8 × 5 inches). Spread 8 of the prepared crepes out on the counter and divide the porcini mixture evenly in the center of each crepe. Fold the crepe around the filling to form a rectangular bundle about 3⅓ × 2 inches. Place 2 of the bundles seam side down in each oiled baking dish. Top each with the remaining sauce and cheese mixture. Bake at 350° for 20 minutes or until hot and bubbly.

COLD MUSHROOMS CREAMED

MAKES ABOUT 4 CUPS

This dish is used in Milan as a salad, a side dish, a sandwich filling. You can use any kind of mushrooms that you have on hand, as long as they are not canned.

1½ pounds mushrooms, sliced ⅛ inch thick	**THE DRESSING**
	¼ cup mayonaisse
	¼ cup sour cream
2 tablespoons olive oil	Salt and freshly ground black pepper to taste
	1 tablespoon chopped parsley

Sauté the mushrooms in the olive oil over high heat a few minutes until just tender. Do not brown too much!

Drain well and cool. (Use the juice in another dish.)

Mix the dressing and toss with the mushrooms. Refrigerate 1 hour.

MUSHROOM SOUP

SERVES 4–6

Mushroom soup is a joy to most of us. To the Italians it is a necessity.

We found something close to this version in a restaurant in Florence, a good place called the White Boar. The soup is a bit unusual as the chef uses potatoes rather than a roux for thickening. Very good!

½ ounce dried porcini
   (page 415)
¾ cup hot water
2 pounds russet
   potatoes
2 tablespoons olive oil
2 cloves garlic,
   crushed
1 pound fresh
   mushrooms,
   thinly sliced
3 cups Chicken Stock
   (page 116)

½ cup dry white wine
1 tablespoon chopped
   parsley
1 teaspoon mushroom
   powder (grind up
   a few additional
   pieces of dried
   porcini in an
   electric spice
   grinder)
Salt and pepper to
   taste

Place the porcini in a water glass and add the hot water. Allow to soak for 45 minutes. Drain the soaked mushrooms, reserving the liquid. Rinse the porcini to be sure they have no sand. Chop the porcini and set aside.

Boil the potatoes with the skin on until they are tender when pierced with a knife, about 35 to 40 minutes. Drain the potatoes and allow to cool. Peel the cooked potatoes and run them through a ricer into a bowl. Set aside.

Heat a large frying pan and add the oil, garlic, and porcini. Sauté for 1 minute and add the sliced mushrooms and sauté until the mushrooms are just tender.

Remove the sautéed mushrooms to a 4-quart pot. Pour the reserved porcini liquid through a fine strainer into the pot. Add the riced potatoes and the remaining ingredients except the salt and pepper to taste. Bring the pot to a boil, cover, and simmer 1 hour. Add salt and pepper to taste. This soup is richer and more flavorful the next day!

GRILLED PORCINI OR LARGE MUSHROOMS

It is common in Italy to simply grill a large mushroom and serve it. Talk about a rich steak!

You can do this very easily if you purchase large Portobello mushrooms. Trim off the stems and place the large caps on a hot oiled grill. Use regular olive oil on the grill and remember a grill (page 35) is not a griddle. Grill them just as you would a good steak, but not as long, of course. If you turn the mushrooms once during cooking, it should take about 3 minutes on each side on a hot grill, no more. You might even decide to cook them on the charcoal barbecue grill, but be very careful not to overcook.

I serve mine on a plate and then drizzle a bit of Lemon Olive Oil (page 489) on the top of each. A chopped parsley garnish should be enough. This is very fine eating!

MUSHROOMS AND MARSALA

This is so simple that you will need only a description of the method.

Prepare the fresh mushrooms, any variety that you wish, by cutting off the stems and brushing the fungi clean with a damp towel. Don't ever wash mushrooms as they will absorb tremendous amounts of water.

Heat a frying pan and add a bit of olive oil and chopped garlic. Sauté the mushroom caps until done to taste and then throw in a light splash of dry Marsala. Toss for a moment. Add salt and pepper to taste. Serve with a parsley garnish if you wish.

Do not overcook the mushrooms as you will get a big puddle of juice. Further, remember that the Marsala might flame up a bit if the pan is really hot. Don't worry about it. Just keep the kids out of the kitchen during the preparation of this dish.

The Italian Truffle

One of the great treasures of the food world is to be found in Italy, and only in Italy. The white truffle, *tartufo bianco,* grows in the Piedmont region of the North, and it is shipped throughout the world . . . if you are willing to pay enough.

There are basically two kinds of truffles, one black and the other white—or actually a light tan color. Italy grows both. France has only the black.

The truffle is not really a true mushroom but rather a tuber. Nevertheless, it is classified as a form of fungus so we have included it in this section. The tuber grows on the roots of the trees in the Piedmont forests. The hunter goes into the woods with trained dogs and the dogs sniff out the truffles and dig them up. The French have used pigs, or trained boars, in the past but the Italians have always preferred dogs, usually females, because the dog is so much more "dolce," sweeter, than an old boar.

We had an opportunity to go truffle hunting with Teresio Vaschetto, the president of the truffle hunters of the Piedmont region. What an experience! I had never even eaten a white truffle, let alone hunted one. Out came the dogs, dogs who are kept on a very slim diet during the hunting season, a diet so slim that they will work like crazy for a tiny crust of bread. No, it is not unkind, and yes, the truffle hunter loves and cares for his dogs. It is actually a very beautiful thing to watch.

Off we went into the forest with the dogs jumping about and sniffing the ground and the bushes. Once they find the scent they begin to dig, and the truffle hunter assists with a special hunting and walking stick. It is a team effort as the two of them go after the tuber. If the hunter is not very careful the dog will find the truffle and eat it himself! Sometimes there is a great deal of work involved in finding these delicacies as they may be four or five feet down in the soil.

Once a truffle is located, the hunter begins to smell the soil, just as the dog is doing. When the treasure is unearthed, and I will never forget this, ever, the perfume of the truffle explodes into the air. I was six feet away from the digging and I was astounded at the potency of this little child of the soil, not much bigger than a filbert. The aroma is sort of halfway between that of a dark and earthy mushroom and Gorgonzola cheese. As a matter of fact, the dogs are taught to hunt by sniffing out Gorgonzola that has been hidden from them in the earth.

If all of this sounds very romantic, get ready for the meal. Craig found three truffles, along with the assistance of Mr. Vaschetto, of course, and we took them to a favorite restaurant in Parma where Craig and the chef cooked a batch of creamy risotto . . . and then shaved the truffles over the top. I will never forget that dish.

White truffles can be purchased canned and even frozen, but expect to pay a fortune. I saw one truffle in Milan about the size of a baseball, and it sold for seven hundred dollars. No, I did not buy it, but I did stand there and smell it for a few minutes.

We have included recipes in this section for both the white and black truffles. There, aren't you relieved?

You will also note our use of truffle oil on pasta and polenta. The oil is a blend of olive oil and the essence of the white truffle and can be found in any large Italian market. You will not need much as it is to be used like a perfume on your food, not as a cooking oil.

TAGLIOLINI WITH BUTTER AND WHITE TRUFFLES

This is simple to prepare but very costly because of the white truffles.

Cook the fresh tagliolini in fresh Chicken Stock (page 116), not in water. Add a bit of salt to the stock. Drain, reserving the stock for another use, and toss the pasta with a bit of butter. Place the pasta on separate serving plates and grate a bit of white truffle over each.

You will not need cheese or parsley—none of the usual garnishes. Let the truffle speak for itself.

RISOTTO WITH WHITE TRUFFLES

This is the best way to show off your fresh white truffle, or your canned one, for that matter. The season for white truffles is from October through the first week or so of December. You can buy fresh white Italian truffles in any American city that has a large Italian community such as Boston, New York, Philadelphia, San Francisco, or Seattle.

Prepare a batch of Basic Risotto (page 239) and place on individual serving dishes. Shave the white truffle over the top. Use a truffle shaver (page 36) for this or a potato peeler.

This is a wonderful celebration of that one food product that no one else in the world seems to have ... just the peoples of Piedmont. No wonder they are so arrogant and proud about the quality of their food.

FISH AND SEAFOOD

The pride that Italians feel when it comes to discussing the seafood in their own regions is certainly understandable. Here in America we talk about seafood from the Pacific or the Atlantic. In Italy you can talk about special fish that comes from the Adriatic on the eastern shores or the Ionian, which is between the heel and the toe of the Great Boot. If you live in Liguria, where Genoa is to be found, then you know that the Ligurian sea has special creatures that delight. The west side of the country fishes in the Tyrrhenian Sea, and to the south one dines from the Mediterranean. Each region claims that its sea is the best. Good old Italian pride even when it comes to fishing.

If you are a seafood lover, then you understand one of the glorious things about this long and narrow country that is entirely surrounded by water except at the top of the boot where it connects to the rest of Europe. No matter where you live in Italy you are just a short drive from one of the several seas. Therefore every city market has seafood stands offering fresh and varied delicacies.

It is not hard for me to tell you which region I prefer when it comes to fish and seafood. It is the Veneto, and the city is Venice. The varieties that come in from the Adriatic just amaze me; they are so very different from those fish that we see on the West Coast of America. The eel, the live baby crabs for soup, the squid everywhere, the many varieties of shrimp, sea snails, several kinds of fresh flatfish . . . all of these really excite me.

I must not forget the cats. They are respected in this city of islands because they keep the place free of any kind of rodents. So when you go to the fish market behind the Rialto Bridge, be prepared to see several cats sitting under the display tables quietly eating first-class seafood. No, it will not be a leftover, or something mistakenly dropped to the wet stone floor. It will be a whole but small delicacy offered by the fishmonger to the local cats out of appreciation. Hey, this is Venice!

In this section I want you to be sure to try Fulvia's Salmon Baked in Foil. The Seafood Couscous from Sicily is wonderful and Craig's Steamed Clams with Vermouth and Cream will tickle everyone.

When buying fresh fish remember that the eyes should appear clear and bright, the flesh firm, the gills bright pink, and the fish should not smell "fishy." Go ahead and pick the thing up and check it over. The fishmonger will understand that you are serious. The idea of buying a fish in Italy without checking it over first would never occur to anyone in any of the regions.

CIOPPINO

SERVES 4–6

This wonderful fish stew is heavy with fresh tomato sauce and it is particularly popular in the Southern regions. In Venice a fish soup would have little tomato sauce in it but in Naples the tomato hand is heavy. I like both varieties, though this one is closer to a stew than a soup. The sauce that is left over after this dish is celebrated is just wonderful.

1 pound clams
    (Manila clams
    are best)
1½ pounds mussels
2 tablespoons olive
    oil
4 cloves garlic,
    peeled and sliced
½ cup dry vermouth
½ cup Chicken Stock
    (page 116)
½ cup bottled clam
    juice
4 tablespoons butter

¼ cup chopped
    parsley
1½ cups Fresh Tomato
    Sauce Sicilian
    (page 139)
1½ pounds fresh cod
    fillets, cut into 1-
    inch pieces
1 pound medium
    shrimp, peeled
Salt and pepper to
    taste (you may
    not need salt)

Rinse the clams and place in a bowl. Cover with plenty of cold water and allow to stand for 1 hour. Drain the clams. Remove the fuzzy beards from the mussels and discard. Cover with plenty of cold water and allow to stand for 1 hour. Rinse the mussels well and drain.

Heat a 6- to 8-quart pot and add 1 tablespoon of the oil and 2 cloves of the garlic. Sauté for 10 seconds and add the drained clams. Add ¼ cup of the vermouth and cover and simmer about 5 to 7 minutes until the clams just open. Strain the clams, reserving the nectar. Set the clams aside, loosely covered, to cool but not dry out.

Cook the mussels in the same pot, using the remaining oil, garlic, and vermouth. The mussels will take a little less time to cook. Strain and reserve the same as the clams.

Return the pot to the burner along with both reserved nectars and add the Chicken Stock, clam juice, butter, parsley, and fresh tomato sauce. Bring to a boil and simmer, uncovered, for 3 minutes to reduce a bit. Add the cod and simmer 1 minute. Add the shrimp and simmer 2 minutes more. Add the reserved clams and mussels in their shells and heat through. Add salt and pepper to taste and serve in bowls.

CIOPPINO OVER BRUSCHETTA

SERVES 4–6

Things go better with Bruschetta! That is the theme of the peasant cook in Italy. Rich soups of any kind are just great over garlic toast. Cioppino is no exception.

Prepare 4–6 slices Bruschetta (page 261) and place in large shallow bowls. Serve Cioppino (page 430) over the toasted bread.

CREAMED BACCALÀ OVER POLENTA CROSTINI

SERVES 6–8

The love of salted fish is an acquired taste, I will admit. However, this creamed dish is very typical of Venice and the Veneto region, and I think it is worth your try. It is very rich and if you are careful to drain the baccalà several times while you are refreshing it, the dish will not be too strong or salty.

    Do not expect a good dish if you buy cheap baccalà. Talk to a good Italian merchant and tell him what you are doing. He will be your guide.

¾ pound baccalà (page 21) (Rinse the cod several times in cold water and place in a medium-size bowl. Cover with plenty of cold water and allow to soak 24 hours. Refresh the cold water several times while soaking.)
1 tablespoon olive oil
2 cloves garlic, crushed

½ cup thinly sliced yellow onion
¼ cup dry vermouth
¼ cup Chicken Stock (page 116)
½ cup half-and-half
2 tablespoons butter
4 tablespoons flour
Salt and pepper to taste
1 recipe Hard Polenta (page 225)

GARNISH
Chopped parsley

Drain the soaked cod and place in a medium saucepan. Add fresh cold water to cover and simmer gently for 10 minutes until tender. Drain and allow the fish to cool. Debone and flake the fish; set aside covered.

Return the pot to the burner and heat the oil. Add the garlic and onion and sauté until the onion is clear. Add the vermouth and Chicken Stock and simmer gently for 1 minute. Add the half-and-half and set aside on a gentle simmer.

Melt the butter in a small frying pan and add the flour. Cook together over low heat for a few minutes to form a roux. Do not brown! Whisk the roux into the hot liquid and stir and simmer until smooth and thickened, about 3 minutes. Add the flaked fish and simmer gently for 2 minutes more. Add salt and pepper to taste.

Serve over the pan-fried polenta slices, and garnish with the parsley.

GRILLED FISH WITH
LEMON OLIVE OIL

Grilled fish is popular all over Italy. Fresh sole on the grill became a favorite during our several trips to Venice.

Please note that we are not talking about a griddle, which is flat, but rather a grill, which will leave dark lines on the fish. The grill is explained on page 35.

Lemon Olive Oil enhances the flavor of just about any fish.

Rub fish fillets or steaks (salmon, snapper, swordfish) with salt and pepper to taste. Rub the fish with Lemon Olive Oil (page 489) on both sides. Grill over high heat a few minutes on each side to taste. Do not overcook. Serve with chopped parsley and additional Lemon Olive Oil drizzled on top of the fish.

STEAMED MUSSELS WITH
BAGNA CAUDA SAUCE

SERVES 4–6 AS AN APPETIZER

I love mussels, and the blending of flavors offered by the mussels and the anchovy sauce is quite profound. No, we did not see this in Italy but it is a fine dish nevertheless.

2 pounds mussels (the Penn Cove type is best)
1 tablespoon olive oil
¼ cup dry white wine
¼ cup Bagna Cauda (page 78), warm

Rinse the mussels well in cold water and remove the fuzzy beards. Just pull them off using a kitchen towel. Drain well. Heat a 6- to 8-quart pot and add the oil, mussels, and wine. Cover and simmer 5 minutes or until the mussels open. Strain the mussels and reserve the broth for another dish.

Immediately return the strained mussels to a large hot frying pan and add the Bagna Cauda. Toss together over medium-high heat until the Bagna Cauda coats all of the mussels, about 1 minute.

SCAPECE

SERVES 6–8 AS AN APPETIZER

This bit is somewhat unusual. What you have here is a fried fish pickled in vinegar and saffron. It comes from the Abruzzi region, the only region in Italy where saffron grows. The flavors are somewhat startling, but very delicious. You should try this one.

THE MARINADE
1 cup white wine vinegar
2 cloves garlic, peeled and sliced
1 cup peeled and sliced yellow onions
Pinch saffron
½ cup water
2 tablespoons fresh lemon juice

FOR FRYING
1½ pounds fresh cod fillets, boneless and skinless
Salt and pepper to taste
1 cup flour
2–3 cups olive oil for frying

Combine the ingredients for the marinade in a small saucepan and bring to a boil. Simmer, uncovered, for 2 minutes and remove to a medium-size bowl to cool.

Cut the fish crosswise into 1½-inch pieces. Season the fish lightly with salt and pepper to taste. Dredge the fish in the flour and pat off the excess flour. Fry the fish in about 1 inch of olive oil at 375° until golden brown on all sides (an electric frying pan works great for this). Remove to paper towels to drain.

Add the fried fish to the marinade and carefully toss together. Cover and refrigerate for several hours or overnight. Drain and discard the marinade. Serve garnished with lettuce leaves, sliced red onions, and capers.

BACCALÀ SALAD

Serves 6

Too much of a good thing is too much of a good thing! I had never had a salad made with this basic fish commodity of Italy until I ate at the Piccola Venezia restaurant in Boston. This is just a wonderful dish but you must remember to be patient and refresh the baccalà properly. I was amazed at what the mama can do with baccalà at this particular old Italian restaurant in Boston town. It is good!

1 pound baccalà (page 21)
½ cup diced ripe tomato
¼ cup chopped parsley
5 green onions, chopped
½ cup thinly sliced white onion
Juice of 1 lemon
⅔ cup olive oil
Salt and pepper to taste (easy on the salt!)

GARNISHES
Lettuce leaves for serving
2 hard-boiled eggs, grated

Cut the salt cod crosswise into 2-inch-wide pieces and place in a large bowl. Run cold water over the cod several times and drain. Cover the rinsed cod with plenty of fresh cold water and allow to soak at least 24 hours on the countertop. Drain and refresh the cold water several times while soaking.

Drain the fish and place in a large-enough saucepan and cover with fresh cold water. Bring to a boil and simmer gently for 10 minutes. Drain and allow to cool. Flake the fish and discard any bones.

Place in a medium-size bowl and add the tomato, parsley, green onions, and white onion. Whisk the lemon juice and olive oil together and add to the bowl. Fold together and season with salt and pepper. (Don't add too much salt as the dried cod is salty already.) Allow to marinate for 1 hour in the refrigerator. Serve on lettuce leaves and garnish with grated hard-boiled egg.

BACCALÀ IN TOMATO SAUCE OVER POACHED POLENTA CUBES

SERVES 6

You have got to be a fan of baccalà to get in on this one. I have met the children of Italian immigrants who will not even discuss baccalà, and then I have met others who simply love this dish and the memories that it offers.

I like it very much, but not as often as grilled spare ribs.

1½ pounds baccalà (page 21) (buy nice thick pieces)	1 recipe Poached Polenta Cubes (page 233)
1½ cups Fresh Tomato Sauce Sicilian (page 139)	**GARNISH**
¼ cup dry white wine	Chopped parsley

Cut the baccalà into serving pieces and place in a large bowl. Rinse with cold water several times and cover the baccalà with plenty of cold water. Allow to soak for 24 hours. Refresh with cold water several times while soaking. Drain very well.

Fill an 8-quart pot two thirds full with fresh cold water and bring to a boil. In another pot bring the fresh tomato sauce and the wine to a simmer.

Poach the drained baccalà in the boiling water for 2 minutes. Remove with a strainer and add to the pot of sauce. Save the boiling water for cooking the polenta. Cover and simmer the sauce gently 20 minutes or until the baccalà is quite tender.

Poach the polenta cubes in the reserved boiling water with a pinch of salt. Strain the polenta cubes and place on warm plates or a platter. Serve the baccalà over the polenta and garnish with parsley.

STEAMED CLAMS WITH VERMOUTH AND CREAM

SERVES 6–8 AS AN APPETIZER

Clams and vermouth seem to have always been lovers. This blend of flavors is really profound, and it is common among the Italian cooks in this country. Throw a little dry vermouth around the kitchen and the results will always be delicious.

4 **pounds clams** (Manila clams are best)	½ **cup bottled clam juice**
4 **tablespoons butter**	1 **tablespoon lemon juice**
½ **cup peeled and minced yellow onion**	3 **tablespoons parsley**
5 **cloves garlic, peeled and thinly sliced**	½ **cup dry vermouth**
	½ **cup whipping cream**
	Black pepper to taste

Rinse the clams in cold water and place in a large bowl. Cover with plenty of cold water. Allow to soak for 1 hour and drain well.

Heat a 12-quart kettle and add the butter and onion. Sauté for 2 minutes and add the garlic, clam juice, and lemon juice and simmer, covered, 3 minutes until the onion is just tender. Add the drained clams, parsley, and vermouth. Bring to a simmer and cook, covered, 2 minutes. Add the cream and black pepper to taste and continue simmering a few minutes more until the clams open. Serve in bowls with plenty of the broth and some good bread.

BACCALÀ IN VEGETABLE SAUCE

SERVES 4–6

This is real Italian peasant cooking. The cod was salted during the fishing season and left to dry for the winter. There were some winters during which you ate so much of this stuff that you prayed for spring. Now it is enjoyed year-round since it is no longer a necessity.

Craig developed this dish, which is typical of Southern cooking, and I think it is an excellent dish indeed.

1½ pounds baccalà
(page 21) (buy
nice thick pieces)

4 tablespoons olive
oil

3 cloves garlic,
peeled and
chopped

½ cup thinly sliced
celery

1 medium yellow
onion, peeled
and diced

½ cup peeled and
minced carrot

2 medium ripe
tomatoes,
chopped

3 tablespoons
chopped parsley

1 cup Chicken Stock
(page 116)

½ cup dry white wine

3 tablespoons tomato
paste

Salt and black
pepper to taste
(add salt at the
very end if
needed)

Cut the baccalà into serving pieces and place in a large bowl. Rinse with cold water several times and cover the baccalà with plenty of cold water. Allow to soak 24 hours. Refresh with cold water several times while soaking. Drain very well.

Heat a shallow 4-quart pot and add 1 tablespoon of the oil, the garlic, celery, onion, and carrot. Sauté until the onion is tender. Add the tomatoes and sauté 3 minutes more. Add the parsley, Chicken Stock, wine, and tomato paste. Simmer gently, covered, for 1½ hours. Add black pepper to taste but no salt yet. Add the drained baccalà and the remaining 3 tablespoons of oil. Simmer, covered, 20 to 25 minutes. Add salt to taste if needed. You probably will not need salt at all.

Serve with a pasta as a side dish or as a fish course on its own.

TINY CLAMS IN TOMATO SAUCE AND WINE

SERVES 3–4 AS A FISH COURSE

This sort of tomato and seafood cooking is common all over Italy. We had a fine version of this dish in Bologna but a better one was found in Venice. Be sure that the clams are small and very fresh.

3 pounds clams (Manilas, small ones)	3 cloves garlic, chopped
2 tablespoons cornmeal	¼ cup dry white wine
2 tablespoons olive oil	¾ cup Fresh Tomato Sauce Sicilian (page 139)

Clean the clams by soaking them in fresh water along with the cornmeal for about one hour. Rinse well and set aside.

Heat a 6-quart kettle and add the oil and garlic. Sauté for just a minute or so, being careful not to burn the garlic, and then add the clams, wine, and ½ cup of the tomato sauce. Cover the pot and simmer until the clams open. Do not overcook as they will become tough. Discard any clams that do not open.

Strain the clams, reserving the stock. Return the stock to the kettle and reduce the stock by a third, adding the remaining ¼ cup tomato sauce at the end of the reduction.

Return the clams to the kettle and bring up to serving temperature. Serve immediately.

SEAFOOD AND SAFFRON RICE SALAD

SERVES 6–8

Saffron and seafood just belong together. This very colorful dish will probably become a summer favorite for you. Do not be surprised by the use of a little mayonnaise as such a blending is quite common among the fancy food shops of

Milan, Parma, and Bologna. No, I don't think that you would find such a dish in the South.

2 cups Uncle Ben's converted rice	1¼ cups thinly sliced celery
4 cups Chicken Stock (page 116)	½ cup peeled and thinly sliced white onion
¼ teaspoon saffron threads	
2 pounds mussels (the Penn Cove type is best)	**THE DRESSING**
	½ cup olive oil
4 tablespoons olive oil	2 tablespoons lemon juice
¾ pound medium shrimp, peeled	¾ cup mayonnaise (use a good-quality brand)
½ pound large scallops, sliced in half	½ cup sour cream
	Salt and pepper to taste
½ pound fresh tuna or swordfish, cut in ½-inch chunks	**GARNISHES**
	Lettuce cups for serving
2 tablespoons chopped parsley	Ripe tomato wedges

Prepare the rice as instructed on the box but use the Chicken Stock along with the saffron instead of cooking the rice in plain water. When the rice is done spread it out on a sheet pan to cool completely.

Trim the beards off the mussels, wash them well, and drain. Heat a 4-quart pot and add 1 tablespoon of the oil. Add the clean mussels and ¼ cup water. Cover and steam the mussels over medium-high heat until they open, about 3 to 4 minutes. Stir the mussels once while cooking. Drain and allow to cool, saving the mussel nectar for another use. Remove the meat from the opened shells and set aside covered.

Heat a medium-size frying pan and add 1 tablespoon of the remaining oil. Add the shrimp and sauté quickly over high heat until barely cooked, 1 to 2 minutes. Remove and allow to cool. Sauté the scallops and the tuna or swordfish separately using the remaining oil. (The fish will take a bit longer than the scallops or shrimp.) Remove and cool. Place the cooled rice and the cooked and cooled seafood in a large bowl along with the parsley, celery, and onion.

In a small bowl, whisk together the olive oil and lemon juice for the dressing. In another small bowl whisk together the mayonnaise and the sour cream. Slowly whisk the oil and lemon into the mayonnaise and sour cream until smooth. Add salt and pepper to taste. Add to the rice and seafood mixture and fold everything together with your hands. Cover and allow to chill for 4 hours or more. Fold the salad a couple of times while chilling. Serve in lettuce cups with tomato wedges.

CRAB VENETIAN STYLE

I need only explain this one. Venice has such wonderfully fresh seafood that you can live on the stuff and not feel deprived of beef at all.

We had fresh crab one evening in Venice at Alla Madonna restaurant. It is right next to the Rialto Bridge on the Grand Canal, so I suppose you are now thinking of it as a tourist restaurant. No, the tourist places that one must avoid are right on the edge of the Canal. Alla Madonna is down one of the back streets or alleys . . . and it is a favorite among real Venetians.

I had this crab dish as a first course and then a pasta dish and I closed out with grilled eel. I ate the same menu three times at the same restaurant. You should go.

To prepare the crab dish you must be sure that you have fresh crab. In Seattle I buy Dungeness crab, freshly cooked. The crab is cleaned and all of the meat removed and set aside. The back of the crab serves as the bowl. In Venice you sprinkle a tiny bit of white pepper on the crab-back bowl of meat . . . and then drizzle with extra virgin olive oil. It is served at room temperature or slightly chilled.

This is one of the best seafood dishes that I know. You may use either East Coast or West Coast crabs. It will be great either way.

SHRIMP AND RAGÙ OVER PASTA

SERVES 4 AS A PASTA COURSE

Shrimp in a meat sauce sounds a bit strange at first but it works very well. This sort of thing is especially common throughout Northern Italy, though it can be found throughout the nation. Remember that since the country is so long and narrow, no matter where you live you are not far from the sea.

½ **pound fresh medium shrimp, peeled**
Salt and pepper to taste
1 **cup Ragù (page 144)**
¼ **cup dry white wine**

½ **pound penne pasta**
2 **tablespoons olive oil**
2 **cloves garlic, chopped**

GARNISH
Chopped parsley

Season the peeled shrimp lightly with salt and pepper to taste.

Simmer the Ragù and the wine in a small pan for 5 minutes. Set aside and keep hot.

Bring a kettle of lightly salted water to a boil and cook the pasta until al dente and drain well. While the pasta is finishing cooking, sauté the shrimp in the oil and garlic for 1 minute. Don't overcook! Toss the drained pasta with the hot sauce. Serve with the sautéed shrimp on top of the pasta and garnish with parsley.

ZUPPE DI PESCE VENETIAN

MAKES 3½ QUARTS, ENOUGH TO SERVE 8–10, DEPENDING ON THE AMOUNT OF SEAFOOD IN THE FINAL BROTH

This is a very rich version of good old fish soup, not to be confused with Cioppino, which is also delicious but very

*heavy with tomato. In Venice a heavy tomato sauce is sel-
dom used in soup, and I think this version is terrific. I had
something like it at a restaurant called Antica Carbonara.*

STEP 1
- 2 tablespoons butter
- 2 tablespoons olive oil
- 1 head garlic, chopped
- 3 medium yellow
  onions, chopped
- 3 carrots, peeled and
  sliced
- 3 cups cleaned and
  chopped leeks
- 4 cups chopped tomato

STEP 2
- 1 bunch parsley, whole
- 2 cups dry white wine
- 1 quart Chicken Stock
  (page 116)
- 2 quarts cold water
- 1 tablespoon dried
  orange peel

- 1 teaspoon fennel seed
- 5 pounds fresh fish
  heads and bones
- 8 black peppercorns
- 2 cups chopped fresh
  fennel tops

STEP 3
Whole shrimp
Clams in their shells
Mussels
Crab pieces in the
  shell
Scallops
White fish of any
  kind, fresh, cut
  into
2-inch chunks

Place all the ingredients in Step 1 in a 12-quart heavy stock
pot and cook over medium heat, stirring, until things begin
to brown a bit, about 15 minutes.

Add all the ingredients in Step 2 to the pot and bring to
a boil. Turn down to a simmer and cook, uncovered, for 1
hour. Drain the stock from the kettle and discard all the
ingredients, returning the stock to the pot.

When ready to serve, bring the stock to a boil and add
any or all of the seafoods in Step 3. Use any amount you
wish, the more the better. Simmer until the clams and mussels are open, the shrimp pink, and all is tender but not
overcooked, about 10 to 15 minutes. You might want to
add the scallops and fish last. Start with those creatures in
the heavy shells, and move along to the lighter seafood.

Try serving this rich broth over Bruschetta (page 261). All you need is a salad and a dry white wine and you are set.

I like this version better than the French bouillabaisse, though the two dishes are similar.

SEAFOOD COUSCOUS

SERVES 6-8

Couscous is a dish from Morocco, of course. What is it doing in Italy? When the traders from North Africa moved into Sicily, their food became popular in the great island. This is one of my favorite seafood dishes and it is certainly one of the best blends of two cultures that you could ever imagine.

1 pound squid
(Remove the
heads with
tentacles and
discard. Remove
the clear cuttle
bone inside the
body. Rinse the
inside of the
body or tube
and drain well.)

1¼ pounds swordfish
or firm white
fish (boneless)

2 tablespoons olive
oil

3 cloves garlic,
chopped

1 medium yellow
onion, chopped

2 ribs celery, thinly
sliced

2 tablespoons parsley

2½ × 2-inch pieces of
orange peel with
no pith

3 cups Fish Stock
(page 117)
Pinch of saffron
(page 24) (a
good stiff pinch!)

½ pound scallops
(sliced in half if
they are large)

½ pound medium
shrimp, peeled

1 tablespoon butter
Salt and pepper to
taste

THE COUSCOUS

Prepare the couscous as in the recipe for Meatball and Cabbage Couscous (page 340). Have the couscous ready as the seafood finishes cooking.

GARNISH
Chopped parsley

Cut the cleaned squid crosswise into ½-inch rings, rinse them carefully in cold water, and set aside. Cut the swordfish or white fish into ¾-inch chunks and set aside with the other seafood.

Heat a 6-quart pot and add the oil, garlic, onion, and celery. Sauté for 5 minutes and add the parsley, orange peel, Fish Stock, and saffron. Cover and simmer 45 minutes. Add the swordfish or white fish and simmer 1 minute. Add the scallops and shrimp, and simmer 2 minutes more. Add the squid and simmer 1 to 2 minutes more until hot throughout. Do not overcook! Serve over the couscous and garnish with parsley.

FULVIA'S SALMON IN FOIL

SERVES 6-8 AS A FIRST COURSE OR FISH COURSE

Fulvia Sesani knows everyone in the food world. She has studied for years and now runs a most elegant cooking school in Venice. She calls her school Venetian Cooking in a Venetian Palace. Her family has lived in this palace on the edge of the Venetian canals for seven generations. She is terribly gracious and elegant and time spent in her kitchen will never be forgotten.

If you wish to study with her in one of the great food cities of the world you may write her:

Fulvia Sesani
Castello Sessantuno Quaranta
Palazzo Morosini
S. Maria Formosa 6140
Venice, Italy

She claims that Venetian cooking is not at all complex, but you must have very fresh fish. She offered the following recipe on one of our Italian shows.

1 salmon fillet, skinless
    and boneless, cut
    from the large end
    of the fish (about 3
    pounds)
6 or 8 12-inch-square
    aluminum foil
    pieces

3 Roma tomatoes,
    peeled, seeded, and
    sliced into ¼-inch
    strips, the long
    way
Kosher salt
Extra virgin olive oil

Cut the salmon into 1½-inch pieces, crosswise. You should
have about 16 pieces, each about 3 ounces.

Arrange 2 of the slices on a square of aluminum foil.
Place them right together, cut side down. Place 2 or 3 tomato strips atop the fish and sprinkle with a bit of kosher
salt. Drizzle with a bit of olive oil and wrap up the fish by
forming a sealed envelope, leaving a bit of space above the
fish. Crimp the edges of the foil to seal.

Place on a baking sheet and bake for ten minutes in a
400° oven. Do not overcook.

You may serve this dish right out of each individual foil
wrapper.

FULVIA'S SWEET AND SOUR FISH

SERVES 3–4 AS A LIGHT FISH COURSE OR ELEGANT SNACK

*This is another wonderful dish from our friend Fulvia from
Venice. The dish is actually very old since the use of pine
nuts, currants, and vinegar points to early Roman influ-
ences. The dish is called sweet and sour because the natural sugar in the sautéed onions blends with the vinegar
and wine to create a true sweet and sour sauce. In Venice
it is pronounced "saor."*

*One hint. Have all of the garnishes prepared before you
jump into this very contemporary version of a very old dish.
You don't want to let things get too cold before you serve,
so have the parsley stems all cleaned and ready, etc.*

This dish will delight your friends if you are creative with the presentation. If you do not want to bother arranging things in such a way, or if you lack Fulvia's wonderful artistic style, then just serve the fish with the garnishes placed about the plate. It will be delicious either way.

THE ONION SWEET AND SOUR

- 4 medium yellow onions, peeled and thinly sliced
- 2 tablespoons vegetable oil
- ¼ cup white vinegar
- ¾ cup dry white wine
- Salt to taste

THE FISH

- 1 pound fresh small sole fillets, skinless and boneless (Choose Dover sole fillets that run about 4 to 5 ounces each. They would be ideal for this dish.)

- 1 cup flour for dredging
- Vegetable oil for frying (peanut or safflower)

GARNISHES

- Twigs of parsley stems
- Small bay leaves
- Pine nuts, lightly pan-toasted
- Currants or small raisins

In a large lidded frying pan sauté the onions and the 2 tablespoons of oil over low heat, covered, until clear and very tender. Do not brown these but rather "sweat" them down.

Add the white vinegar and the wine to the pan. Simmer gently for about 2 minutes. Add a bit of salt to taste and allow the onion mixture to cool. Puree in a food processor for about 2 minutes. Pour the mixture onto a large serving platter and spread it out with a rubber spatula. Cover only the center of the plate, not the rim. Cover with plastic wrap and set aside.

Cut the fillets lengthwise into 2-inch-wide strips. Roll up each, beginning with the tail end, and secure with a toothpick. Flour and then gently shake off the excess flour by placing the rolls, a few at a time, in a kitchen strainer. Shake very gently.

Heat enough oil for frying in a 12-inch frying pan to bring the oil up to about ¾ inch deep. Heat to 375°. You may want to use an electric frying pan for this. Fulvia puts a regular toothpick in the oil. If it bubbles, the temperature is just right. Carefully place half the rolls into the oil and fry on each side until just barely golden brown. Turn only once. This should take about 3 minutes total time. Remove and drain on paper towels. Bring the oil up to temperature and fry the second half of the rolls.

Remove the toothpicks and cut each roll in half so as to form pinwheels.

Garnish the plate of pureed onion with the parsley twigs and then add the small bay leaves so as to make a flower or shrub pattern. Place the pinwheels on the branches so that they appear as flowers on the branch. Garnish with the pine nuts and currants by just sprinkling them about on the plate.

Serve with a great deal of pride.

EGGS

What more can be said about the beautiful egg? When we say "egg" in the American culture, we generally mean chicken eggs. But from the earliest days of Rome, eggs of all kinds were appreciated. Chicken eggs, duck eggs, peacock eggs, ostrich eggs, and quail eggs. This affection for exotic eggs occurred because the Romans traveled everywhere and returned to glorious Rome with the most unusual of birds.

The appreciation of eggs has continued in Italy since ancient times.

Please note that when a recipe is called a frittata it begins in a pan, just as the French make an omelet. But the Italians—and this is a common practice all over the country—do not turn or fold the egg mixture as do the French. The Italian method is to place the half-cooked egg mixture under a very hot broiler, thus causing the whole to rise and puff and sing. Very different from the French method. The cooked dish is cut like a pie or cut into squares. Italians will eat frittatas cold, warm, hot, whatever. The dish can be a first course, a second course, a main course, whatever.

You will enjoy the Asparagus Frittata, which actually goes back to ancient times. The first century Roman cook Apicius was very fond of this one. Fonduta makes a great topping. I am also fond of the Spaghetti Frittata Marino.

ASPARAGUS FRITTATA

SERVES 4-6

Lovely. This frittata is very different from the omelet in that it is broiled rather than turned. I think it is a fine dish. In ancient Rome, Apicius, the supposed author of a cookbook written during the first century A.D., offered a similar recipe and I really see no reason for trying for improvements. This is luscious.

STEP 1

½ pound fresh asparagus, rinsed and with the tough ends broken off (This will probably take ¾ pound whole asparagus in order to yield the amount necessary for this recipe. Cut into ¼-inch pieces.)

1 tablespoon olive oil

STEP 2

½ medium onion, sliced
1 tablespoon olive oil

STEP 3

6 eggs, beaten
Salt and pepper to taste
½ cup freshly grated Parmesan cheese

Blanch the asparagus in boiling water for about 2 minutes along with the tablespoon of oil. Drain and rinse under cold water. Set aside.

Turn on the broiler in your oven.

Sauté the onion in the second tablespoon of olive oil until tender. Use a 12-inch nonstick frying pan.

Season the eggs with the salt and pepper and stir in half the cheese. Add this mixture to the heated frying pan along with the asparagus and prepare as an omelet. Do not stir. Top the mixture with the remaining cheese and place under the broiler until light and puffy, just beginning to brown.

Cut into wedges to serve.

ASPARAGUS FRITTATA WITH FONDUTA

Just a description, that is all you will need. But get ready for a very rich and enjoyable meal.

First, prepare a batch of Fonduta sauce (page 80). Then prepare an Asparagus Frittata (page 458). Simply top the frittata with some of the sauce and serve in wedges.

It is difficult to think of a more wonderful summer morning breakfast—or lunch or dinner, for that matter.

FOLDED CANNELLONI WITH
CHEESE AL FORNO

SERVES 4–5, TWO CREPES EACH

This dish is common in Reggio Emilia. I need only describe it as it is very easy to prepare. This works as a pasta course or a main course, depending on how involved you want the dinner to be. If you have small individual porcelain baking boats, you are set for anything.

Prepare a batch of Basic Cannelloni Crepes (page 207). Cut a little slice of imported Italian Fontina cheese that will just cover one quarter of the circle of the cannelloni. Fold the pasta in half, thus covering the cheese. Place a slice of regular mozzarella on one half of the pasta and fold it over. You now have a round noodle folded into fourths and filled with cheese.

Place one or two into individual baking boats. Be sure to oil the dishes first. If you wish to bake all of these in one dish, choose a large one.

Top each with a splash of Fresh Tomato Sauce Sicilian (page 139) and then with some additional cheese.

Bake at 375° for 20 to 25 minutes.

SPAGHETTI FRITTATA MARINO

SERVES 6 AS A SIDE DISH

You would love Marino. He is from Naples and, typical of the people from the South of Italy, he feels that the Northerners do not really know how to cook. Too fancy and too much fooling around! He is the bartender at our hotel in Milan . . . a Southerner moved North. Italians are always anxious to give you a recipe when they find that you are composing a cookbook. Marino gave us this recipe while we were sipping a gin at his bar. Such a sweet guy. The recipe was free and so were the drinks!

STEP 1	STEP 2
1 tablespoon olive oil	3 eggs
2 cloves garlic, crushed	½ pound dry spaghetti cooked al dente
½ cup chopped tomato	2 tablespoons freshly grated Parmesan cheese
¼ cup sliced black California pitted olives	
1 teaspoon chopped pickled capers	

Use a nonstick 12-inch frying pan for this one. Heat the pan and add the olive oil and garlic. Barely cook the garlic and then add the rest of the ingredients for Step 1. Simmer for a few minutes.

Remove the pan ingredients to a bowl and mix in the ingredients for Step 2. Heat the frying pan and add all. Lightly brown on one side and then turn. Brown on the second side and serve.

ONION OMELET WITH BALSAMIC VINEGAR

MAKES 1 OMELET

This is a gift to us from our dear friend in Rome, Dr. Micaela Balzoni. She traveled all over Italy with us and I have never known any other person who could move the strange political structures of that country as she can. Everything from the police to the local park department!

She is from Sicily, raised in Germany, and married to a beautiful man from Modena, thus her affection for balsamico. She described this dish to us one afternoon while we were racing along an Italian freeway. The dish is delicious and it is perfect for an evening meal along with a nice salad and a good wine . . . and good friends, of course.

3 tablespoons olive oil
1 cup peeled and thinly sliced yellow onion
1 tablespoon balsamic vinegar (use good stuff or a blend)

3 eggs, whipped
1 tablespoon water
Salt and freshly ground black pepper to taste

Heat a 10-inch nonstick frying pan. That is what you will need for a good omelet. Add 2 tablespoons of the oil and sauté the onion, gently, on medium heat, until it just begins to lightly brown. Add the vinegar and remove all to a dish and set aside.

Whisk the eggs well. Heat the frying pan and add the remaining oil. Whisk the water into the eggs and pour into the pan. They should immediately begin to set up but not brown. The secret is not to have the temperature too high. As the omelet sets up, use a wooden spatula to lift an edge of the omelet and allow the still-fluid eggs on top to flow under and thus finish the cooking. Do not overcook an omelet. I like mine very moist.

Top the omelet with the onion and add a bit of salt and pepper. Never put salt in the egg mixture prior to frying as it will toughen the eggs. Fold the omelet onto a plate and enjoy.

This will produce one omelet just right for one person. When eating this delight be sure to silently thank Micaela.

COLD FRITTATA WITH ONIONS AND HERBS

A cold frittata is seen very often on the antipasti tables in Northern Italy. All right—not cold, just room temperature.

Prepare an Asparagus Frittata (page 458) and allow it to cool. Drizzle some extra virgin olive oil on the dish and cut it into small pie-shaped wedges. Serve on the antipasto buffet.

You may wish to omit the asparagus and substitute some clever flavoring of your own. Try one made with ricotta cheese or one with several fresh herbs. Mushrooms would be delicious.

CHEESES

Cheese is one of the five major ingredients in the Italian kitchen. Pasta, bread, wine, olives, and cheese. While the French generally eat cheese as a separate course, the Italians are more likely to cook with it. And good cheese is absolutely necessary to a good Italian kitchen.

Parmigiano-Reggiano

There are many fine cheeses to be found in the regions of the land, but the most important cheese for the kitchen, as far as I am concerned, is real Parmigiano-Reggiano.

The production of this great cheese has changed little during the past seven hundred years. Further, the controls placed upon the some nine hundred small cheese factories in the region are so strict that I doubt that much will change during the next hundred years. These people will convince you that the way to keep a good thing going is to continue as much as possible to make it in the old way.

We visited the small cheese factory called "Spadarotta" in the Reggio Emilia area. Mr. Umberto Iotti and wife, Anna, along with their two children, make ten cheeses every day during the season. Cows don't take Sundays or saint's days off! Further, it is normal for a local Parmigiano-Reggiano factory to be run by a single family. I do not know whether it is tradition or law, but the wife of the cheesemaker is always in on the process.

Milk for the factory is brought in from local cows that have a very carefully controlled diet. They are not even allowed to wander in the fields since they could possibly eat something that would alter the flavor of the milk. The animals stay indoors a great deal of the time and are milked once in the morning and once in the evening.

A shipment of milk is delivered to the Iotti family late each day. The milk is allowed to separate overnight in large stainless-steel trays. In the morning the separated milk is drained into a large cheese-making kettle, the cream being kept aside and sold to a butter maker. Upon the arrival of the morning shipment of milk, which is still warm from the cow, the cheese-making kettle is filled with the new whole milk.

The cheese vats are most ingenious. They are large copper kettles in the shape of a cone. Each holds 1,100 liters (about 290 gallons) of milk. They are so deep that the bottom of the cone is built down into the floor so that one can work the top of the vat at about waist height. In the old days a wood fire was built under the vats but in our time the vats are covered with a steam jacket so they work much like a double boiler.

The milk is heated to 35° centigrade (about 95° Fahrenheit) and rennet is added. This is a natural extract from the stomach of young cows and it causes the milk to form into a curd, much like a light gelatin. Once the curd has formed, it is cut up into tiny chunks the size of small grains and the heat is increased to 55° centigrade (about 135° Fahrenheit). The curds are cooked thus for a short time, stirring all the while, and then allowed to settle into the small base part of the cone-shaped vat. Before this great ball of compressed curd is removed from the bottom of the vat the cheese maker takes an eight-foot-long wooden paddle and makes the Sign of the Cross over the cheese vat. Now you know you are in Italy.

Using the paddle the cheese is brought up to the surface, drained a bit, and cut in half. Each vat of 290 gallons of milk will produce two cheeses, each weighing between 85 and 90 pounds. The cheeses are placed in molds and allowed to dry and cure for a few days. A natural rind forms on the cheese and then each is cured in a saltwater bath for about two weeks. The cheese maker ages the cured cheeses for several months in his own warehouse. And just so that you know this whole process is frugal, nothing is wasted.

The whey that is left over from the vats is saved and fed to the pigs from which we get the great Parma prosciutto hams!

Since the Iotti family has five steam-jacketed cheese kettles, they make ten cheeses a day, every day. They work from six in the morning until about seven-thirty in the evening, a long and hard day. But of course, since they are Italian, remember that the largest meal of the day and the best family time occurs in the middle of the afternoon.

I watched this family operate, everyone having his or her hands in the cheese vats, and I had a vision. Patty, my wife, was standing beside me helping with the cooking of the curd. Channing and Jason, our sons, were busily washing out milk cans and scrubbing the floors of the dairy. Suddenly, the vision vanished, and I know why. An argument broke out between the boys and Patty yelled, ''Pazzo!'' (''Crazy!'') She had had it!

I do not know how the Iotti family does it, but it is Italian tradition and the family seems firm and well.

Incidentally, nothing other than fresh milk, rennet, and salt is allowed in the dairy. That is the law of the region, so the nine hundred or so families who make these cheeses produce a consistent and delicious product. And only fresh water and steam can be used in cleaning.

After several months of aging in the dairy, the cheeses are sent to one of several central aging houses, carefully controlled by the laws of the region. Each cheese bears the number of the family dairy that produced it, and each cheese then comes under the authority of the master cheese taster. The Magnani Aging House has at least fifteen thousand cheeses aging at any one time. The cheeses are turned and polished every two weeks, and aged until they are eighteen months to two years old. The master cheese man, Mr. Rino Alvisi, tastes each cheese as it comes to the ripening point. This is done using a tiny corkscrew device that is poked into the cheese and withdraws a tiny bit of cheese. Mr. Alvisi, who sports one of the largest and most beautiful noses that I have ever seen, then smells the cheese and checks for the proper graininess. Only after he gives the proper sign is the cheese branded and allowed to go to market.

Mr. Alvisi has been tasting Parmigiano-Reggiano for forty-five years, like his father before him. He started his job in the cheese house when he was eighteen years old, and he is now over seventy. I asked him when he was going to retire and he said softly, "I cannot retire. Parmigiano-Reggiano is a drug, and I am totally addicted!"

Please do not confuse this cheese with the pre-grated, plastic-wrapped, cardboard-tasting cheese that we find on the shelves of local markets in this country.

The tiny hammer that Mr. Alvisi uses to tap the cheese when checking for air spots, and the tiny corkscrew used for tasting, make up the tools of his trade. He has had his set for decades and he claims that the set will be buried with him.

I am amazed that the Italian culture takes so much care and concern over the making of a single cheese but cannot get a telephone call from Parma into Rome! First things first, I guess.

Other Famous Italian Cheeses

Fontina

This very rich and creamy cheese is made from cow's and sometimes goat's milk. It is used in cooking great sauces or in fine sandwiches. A great melting cheese. Buy the imported Italian cheese, called Fontina d'Aosta. The Danish version is much more firm and not as rich.

Gorgonzola

Italy's wonderful version of blue-veined cheese. Imported, it is beyond belief in terms of flavor and it is great in sauces for pasta, et cetera.

Asiago

A firm aged cheese made of cow's milk. Very distinctive flavor, a bit sharp.

Pecorino-Romano

A hard, fully cooked cheese made from sheep's milk. Excellent grating cheese for pasta if you like the strong sheep flavor. I do!

Mozzarella

Fresh mozzarella is made in Italy from the milk of the water buffalo. Really! It is only a few days old when you eat it. A second kind is aged a bit and used in cooking and sandwiches. The kind you see in this country is generally made from cow's milk.

Provolone

A firm cow's-milk cheese that is cured in brine and then very lightly smoked. Great for sandwiches and sometimes popular for pizza toppings.

Mascarpone

Really not a cheese as such but closer to a very rich sour cream. Used in many desserts, it is delicious . . . and expensive. Substitute sour cream if you cannot find this one.

Ricotta

A cheese close to our cottage cheese. Easy to find in the markets these days but it might be fun to make your own (page 475).

Dried Ricotta (*Ricotta Salata*)

This is a grating cheese and it is what it says it is. The dried ricotta is terrific on pasta, bruschetta, and salads.

Scamorza

Similar to aged mozzarella. Made from whole cow's milk, it is formed into a kind of pear shape and aged for about two weeks. I think it is delicious sliced and broiled until lightly browned (page 479).

Caprino

A soft, white, rindless fresh goat cheese. French chèvre is the same thing so it is an easy substitute. Spread on bruschetta or use in cooking.

In addition to the recipes in this chapter you may also wish to see:

Fried Radicchio Filled with Cheese (page 73)
Fonduta (page 80)
Fonduta Mayonnaise Vegetable Dip (page 82)

DRIED RICOTTA CHEESE ON BRUSCHETTA

When ricotta is salted and dried it becomes hard enough to grate and it is aged for the wintertime. Originally from Sicily, this potent cheese is great in cooking.

You can find it in any good Italian food market. Ask for ricotta salata.

Try making a bit of Bruschetta (page 261) and grating some dried ricotta on the toast while it is still hot. Terrific!

CHEESE CUSTARD PLAIN

If you wish to avoid the trouble of wrapping the cheese custards in phyllo dough (page 472), do just that! The custard cups can be served warm as a side dish and everyone will love it. The cups can even be served at room temperature or just barely warm.

CHEESE CUSTARD WITH RICE

SERVES 6–8 AS A SIDE DISH

I so enjoyed the cheese custard that I decided to try it with rice. The result is a very tasty rice pudding with cheese for a side dish at the meal, not a dessert. This is very versatile since it goes with almost anything, but you must use fine imported Italian Parmigiano-Reggiano cheese.

¼ cup long-grain rice
1 cup cold water
Pinch of salt
5 eggs
1½ cups milk
1½ cups freshly grated Parmesan cheese
¼ teaspoon lemon zest
Salt and freshly ground black pepper to taste

1 tablespoon butter, melted

GARNISH
2 tablespoons additional grated Parmesan cheese

Place the rice and the water in a small saucepan with a pinch of salt and bring to a boil. Cover and simmer for 15 minutes. Drain in a strainer and allow to cool.

Beat the eggs together in a mixing bowl. Stir in the milk, Parmesan cheese, lemon zest, the cooled rice, and the salt and pepper to taste.

Grease an 8 × 8-inch glass baking dish with the butter.
Add the egg mixture. Bake in a preheated 325° oven for
20 minutes. Sprinkle on the 2 tablespoons of cheese for
garnish and continue baking 10 more minutes. Turn the
oven to broil and lightly brown the top of the custard. (Do
not leave unattended as the top of the custard can burn
quickly.)

CHEESE CUSTARD IN PHYLLO DOUGH

SERVES 6 AS AN ANTIPASTO COURSE

*I was amazed to see the creative ways in which Parmigiano-
Reggiano cheese is used in cooking. At the Gener Neuv
Ristorante in Asti, a fine eating establishment, they wrap
cheese custard in phyllo dough and then cook it a second
time. This dish is glorious!*

THE CHEESE CUSTARD

- 6 eggs
- 1⅓ cups milk
  White pepper to taste (not too much)
  Pinch of salt
- 1 cup freshly grated Parmesan cheese
- 6 ramekins (1½ inches deep by 3 inches in diameter)
- 1½ tablespoons butter for greasing the ramekins

THE PASTRY COATING

- 1 1-pound box phyllo dough (12 × 17-inch sheets)
- ½ cup butter, melted, for the phyllo dough

GARNISH
Freshly grated Parmesan cheese

Preheat the oven to 350°. In a small bowl, beat the eggs well. Add the milk, white pepper, salt, and 1 cup Parmesan cheese and beat again. Grease the ramekins with the butter and divide the egg mixture evenly among the ramekins. Put the molds in a baking pan and carefully place the pan on the center rack in the oven. Pour enough hot water into the pan to come ¼ inch up the sides of the molds. Bake at 350° for 20 minutes or until the custard becomes slightly firm in the center. When the ramekins are cool enough to handle, remove them from the baking pan of water and allow to cool to room temperature on the counter. Since the custard is very delicate you must be gentle from this point on.

Run the back of a table knife around the inside edges of the custard molds to loosen. Invert the ramekins one at a time onto a small sheet pan and tap the bottoms of the molds to pop the delicate custards out. Carefully lay a sheet of phyllo on a clean counter. Brush the sheet lightly with melted butter. Fold the sheet in quarters so that it measures 6 × 8½ inches. Brush with melted butter and place the custard in the center of the buttered phyllo. Fold the phyllo around the custard. Wrap the remaining 5 custards in phyllo. Place the wrapped custard rounds seam side down on a nonstick sheet pan. Brush with additional melted butter and sprinkle with Parmesan cheese. Bake at 375° for 20 minutes until golden brown.

PARMIGIANO-REGGIANO CHEESE WITH A DROP OF GOOD BALSAMICO

This is not a recipe but rather a description of one of the most unusual and delicious ideas I have ever come across. For a middle course or even a dessert, cut a small piece of Parmigiano-Reggiano cheese and put it on a lovely plate. A drop of two of finest-quality balsamic vinegar is placed on the top of the cheese and served.

Unless you have tasted this union of flavors I doubt that

you can ever understand why the people of Modena claim that no one else in the world knows how to eat as they do. I am with them!

IGNUDI AL RAGÙ

SERVES 4

This is really a very clever dish. We are attempting to copy something that we had in Florence at the Buca dell'Orafo, very near the Ponte Vecchio. It is a very small downstairs place and it is usually very busy with foreigners. The food, however, is quite good. They make terrific Tripe Florentine and this delightful Ignudi al Ragù.

This dish is actually the spinach and ricotta cheese filling for ravioli and dumplings. Here the filling is served in little mounds topped with Ragù. No pasta in sight.

1 pound fresh spinach	Salt and pepper to taste
1 tablespoon olive oil	
2 tablespoons butter	1 cup Ragù (page 144), hot
2 tablespoons all-purpose flour	
2 egg whites, at room temperature	**GARNISH**
1 pound fresh ricotta cheese (page 469)	Freshly grated Parmesan cheese

Remove the stems from the spinach and discard. Chop the spinach leaves and wash well and drain. Heat a large frying pan and add the oil and spinach. Sauté until the spinach collapses and the liquid is gone. Remove to a colander and allow to cool. Squeeze out the excess liquid and set the spinach aside.

Melt the butter in a frying pan and add the flour. Cook together to form a roux but don't brown. Beat the egg whites and ricotta together in a bowl and place in a double boiler. Cook the ricotta in the double boiler, stirring all the time, until warm. Whisk in the roux and continue cooking and stirring until thickened like pudding. Stir in the reserved spinach and season with salt and pepper to taste. Serve in attractive little mounds on warm plates (a small ice cream scoop works well for this). Top with the Ragù and garnish with Parmesan cheese.

HOMEMADE RICOTTA

MAKES ABOUT 2 POUNDS

Ricotta is close to what we call a cottage cheese, but it is a bit more dense and not quite as wet. It is used in cooking and baking, with pasta dishes, and for wonderful dessert fillings.

I don't know if you have ever gotten into making your own cheese but I certainly have and I really enjoy it. It is one of those things that you do for relaxation and for personal delight. After you make a few pounds of ricotta, you may just decide that you can relax more by buying it at the market. In any case, here is the method for a decent ricotta.

You must have a cheese/yeast thermometer (page 45) for this process.

1 gallon fresh whole milk	¼ cup fresh cultured buttermilk
8 drops liquid vegetable-based rennet (find in health-food stores)	2 tablespoons distilled white vinegar
½ cup water, barely lukewarm	Kosher salt to taste

Please note that all pieces of equipment used in the production of cheese must be very clean, free from soap and any outside molds, cheeses, or bacteria. I use only stainless steel when I make cheese, except for the small plastic mold, which I wash and rinse very carefully.

Place the milk in a stainless-steel pot and *very gently* heat to 70°. No hotter. Watch this carefully. This will take only a few minutes.

Stir the 2 drops of liquid rennet into the water and stir this, along with the buttermilk and vinegar, into the milk. Stir well and cover with a towel. Leave at room temperature for 12 to 18 hours, until the mixture is like soft gelatin.

Cut the curd into ⅛-inch cubes. Use a stainless-steel knife or an old-fashioned potato masher for this. A bird's nest frying basket will also work well. Do this very carefully or you will soon have too fine a curd.

Place the pot into a bit larger pot on the stove and add water to the outside pot, thus making a bain-marie or double boiler. Stir the curds *very gently* with a stainless-steel spoon in order to separate and gently cure them. Gently heat the curds to 110° and lower the heat, or you might even turn the heat off and on in order to maintain the 110° temperature for 8 to 10 minutes.

Add salt to taste, about ½ tablespoon.

Drain the curd, using a piece of cheesecloth and a colander, saving the whey for use later in a soup. Place the curd in any kind of small basket mold and refrigerate, placing the mold on a deep dish so that any remaining whey does not drain onto your refrigerator floor. A small stainless-steel strainer works well for this. Do not allow the curd to drain until too dry; just drain it to your taste, anywhere from 2 to 8 hours. If it becomes too dry you can always mix it with a small amount of milk. When the cheese has reached the consistency that you wish, remove it from the mold and refrigerate on a plate, covered with plastic wrap, or in a sealed plastic container.

CHEESE PACKED IN OIL

MAKES 12 PATTIES OF CHEESE, ENOUGH FOR 24 SERVINGS

I first saw this cheese at a roadside eating house in Italy called an "Autogrill," part of a chain of places along the Italian freeways. These places are not at all like our roadside eating joints, not at all. They are clean and cheerful and they have a menu that will surprise the driving tourist.

This dish is similar to one that I learned from my Lebanese uncle, Uncle Vic Abdo. This method of preserving cheese must have come to Italy from the Arabs. It is delicious.

Once you get a batch of yogurt going, you can keep it for months, maybe years. It is refreshed each time you make a new batch.

You must have a cheese/yeast thermometer (page 45) for cheese making.

THE CHEESE

1 gallon fresh milk
10 teaspoons dry
   yogurt starter (I
   prefer Bulgarian
   Yougurt starter,
   available in
   health food
   stores.)
2 cups very fresh
   cultured
   buttermilk

THE HERBS AND OIL

1 red bell pepper, cut
   into strips
4 bay leaves, whole
4 garlic cloves, cut
   into slivers
2 teaspoons oregano,
   whole
2 fresh rosemary
   sprigs, each 2
   inches long
   Olive oil to cover
   the cheese (This
   need not be extra
   virgin, but I
   would use virgin,
   page 487.)

Place the milk in a stainless-steel pot and very carefully heat it to between 180° and 190°. Hold it at this temperature for 8 minutes. You may have to turn the heat off and on. After the 8 minutes remove the pot from the heat and cool to 112°.

Remove ½ cup of the warm milk from the pot and put it into a glass measuring cup. Stir into the cup the dry yogurt starter, making a smooth paste. Blend this into the warm milk pot, being very sure to stir until all is very smooth. Add the buttermilk.

Keep this pot warm for between 6 and 12 hours, depending on how strong you wish the flavor of the cheese to be. I keep mine in the stainless pot, covered, in my gas oven overnight, using only the heat of the pilot light. Perfect! If you do not have such a thing, then place the pot on a heating pad set on low. Wrap a large bath towel around the pot and in the morning you will have perfect yogurt.

On the next day remove 2 cups of yogurt and save it sealed in a plastic container in the refrigerator as a starter for your next batch of yogurt.

Place a large stainless colander in a large bowl. Line the

colander with a couple of layers of cheesecloth and very gently pour into it the yogurt. Allow it to drain overnight. You must drain the bowl several times to start with so that the cheese can continue to drain. Save the whey for use in soup.

If the yogurt has not formed into a light and moist cheese, hang the cheese ball by tying up the corners of the cheesecloth and allowing it to hang from a kitchen hook or cabinet knob. Be sure to put a bowl under it.

When you have a cheese something like the texture of cream cheese, mold it into 12 equal patties, each about ¾ inch thick and about 3 inches in diameter. Moisten your hands with cold water now and then when forming these patties so that the cheese does not stick to your hands.

Place the patties on a double-thick layer of flour sack kitchen towels (page 254). Space them apart so that they can dry a bit. Cover with another towel and allow to dry for a day so that they are a bit more firm.

Clean 2 1-quart wide-mouth mason jars. Place six of the patties in each. Add to each jar a few red bell pepper strips, 2 bay leaves, 2 cloves of garlic cut into slivers, 1 teaspoon of the oregano, and a sprig of fresh rosemary.

Top off each jar with enough olive oil to cover, and seal.

Place in the refrigerator and allow to marinate for at least a week. This cheese will keep for a few months, so you do not have to use it all at the same time. Serve it with crackers or bread, along with some of the oil.

Note: The olive oil will cloud up when cold. Not to worry. Just remove the cheese from the refrigerator an hour or two before you are going to serve it. It will be clear and nice at the table.

BROILED SCAMORZA

Don't you just love trying to say the name of this cheese? It is an uncooked cheese, similar to mozzarella, and is made from cow's milk. It is stringy and rich, high in butter fat, and formed into pear-shaped pieces. It is aged for about two weeks. You can find this in an Italian market in any large Italian community. It is worth the search.

We tasted it broiled in L'Aquila, in Abruzzi. They do love cheese in that region! Our driver, Big Giorgio, ordered this for his lunch. Very good.

Purchase a ball of mildly aged scamorza. It will weigh about ¾ pound. Slice it the long way into pieces ½ inch thick. Place on an oiled broiler and broil until the cheese is bubbly and browned a bit on top but still retains its form. Serve as a hot lunch course along with a good salad and red wine.

BAKED RICOTTA

MAKES ABOUT A 2-POUND LOAF
THAT WILL SERVE YOUR HOUSEHOLD
AND THE NEXT THREE HOUSES DOWN THE STREET

Baked cheese does not very often come to the mind of the American cook. It Italy it is common to serve a baked cheese as a first course, and in the summertime as a main part of the meal.

This is simple and delicious. Prepare a batch of Homemade Ricotta (page 475) or drain 2 pounds of commercial ricotta in a small colander. Keep it refrigerated as you drain it and let it firm up for a day or so.

Preheat an oven to 375°. Remove the drained cheese from the mold and place it bottom side up on a nonstick baking pan with rimmed sides—not a sheet, as some liquid may accumulate during the baking.

Bake the cheese loaf until just a few golden spots appear on the surface, about 40 minutes.

Serve either warm or cold on a buffet, offering toast or crackers so that your guests may smear some of the baked cheese on a crunchy bit.

RICOTTA TOAST SPREAD

Sometimes breakfast should be a light and toasty thing. I dislike American breakfasts for the most part as I cannot get going after eating all that heavy food. In Italy breakfast is a cup of good coffee and maybe a tiny pastry or even a light sandwich. This is consumed in a favorite local bar as one marches off to work.

I think this cheese spread makes a splendid breakfast— or evening snack, for that matter.

1½ cups ricotta cheese
1 small garlic clove, crushed
2 teaspoons chopped parsley

Salt and pepper to taste

Mix together all the ingredients in a small bowl. Serve at room temperature as a cheese spread for Bruschetta (page 261).

PASTA WITH DRIED RICOTTA CHEESE

Dried Italian ricotta (ricotta salata) is very similar to what the Greeks call "mizithra." However, ricotta is always made from cow's milk and mizithra is most often made from sheep's or goat's milk. Either will do well for this recipe but the Greek version is much stronger in flavor.

Cook a batch of pasta and drain it. Add enough garlic and olive oil to taste and some grated, dried ricotta. Toss and add salt and pepper to taste.

That's it! This is a great pasta dish that can be prepared in just a few moments. Keep a chunk of dried ricotta about for this very easy dish.

Always buy imported dried ricotta. The stuff from our Midwest just does not have the same flavor.

OLIVES AND OLIVE OIL

I have tried to imagine the Italian kitchen without olive oil. I have had no success, none whatsoever.

Olive oil, and olives, for that matter, are basic to all that goes on in the kitchen, and this seems to have been true since times prior to the Roman Empire. The oil has remained as one of the most important basic ingredients, the others being wine, pasta, bread, and cheese.

The current interest in the healthfulness of the "Mediterranean Diet" stems from the fact that olive oil and wine seem to be so helpful in the prevention of heart problems and cholesterol buildup. So, up with olive oil!

Olive trees go back to prehistoric times, and by 2500 B.C. they were quite common in Syria and Crete. The Greeks were great producers of oil and shipped it around the Mediterranean, certainly into Rome. And, as the Romans have always done, they picked up on a great idea and improved upon it. They invented the screw press for manufacturing olive oil and we have been using their pressing methods in one way or another ever since.

Today olive oil is more widely used in Italy for cooking and dining than all other vegetable oils or animal fats put together. The reason is simple. Olive oil is delicious, just delicious!

We had a meal at an inn high in the hills of Tuscany, just outside Florence. We had visited the olive fields, fields that shared their space with grapevines, and we tasted the Tuscan air. The perfume, the aromas in the air, were rich and heavy with the fall sun. Just as we reached a point of near intoxication we were led to this tiny little restaurant in the inn Albergaccio Niccolò Machiavelli. It was the inn in which Machiavelli had written one of the most important political articles of his time, and I think he must have written it in olive oil.

This inn has always used the finest olive oil in almost every dish. Tall decanters of this wonderful Tuscan oil were on every table and you were expected to use it in a most liberal manner on just about every course. First, a charcoal-broiled toast with olive oil and garlic—bruschetta. Add more oil. Then a fresh tomato soup with garlic, bread, and oil. Add more oil. A steak, grilled with olive oil, was next. Add more oil. I don't remember the dessert because it had no oil in it.

I know that this kind of a meal would frighten some Americans, but these Italians are healthy and hearty and beautiful. Such a meal I have never had! All of the recipes for that luncheon—yes, it was only lunch—appear in this book.

The Pressing

Craig, my chef, and I went into the olive orchards to taste the ancient fruit. I was shocked by the bitterness, just shocked! I was then told that when the olives are pressed, using great round granite wheels that go back a thousand years, the juice that comes from the pressing is a mixture of oil and fruit juice. It is the juice of the fruit that is bitter, not the oil. In the old days the crushed olives were placed in a screw press and the juice and oil thus gained were allowed to separate in large vats. In our time we use a centrifuge, just as we do when separating milk from cream. This centrifuge method is one of the few changes that have been made in the manufacture of olive oil since Roman times.

When you press black olives, or mature olives, you get a rather yellow oil, smooth in flavor. When you use younger olives, green olives, you get a green and fresher-tasting oil with a sort of wonderfully raw and grassy flavor. Both have their uses and both are made in various grades of quality. There are many grades, but for the normal household cook in America, these four are the only ones that you really need know about.

Grades of Oil

Most of us are confused by the grading levels of olive oil. Actually, they are quite simple.

Extra Virgin

This is the best. Not only is it the first pressing but the oil is graded in terms of its very low acid content. This is the most expensive of the grades but you can find a wide price range even in this best grade.

Use for salads, soups, antipasti, etc. Not a cooking oil at all.

Virgin

Very close to the above but the acid content, or the bitterness of the oil, will be just a bit higher. You will still get good results and the price will be lower.

Pure

This is generally a second or third pressing done under heat. It will have less flavor but it is just fine for pan-frying or even deep-frying. Since the flavor is not as bright, you can use it in just about anything. But when you want flavor, go to extra virgin. You are worth it.

Light

A new category that offers a pure oil that is light in flavor. It is *not* light in calories as it contains the same caloric count as do any of the oils above.

Any good Italian market will carry many levels of quality as well as many sources. California, Greek, Spanish, Italian, and French oils will all be represented. I prefer Italian oils, though some Greek oils are just great and not as expensive. Please find an Italian market in your city and talk with the owner about some good buys in all grades of olive oil.

Storage

You will get a much better price if you buy the oil in a gallon tin. Spoilage is no problem as long as you keep the tin or glass closed and in a cool, dark place. I fill a quart wine bottle and leave it on the counter, with the rest staying in the pantry closet. Just keep it cool, or you can refrigerate the oil. It will become very cloudy and sluggish. Just let it come to room temperature and you are all set.

Olives in Cooking

As Americans we should use more olive oil in our diets. All of the current health studies point to that fact. Further, Thomas Jefferson was so in love with olive oil that he tried to grow olives on his estate at Monticello in Virginia. The olives could not take the weather but we can take the olives.

Olives were a regular part of the ancient diet and they seem to have maintained their place. In this section I want to tell you about Lemon Olive Oil and Black Olive Paste. Also the Roast Pork with Black Olive Paste is one of the best pork dishes I have ever eaten!

In addition to the recipes in this chapter you may also wish to see:

Roast Pork with Black Olive Paste (page 345)
Roast Lamb with Black Olive Paste (page 346)
Bread and Tomato Soup with Olive Oil (page 122)
Pinzimonio (page 147)

LEMON OLIVE OIL

MAKES ABOUT 4 CUPS

This is one of the most refreshing uses of olive oil that I have ever tasted. My friend Carlo Middione, a chef in San Francisco, imports this oil from Italy and sells it in his shop. It is very expensive. While I will admit that the imported version is better than this one, you will enjoy this blend very much.

Carlo served this on a green salad, but it is also good on antipasti, pasta, polenta, meats, and so on.

6 large lemons, the ripest you can find	**4 cups extra virgin olive oil**

Peel the lemons, using a potato peeler, making sure that you do not remove any of the white pith. This should yield about 1 cup of lemon peel. Save the peeled lemons for juice in other dishes. Place the peel in a mortar (page 47) along with ¼ cup extra virgin olive oil. With the pestle, pound and rub the peel and oil together for 1 minute. Remove to a 2-quart glass jar or sealed plastic container and add 3¾ cups additional extra virgin olive oil. Allow to marinate 4 days at room temperature. Strain the oil and discard the peel.

STEAK GRILLED WITH OLIVE OIL

The people of Florence and the surrounding hills of Tuscany love beef and pork. The steak that we were served in the Machiavelli Inn had been brushed with extra virgin olive oil and then cooked over coals. It was rare and delicious, better than most beef in Italy, and then we were encouraged to drizzle more olive oil over the steak while at table.

I see two good things here. First, the flavor of the olive oil simply blesses the beef. Second, you can trim the beef fat from the meat and replace the joy of fat with healthy olive oil.

Such a good marriage!

BLACK OLIVE PASTE

MAKES 2 CUPS

This paste will prove to be a wonderful and tasty backup in your kitchen. It takes a bit of work to prepare, but as you can see from the following recipes, it is very versatile and helpful. Such a clever use of this ancient fruit, the olive.

¾ cup pitted dried
   Italian olives
⅓ cup pitted Calamata
   olives
2 small cloves garlic,
   peeled and
   chopped
½ cup coarsely
   chopped yellow
   onion

¾ cup olive oil
1 tablespoon lemon
   juice
   Black pepper to
   taste
2 tablespoons chopped
   parsley
½ teaspoon sugar

Pit the olives using a good olive pitter. If you can find an old-fashioned cherry pitter it will work well for this process. Otherwise, just pour a glass of dry sherry and pit them by hand. It will be worth it, I promise. Remember that the amounts called for in this recipe are for *pitted* olives, not whole olives.

In a food processor, finely chop the garlic, onion, and olives (pulse, pulse). Do not grind too finely. Stir in the remaining ingredients.

PASTA WITH BLACK OLIVE PASTE

SERVES 8 AS A RICH PASTA COURSE

This dish looks a little garish because the pasta will be blackened by the olive paste. Just tell the kids that you are serving "Dirty Spaghetti" and they will love it.

1 pound pasta (penne
    or rigatoni works
    best because they
    are easier to toss
    together)
½ cup Black Olive
    Paste (page 490),
    at room
    temperature

¼ cup virgin olive oil

GARNISHES
Grated Parmesan
    cheese to taste
Chopped parsley

Boil the pasta al dente in lightly salted water. Drain well and return the pasta to the pot. Add the Black Olive Paste and oil and toss together quickly. Serve with the garnish.

BALSAMIC VINEGAR

We call it vinegar . . . but it is not vinegar in the normal sense, not at all. It is closer to a syrup, a perfume, a condiment, a blessing.

The very best balsamic condiment comes from Modena, in Northern Italy.

Balsamic is not a wine vinegar since the pressed grapes are never allowed to ferment and turn into wine. The must, or pressings of very special and rich grapes, is cooked down over low heat. This rich extract is then made into vinegar, a "mother" being added to the cooked pressing. It is never a wine at all.

The process goes back several hundred years and little has changed in terms of the procedure. Americans cannot understand the ritual and cost involved in this process until they taste the final aged product. Since this product is so expensive, few of us in America ever taste it!

Here is the process: The grapes are harvested and pressed, just as in wine, but the must is not allowed to ferment. Instead, it is cooked down until it is very rich and then placed in a wooden vat into which a previous vinegar "bug" is introduced. The must is then added to the first of a series of barrels of previously prepared balsamic . . . and little by little, as the product evaporates, it is moved from an oak barrel to a smaller chestnut barrel, to a smaller cherrywood barrel, to a smaller ash barrel, to a smaller mulberry barrel.

This whole process can take up to twenty years, so you can understand how the original pressings become concentrated and drawn down to the most delicious flavors one can imagine. At the end of the first twelve years of moving small amounts of the precious fluid from barrel to barrel, the maker is finally allowed to draw three liters from the last little barrel. This is considered ready to use, though the condiment maker may extend the time to improve the quality of the finished product. The loss due to evaporation is about 10 percent per year, so after twelve years you may have gone from thirty liters of reduced must to three liters of fine aceto balsamico.

The set of barrels used for this lengthy process most often has been in the family for generations. Count Paolo Giudotti Bentivoglio, president of the Consorzio Produttori de Aceto Balsamico Tradizionale di Modena, has a set of barrels that have been in constant use by his family for two hundred years! They have to be repaired now and then but they are all in use. "The rest of these barrels are new," he explained. "Some are only fifty years old." Oh.

The consortium is a marvel of discipline and tasting skills. Since this process of making true aceto balsamico is so lengthy, one can understand that no one is really in it for the money. It is rather a tradition, an art form, with a wonderful final product. The vinegar maker, after at least twelve years of patience, submits a tiny sample of his final three liters of vinegar to the panel. The panel consists of thirty people who have studied for at least nine years and no fewer then five may judge at any one time.

The judging room has a very large round table divided up by tall boards into a pie with five or six wedges. No one can see anyone else. No one speaks. A tiny bottle of vinegar is given to each taster, who then silently judges it for flavor, bouquet, color, richness, sweetness, acidity . . . twelve characteristics in all. The little sample bottles have no names on them, only numbers. A name cannot be used since the bottle may belong to a friend of a panel member or even a panel member himself or herself. Talk about cloak-and-dagger stuff! They all sit in their private niches with candles and tiny silver spoons and taste up to a dozen different vinegars in the course of a session.

If the panel decides that the sample is really a fine product, then the maker is allowed to put it in a specially shaped bottle of the consortium and may sell it in amounts of just less than half a cup . . . the cost being somewhere around

$120. I cannot think of any liquid condiment that is more expensive, but then you do not just slosh it around. It is so rich and the flavor so bright and overwhelming that overuse will ruin a dish. It is used by the teaspoonful, or by the drop.

There are many levels of quality on the market so you need not panic. Good balsamic vinegar can be purchased for about fifteen or twenty dollars a pint and it is fine for cooking. Certainly it is nowhere near as rich as the fancy stuff but very usable nevertheless. A cheaper salad version is readily available in any Italian market.

Incidentally, the term *balsamico* means "healing," and the vinegar is so named because during the plague people threw it on hot coals to inhale the smell and attempt to avoid the vile disease.

Balsamico is used throughout this book. In addition to the recipe for the salad dressing you may wish to see:

Chicken with Balsamic Vinegar (page 301)

Beef with Balsamic Vinegar Sauce (page 342)

Onion Omelet with Balsamic Vinegar (page 461)

Cold Chicken with Green Sauce Balsamic (page 311)

Parmigiano-Reggiano Cheese with a Drop of Good Balsamico (page 473)

Strawberries and Balsamic Vinegar (page 517)

LEMON OLIVE OIL AND
BALSAMIC VINEGAR DRESSING

Patty, my wife, will kill for this stuff! It is so easy and so mild and light and . . . well, do not try to take her salad from her when I have dressed it with the following.

½ cup Lemon Olive Oil (page 489)
2 tablespoons balsamic vinegar (page 495)

Salt and freshly ground black pepper to taste

Blend together and toss with fresh greens or use as a marinade for vegetables.

DESSERTS

Now we are really talking about two different eating systems. In Italy sweets, pastries, the kind of things that we call desserts in this country, are consumed at breakfast and at breaks throughout the day. We do that as well. However, when dinner is over in the evening, we look forward to another sweet of some sort. It seems to me that the Italian is done for the day and would just as soon eat a bit of fruit or close out with a salad.

I talked with Craig about this and he came up with a great line. "Clean your plate so that you can have some chocolate cake!" That is very American. Italians don't seem to think that way. Dinner is not a means to a sweet. Oh, don't let me mislead you. If there are guests in the house for the evening meal, the household may very well finish dinner and then wander down to the public square for a sweet bit and some wine and coffee. But note that this is a different event. It is not dinner; it is time with your friends in the square.

I have included a Bellini cocktail in this section because it is a dessert for me. I could not possibly drink one or two of these and then order dinner. Patty, my wife, can and does. Enough is enough!

I will put Craig's Tiramisù up against any I have ever tasted, and the Torroncino is just wonderful. The Sweet Tagliarini Tart from Lynn Rossetto Kasper will bring you to tears. Just don't bring it to me after a full Italian meal. Better in the morning or in the late afternoon with coffee or espresso.

BELLINI COCKTAIL

MAKES ONE DESSERT COCKTAIL

This is sort of Venetian fun. Years ago Harry Cipriani served such a drink in his famous Venetian bar, a hangout for Americans. I have been in the place (it is just off Saint Mark's Square) but I really didn't get into the whole thing like some American tourists seem to. Stories are told about Ernest Hemingway sitting about the place and drinking Bellinis. I have no way of knowing whether or not this is true.

Patty, my wife, tells this story. The old recipe called for a nectar made from white peaches, lovely white Italian peaches. These are a very fragile fruit and the season is short. Patty went into Harry's Bar and ordered a Bellini and loved it. The next day she did the same. On her third day in Venice she ordered the same drink from the same bartender and he replied, "No!" When my wife asked why no Bellini today she was told that the season ended last night. These Venetian bartenders must be serious!

Since we seldom ever see a white Italian peach in this country we have developed the following variation on the Venetian version. It is really quite good and you can enjoy it all the year round.

2 ounces peach nectar
  (Kern's is a good
  brand and it
  contains no
  additives. Find it
  in any good
  supermarket.)
1 teaspoon fresh lemon
  juice
1 ounce peach
  schnapps (the
  liquor store)

3 ounces Prosecco
  (Italian
  champagne),
  chilled, or dry
  champagne,
  chilled, or Asti
  Spumante, chilled

Mix the peach nectar along with the lemon juice and schnapps in a cold glass. Add a bit of crushed ice and stir. Then add the Prosecco or champagne.

TIRAMISÙ

SERVES 6

While some Italian writers claim that this dish is actually quite old, it seems to have become really popular in this country just during the last few years. In any case you can find it now in any Italian coffee shop here in America and in many bars in Italy.

Since I am not a sweets man, and since Craig spent a good deal of time studying with a French pastry chef, I told him to go at this one. It is a fine version and much more moist than the usual. Even I enjoy this sweet dish, but I must warn you that this is wonderfully rich!

THE FILLING

1½ cups espresso or
 triple-strength
 regular coffee at
 room
 temperature
½ cup sugar
¼ cup brandy
2 egg yolks
1 pound mascarpone
 cheese (find in
 Italian markets;
 the weight may
 be ½ or 1 ounce
 less)
1 8-ounce package
 ladyfingers (find
 in Italian
 markets)
4 ounces semisweet
 chocolate, shaved
 (use a box grater
 or a truffle
 cutter, page 36,
 for this)

THE ICING

1 cup fresh whipping
 cream
¼ teaspoon vanilla
2 tablespoons
 confectioners'
 sugar

GARNISHES

Cocoa powder for
 dusting
Additional shaved
 chocolate

Stir the espresso, sugar, and brandy together in a mixing bowl until the sugar dissolves. Remove ⅓ cup of the coffee mixture to another bowl and set the remainder aside. Whisk the egg yolks into the ⅓ cup of coffee. Add the mascarpone and whisk together just until smooth. Do not overmix or it may begin to separate.

Line the inside of a 9½ × 5½-inch loaf pan with a large sheet of wax paper. Tuck the wax paper into the corners of the pan, being careful not to tear it. If you have another identical loaf pan, carefully press it inside the lined pan so that the wax paper will take the shape of the pan.

Dip the ladyfingers one at a time into the reserved coffee

mixture and begin to place them crosswise in the lined pan. The ladyfingers should be soaked with the coffee and will expand a little. This will take only a few seconds; be sure not to soak them so long that they fall apart. Continue with more ladyfingers, lining the bottom of the pan lengthwise with them. You can trim them if they don't fit exactly. Spread on half of the cheese mixture. Sprinkle with 2 ounces of the shaved chocolate.

Layer again in the same manner with 7 more ladyfingers, the remaining cheese mixture, and the remaining shaved chocolate. Top the loaf pan off with the remaining soaked ladyfingers. Fold the wax paper up around the top of the pan and cover the pan tightly with plastic wrap and refrigerate for 6 hours.

Invert the chilled loaf pan onto a serving platter and tap the bottom of the pan to remove the loaf. Remove the wax paper. Place the cream, vanilla, and confectioners' sugar in a bowl and whip until stiff. Spread the whipped cream all over the inverted cake in an attractive manner. (You may want to use a pastry bag to decorate it with the whipped cream.) Place the cocoa in a fine strainer and dust the top of the cake. Sprinkle with additional shaved chocolate. Slice and serve.

CHERRIES IN BRANDY OR GRAPPA

SERVES 4

This is a quick way to prepare cherries packed in brandy, a favorite in Italy. These go well over ice cream and make a rather flashy dessert.

1 16-ounce can Bing cherries in heavy syrup	½ cup brandy or grappa (page 23) 1½ tablespoons sugar

Drain the cherries, reserving the syrup. Place the drained cherries in a small bowl and add the brandy or grappa; set aside. Simmer the reserved syrup and the sugar in a small saucepan until reduced by half. Allow to cool and add ¼ cup of the reduced syrup to the cherries. Cover and allow to marinate in the refrigerator overnight. Serve plain in little bowls along with the juice or serve over vanilla ice cream.

TORRONCINO

SERVES 12–14

There is a fine restaurant in Treviso called Alla Pasina. The chef is most cordial and he was anxious to have us taste this glorious dessert. When he saw how pleased I was, he marched out to the kitchen and came back with a recipe for me. These Italian chefs are so willing to share!

It was translated by our dear friend Carmine who owns one of the best restaurants in Seattle, Il Terrazzo.

4 eggs
4 tablespoons sugar
1½ tablespoons brandy
1 pint whipping cream
1 cup coarsely chopped torrone (nougat) candy (find in Italian markets)
½ cup crumbled amaretto (almond) cookies (find in Italian markets)

THE SAUCE
3 egg yolks
⅓ cup sugar
1¼ cups milk
⅓ cup shelled pistachios (not salted)

GARNISH
Additional slivered pistachios

Separate the 4 eggs and place the yolks in one bowl and the whites in another. Add 2 tablespoons of the sugar to the yolks along with the brandy and whisk until thick, and set aside.

Whip the egg whites until they form soft peaks and slowly whip in 1 tablespoon of sugar. Whisk until thick and glossy and set aside.

In another bowl whip the cream with the remaining 1 tablespoon of sugar until fluffy. (Don't overwhip the cream to the point that it begins to turn yellow or curdles.) Fold the whipped cream into the egg yolks until smooth, along with the candy and cookies. Fold the meringue into the whipped cream mixture until smooth. Do not stir this or it will begin to collapse. Remove to a sealed container and freeze for several hours.

Place the egg yolks and sugar for the sauce in a bowl and beat together well. Bring the milk and pistachios to a simmer in a saucepan. Slowly whisk the hot milk and nuts into the egg yolks and sugar. Return to the saucepan and cook over low heat, whisking constantly, until the sauce thickens enough to coat the back of a spoon. Strain the sauce, discarding the pastachios, and allow to cool to room temperature.

Remove the semifreddo from the freezer for 10 minutes before serving. To serve, scoop the semifreddo out onto serving plates and ladle some of the sauce over the top. Garnish with slivered pistachios.

LEMON SHERBET WITH VODKA

SERVES 8

A good chef can take simple things and blend them in such a way that they give us new tastes and new gifts. The chef at Alla Pasina in Treviso makes his own lemon sherbet (a Donvier ice cream maker works great for this) and then dowses it with good vodka. That's it. Just lovely.

We can give you a recipe for a good lemon sherbet, but you might want to just buy it from a good market and splash away with the vodka.

1 cup sugar
1 cup water
    Juice of 3 lemons
2 cups dry white wine
2 teaspoons lemon
    zest (use the peel
    from the above
    lemons)

½ cup whipping cream
    (cold, and not
    whipped)

GARNISH:
Good quality vodka
    to taste

Freeze the inside cylinder of a Donvier ice cream maker overnight.

Boil the sugar and water in a small saucepan for 5 minutes. Remove to a metal bowl and stir in the lemon juice, wine, and lemon zest. Refrigerate until cold. Stir the cold cream into the bowl and chill several hours or overnight. Pour the cold sherbet mixture into the frozen Donvier cylinder. Immediately reassemble the machine and follow their instructions for making ice cream (or follow the instructions on other ice cream makers.)

When the syrup mixture has turned into ice, scoop out little balls and place in fancy glasses. Drizzle with the vodka. This sherbet is great between courses at formal dinners.

FRUTTA FOR DESSERT

Americans rarely order fresh fruit at the end of a meal. Something sweet and heavy is generally preferred.

Throughout the North of Italy it is very common to see a waiter march over to a table with a big bowl of assorted fresh fruit . . . and a good-sized bowl of ice water. When I saw this the first time I was confused as to what the water was for. Micaela, our dear friend and guide, ate fruit all day long, and for dinner she would have another bowl of fruit along with the ice-water bowl. She explained that Italians are so fussy about fresh fruit that the fruit is not washed ahead of time as the washing will discolor the fruit if it sits around a bit after being cleaned. So the client is given ice water so that he may clean his own fruit at the table, just as he is about to eat it.

One of the most elegant dessert eaters I have ever seen is Fulvia Sesani, of Venice. This very attractive and sophisticated lady sat in the garden of a restaurant on the edge of the canal and dipped grapes into ice water. It was done with such grace that I was fascinated.

Try this at home sometime. Grapes of all kinds, pears, figs, fresh dates, Sicilian blood oranges—all can be arranged for your guests and each gets his own bowl of ice water. This sounds like such a simple thing, but if the fruit is in perfect shape and is properly ripened, an Italian woman can turn this simplicity into quite a dramatic production.

SWEET TAGLIARINI TART

SERVES 8–10 AS DESSERT

Lynne Rossetto Kasper marched into our television kitchens armed with her wonderful cookbook, The Splendid Table, her amazing knowledge of the Emilia-Romagna region, and her sense of humor. We all fell in love with her. Then she presented us with this cake. The cake takes a bit of doing since it is very much like Lynne, rather complex. But the result is well worth the effort.

THE SWEET PASTRY

1 cup (4 ounces) all-purpose unbleached flour (organic stone-ground preferred)

½ cup plus 2 tablespoons (2½ ounces) cake flour

½ cup (3½ ounces) sugar

Pinch of salt

½ teaspoon grated lemon zest

8 tablespoons (4 ounces) unsalted butter, chilled, cut into chunks

3 egg yolks, chilled

1 to 2 tablespoons cold water

1 tablespoon unsalted butter (for greasing pan)

THE FILLING

2 quarts salted water

2 ounces fresh tagliarini, cut as thin as possible, or 3 ounces imported dried fidelini or cappellini

1½ cups (6 ounces) blanched almonds, toasted

1 cup (7 ounces) sugar

3 tablespoons all-purpose unbleached flour

9 tablespoons (4½ ounces) unsalted butter, melted

½ teaspoon almond extract (see Note)

2 tablespoons Strega, Galliano, or liqueur of Moscato

3 tablespoons water

3 egg yolks

6 egg whites

GARNISH

⅓ cup powdered sugar

WORKING AHEAD: The pastry can be mixed 1 day ahead; wrap it and store in the refrigerator. Bake the tart 8 hours before serving. Tightly wrapped, the tart keeps in the refrigerator several days.

MAKING THE DOUGH BY HAND: Stir the dry ingredients together in a large bowl. Using your fingertips, rub in the butter until the mixture looks like coarse meal with a few large shales of flour-coated butter still intact.

Make a well in the center and add the egg yolks and 1 tablespoon water. Beat the egg yolks and water with a fork until smooth. Then toss with the dry ingredients until everything is moistened. Do not stir or knead because the dough can toughen. Gather the dough into a ball. If it is too dry, sprinkle with the remaining tablespoon of water, toss for a few seconds, and then gather into a ball, wrap, and chill at least 30 minutes.

MAKING THE DOUGH IN A FOOD PROCESSOR: Put the dry ingredients and the lemon zest in a food processor fitted with the steel blade, and blend for a few seconds. Add the butter and process until the mixture resembles coarse meal. Add the egg and 1 tablespoon of the cold water, and process with the on/off pulse until the dough barely gathers into small clumps. Turn the dough out onto a sheet of plastic wrap, gather it into a ball, wrap, and chill at least 30 minutes.

MAKING THE CRUST: Sprinkle a work surface with flour. Thoroughly grease a 9-inch layer cake pan with removable bottom and 1¾-inch sides with the tablespoon of butter. Roll out the dough to form a large round about ⅛ inch thick. Make sure the pastry is all of even thickness. Fit into the cake pan, bringing the dough up its sides and neatly trimming it around the pan's rim. Because of its high sugar content, this pastry breaks easily. Just press it into the pan a piece at a time. Chill about 1 hour.

Preheat the oven to 400°F. Line the crust with foil and weight it with dried beans or rice. Bake 12 minutes. Then remove the liner and weights, prick the bottom of the crust with a fork, and bake another 8 to 10 minutes, or until it is barely beginning to color. Remove from the oven and allow to cool.

MAKING THE FILLING: Preheat the oven to 375°F. Have a 10-inch round of parchment paper handy. Bring the salted water to a vigorous boil. Drop in the pasta. Cook fresh pasta only about 10 seconds. Allow 1 minute for dried pasta. It should be tender enough to eat but still quite firm. Drain, rinse under cold water, and shake dry. Spread the pasta out on paper towels.

Coarsely chop one quarter of the almonds. Set aside. Combine the remaining almonds with the sugar and flour in a food processor, and grind to a powder (or use a hand-operated nut grater). Add 6 tablespoons of the melted butter, the almond extract, liqueur, water, and egg yolks to the food processor. Blend thoroughly. Turn into a large bowl. Beat the egg whites to form soft peaks. Lighten the almond mixture by stirring in a quarter of the whites. Then gently fold the rest of the whites in, blending thoroughly but keeping the mixture light. Slather half the filling over the bottom of the crust. Spread half the pasta over it. Then top with the remaining filling. Sprinkle the reserved almonds over the filling, top with the rest of the pasta, and drizzle with the remaining melted butter.

BAKING THE TART: Lightly cover the tart with a round of parchment paper, and bake 20 minutes. Uncover and bake another 30 to 35 minutes, or until a knife inserted about 2 inches from the edge comes out clean. Cool the tart on a rack.

SERVING: Slip off the side of the pan, and serve at room temperature. Sift a generous dusting of powdered sugar over the tart just before presenting.

Note: ALMOND EXTRACT: Almond extract replaces the traditional bitter almonds, used for centuries to accent almond dishes. Bitter almonds, which can form harmful prussic acid, are banned in the United States. If available, the kernel found inside a peach or apricot pit can be toasted and ground with the almonds to attain a bitter almond flavor.

CORNETTI

SERVES 6

This very simple dessert is common in the coffee bars and pastry shops of Northern Italy. Our version is a quickie, since we doubt that you are going to make your own lemon custard from scratch. This works well and will delight the kids.

1 envelope Bird's
  Custard/Dessert
  Mix*
3 tablespoons sugar
1½ cups cold milk
1 tablespoon finely
  grated lemon
  rind

2 tablespoons
  brandy
6 fresh breakfast
  croissants

GARNISH
Powdered sugar

Prepare the custard mix according to the instructions on the envelope, adding the lemon rind and brandy when finished with the cooking of the custard. Allow to cool.

Cut each croissant down the back and, using a piping bag, fill each with a bit of the custard. Sprinkle with powdered sugar and serve.

*Use Jell-O pudding mix if Bird's is not available in your area.

MACEDONIA

SERVES 4–6

This popular dish is simply fresh fruit salad marinated in a sweet wine or liqueur. It is found throughout Italy, though its origins are in the South where fresh fruits are grown and prized. Use only fresh fruit, freshly cut up, and then marinate in sweet Marsala.

1 cup grapes	¼ cup fresh whole
1 cup pineapple	mint leaves
1 cup cantaloupe	½ cup sweet Marsala
1 cup honeydew	wine

In addition to the above recipe you might wish to throw in a splash of grappa (page 23). That would certainly make the dessert salad stand up!

WINE GELATIN WITH FRESH FRUIT

SERVES 8

When I was a child the neighbor lady was always trying to unload a gelatin mold filled with canned mixed fruit. And she always used green gelatin. Even my mother tried to pass this off on me as food! You remember, as I am sure it also happened to you.

This version is common in Milan where one of these wine gelatin molds goes for about five dollars, and that is for take-out! Our version is not at all expensive but you must use fresh fruit. None of that canned stuff!

2 envelopes unflavored gelatin (Knox brand)	¼ cup sugar
	¼ cup dry red wine
	1 cup fresh blueberries
1½ cups cold water	1 cup fresh raspberries
1½ cups dry white wine	

In a small saucepan stir the gelatin and the cold water together. Add the white wine and the sugar. Bring to a simmer, stirring constantly until clear and dissolved. Remove from the heat and add the red wine. Allow to cool to room temperature.

Divide the berries alternately among 8 4-ounce timbale molds (approximately 2½ inches on the open end by 2 inches tall). Fill the molds with the cooled wine gelatin to about ⅛ inch from the top. Carefully place the molds on a level shelf in the refrigerator and chill overnight.

To serve, dip the outside of each mold into a bath of warm water a few seconds. This will barely loosen the gelatin on the inside. (Don't leave the mold in the warm water too long or it will melt the gelatin.) Immediately invert the molded wine gelatin onto a chilled serving plate or platter.

PIZZELLE

MAKES 36 PIZZELLE

This is a sort of Italian waffle cookie. I eat them now and think back to my old neighborhood in Seattle. Mrs. Petosa lived next door to us, and when she needed a last-minute item from the grocery, she would call over the fence and bid me run the errand. When I returned she would give me a 25-cent piece and some pizzelle filled with ricotta or cream. She was always so sweet to me. I sat by that fence some days just waiting for her to call. I miss the waffle cookies, but I miss her more.

When the cookies come hot from the iron they can be rolled or turned into a cone. They are then filled with flavored whipped cream or sweet ricotta cheese. (Sweeten 1 cup of ricotta with ¼ cup powdered sugar and a touch of vanilla.)

Italian grandmas use a stove-top iron for these cookies but you can buy an electric pizzelle maker from the Vitantonio Company. This recipe is from them.

6 eggs	2 tablespoons vanilla
1½ cups sugar	or anise extract
1 cup margarine, melted and cooled a bit (do not use more than 1 cup)	3½ cups all-purpose flour
	4 teaspoons baking powder

Beat the eggs and sugar together until thickened and pale. Add the cooled melted margarine and vanilla or anise. Sift in the flour and baking powder and mix until smooth.

These can be cooked on the top of the stove if you have an old-fashioned pizzelle iron. You can also use an electric iron. Place a heaping tablespoon of the batter in the top half of the iron. Close and cook about 30 seconds, until light brown. Remove carefully with a fork and cool flat, or roll into cones while warm. Sprinkle powdered sugar on top.

STRAWBERRIES AND BALSAMIC VINEGAR

SERVES 4

I first tasted this dish in a very good Italian restaurant in Chicago, La Strada. I thought the whole concept quite odd, but that was in 1985. Now this dish is understood and quite common. You might try the same thing with other fruits such as cantaloupe, blueberries, raspberries—anything fresh.

1 pint ripe strawberries	2 tablespoons balsamic vinegar (page 495), good quality
1 tablespoon sugar (or more to taste)	

Hull the strawberries and cut them in half lengthwise. Place in a bowl and carefully toss with the sugar and vinegar. Toss just before serving and offer them in fancy glasses.

ITALIAN WINES
MUCH MORE THAN JUST SPAGHETTI WINE

My wife, Patty, is a serious lover of Italian wines, and the whole culture for that matter. When I asked her to do an article for me on Italian wines she agreed . . . but only after I promised her several cases of wine. Such a deal! So, this is her article, and I enjoyed buying the wine and reading her comments. She has a fine mind and a first-class wine tongue.

Soave, Dolcetto, Barolo, Chianti . . . such a litany of beautiful names of Italian wines. But the variety of names can seem a little intimidating when one needs to choose a wine for dinner. With over two hundred recognized zones of origin (DOC), Italian wines seem almost as chaotic as Italian political parties. The amazing thing in both cases is that it all seems to work.

Since the establishment of DOC in 1963, the Italian wine industry has made steady improvements in labeling, marketing, and exporting. Most of the wine that comes to the United States is very drinkable and affordable. Some is exceptional and priced accordingly, but the good news for those of us who love Italian food is that we have easy access to dependable, delicious Italian wine to enjoy with that food.

Just as most of us have moved beyond spaghetti with red sauce to a variety of regional Italian dishes, so we have moved on from Chianti in wicker-covered bottles to some lovely Pinot Grigio with fish dishes and sturdy Barbera with osso bucco.

Perhaps the easiest way to learn about putting Italian wines and foods together is to remember the importance of regional cooking in Italy. Do not be a slave to geography, but looking at a map and learning a little about which wine grows where in Italy will help you team wine with appropriate regional dishes. When you are traveling in Italy this is easy to do, as Italians are fiercely loyal to their regional cuisines and will offer you the wine to go with them. But at home just take a little time to do research on the region of the dishes you are cooking, or think about the ingredients in a particular dish or sauce and try to team them up with a complementary wine.

The map will be invaluable. Wines produced in Tuscany where cattle graze and hearty beans are eaten tend to be hearty to accompany them. Wines produced near the coasts, big lakes, or Venice tend to go very well with seafood.

Most people immediately think ''red'' when thinking of Italian wines. The whites are not as complex as the reds, but there are many excellent whites available. Many pastas with lighter sauces, and most seafood and poultry dishes, benefit from the clean crispness of cool white wine. As several of Italy's Northern provinces are close to Austria and Switzerland, there seems to be a slight Germanic touch to some of the whites. This means that the Riesling-style whites, although fruity, are dry, in contrast to the sweet American-style Rieslings. Soave, a white Italian wine very popular in the United States, is also a fruity, light wine but less Germanic. Most Soave comes from the Veneto area, is excellent with risotto (rice grows along the Po River), and is a delicious summer sipping wine.

Pinot Bianco and Pinot Grigio also come from Veneto and from Alto Adige, but probably the most exciting come from Italy's easternmost region, Friuli, close to Yugoslavia. These can be delicious wines and go very well with poultry, fish, and small game birds.

The white wines of Tuscany, Umbria, and the areas near Rome seem a little bigger and fuller than those of the North.

Vernaccia di San Gimignano is a favorite, excellent with bean soup or bread salad from the Tuscan hills.

From the Northwestern corner of Italy come some strong reds such as Barolo and Barbera. Also from that region, but somewhat smoother are Dolcetto and Spanna. These are excellent with stews of beef or veal and also fonduta and bagna cauda. The Northeastern corner also produces reds, especially the lighter reds of Veneto Bardolino and Valpolicella. Merlots from Friuli and the Northeast are delicious with veal and many pasta dishes.

Chianti is, of course, the wine of Tuscany. The very best are the riservas which have been aged the longest and come from designated areas. Also from specific zones are the classicos which are also complex and full-bodied. Both of these Chiantis cost above average and you should check a vintage chart or talk with a wine merchant before purchasing. But they are delicious, perfect with beef, pork, and other stronger, full-flavored foods.

The Chiantis that are produced elsewhere in Tuscany are also frequently delicious and full bodied. Taste a few with well-known names and find a moderately priced bottle (four to eight dollars) that keeps you happy. It goes into tomato sauce and can be drunk along with tomato-sauced pastas. It is also good with roasted or grilled meats.

There are, of course, many, many other wonderful Italian wines. Some of my favorites were a little too pricy or not particularly appropriate for mealtimes, so they are not included here. My very favorite red is from near Verona, called Amarone. It is slightly bitter, very full-bodied and getting more expensive as you read this.

Another favorite is Bartolomiol's Prosecco, fizzy but not quite champagne. It is glorious mixed with fresh peach juice to produce a Bellini . . . and as you can tell, we have gone way beyond spaghetti wine.

Patty Smith

Epilogue

Now we better understand the Italian table. A family celebration at the table is even more important than the celebration of the Church, though in Italy the two tables become one and the same. The feast of the family becomes the feast of the Church. The wonderful bread and wine become the Body and Blood. Communication becomes Communion. Affection becomes Eucharist and thanksgiving. And the family becomes Mother Church and Father God.

Consider the gifts of such an understanding of the table. Pasta from ancient wheat fields. Bread from history. Mushrooms from the rot of the forest. Wine from the genius of the Creator. Time to relax and enjoy such gifts as befits a beloved child. Traffic jams that point to the presence of the Demonic. And cheese that points to the constant presence of Grace.

The Holy and the Secular meet head-on at the Italian table. Historically this seems to have always been the case, as if this special people were endowed with an insight that helps them see a profound joy in living and eating and loving. And to hell with the government!

Bibliography

Anderson, Burton. *The Simon and Schuster Pocket Guide to the Wines of Italy.* New York: Simon & Schuster, 1987.

Baedecker's Italy. New York: Prentice Hall, no date.

Barzini, Luigi. *The Italians.* New York: Atheneum, 1964.

Bastianich, Lidia, and Jay Jacobs. *La Cucina di Lidia.* New York: Doubleday, 1990.

Cooking of Italy, The New York: Time-Life, 1986.

Cronin, V. *Horizon Concise History of Italy.* New York: American Heritage, 1972.

Del Conte, Anna. *Gastronomy of Italy.* New York: Prentice Hall Press, 1987.

Edwards, John. *The Roman Cookery of Apicius.* Point Roberts, Wash.: Hartley and Marks, Inc., 1984.

Fodor's Italy. New York: Fodor's Travel Publications, 1992.

Hazan, Victor. *Italian Wine.* New York: Knopf, 1984.

Ingle, Schuyler. *Vintage Pellegrini.* Seattle, Wash.: Sasquatch Books, 1991.

Insight Guide to Italy. APA Productions, 1985.

Kasper, Lynne Rosetto. *The Splendid Table.* New York: William Morrow and Co., Inc., 1992.

Liberty of Nations: Italy. New York: Time-Life, 1986.

MacGregor, Ian T. *Let's Go Italy.* New York: St. Martin's Press, 1991.

May, Tony. *Italian Cuisine Basic Cooking Techniques.* Italian Food and Wine Institute, 1990.

Middione, Carlo. *The Food of Southern Italy.* New York: William Morrow and Co., Inc., 1987.

Nagel's Italy. Nagel Publishers, 1987.

Off the Beaten Track—Italy. New York: Harper and Row, 1988.

Rivkin, Bernard. *The Gourmet's Companion Italian Menu Guide & Translator.* New York: John Wiley & Sons, Inc., 1991.

Root, Waverley. *The Food of Italy.* New York: Random House, 1971.

Sack, John. *Report from Practically Nowhere.* New York: Harper and Brothers, 1959.

Wine Spectator, The, September 15, 1992, ''Special Report: Italy.''

Index